D0891977

The Smarter Bomb

The Smarter Bomb

Women and Children as Suicide Bombers

Anat Berko
Translated by Elizabeth Yuval

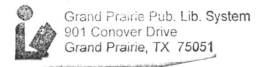
ROWMAN & LITTLEFIELD PUBLISHERS, INC.
Lanham • Boulder • New York • Toronto • Plymouth, UK

Published by Rowman & Littlefield Publishers, Inc.
A wholly owned subsidary of The Rowman & Littlefield Publishing Group, Inc.
4501 Forbes Boulevard, Suite 200, Lanham, Maryland 20706
www.rowman.com

10 Thornbury Road, Plymouth PL6 7PP, United Kingdom

British Library Cataloguing in Publication Information Available

Library of Congress Cataloging-in-Publication Data
Berko, Anat.
  The smarter bomb : women and children as suicide bombers / Anat Berko. — 1st ed.
       p. cm.
  Includes bibliographical references and index.
  ISBN 978-1-4422-1952-6 (cloth : alk. paper) — ISBN 978-1-4422-1954-0 (electronic)
  1. Women suicide bombers.   2. Child suicide bombers.   3. Suicide bombers—Psychology.   4. Martyrdom—Islam.   5. Arab-Israeli conflict—1993–   I. Title.
  HV6431.B477 2012
  363.32501'9—dc23

                                                              2012024452

∞™ The paper used in this publication meets the minimum requirements of American National Standard for Information Sciences—Permanence of Paper for Printed Library Materials, ANSI/NISO Z39.48-1992.

Printed in the United States of America

This book is dedicated to my mother, Claire Aslan, who, with the rest of her family, was forced out of her home in Baghdad and became a refugee at the age of ten. She and my late father, Edward, both Jews expelled from Arab countries, found refuge in the State of Israel. They raised a family and devoted themselves to building their new country and rebuilding their own lives.

Rosh Hashanah [Jewish New Year] 5773/September 2012

Contents

Foreword by Daniel Pipes ix

Preface xiii

Introduction: "Good Enough to Die, Not Good Enough to Marry" 1

1 "Just As Long As the Girl Doesn't Make a Mistake" 15

2 Hamas Deputy Prime Minister: "Whoever Sends a Woman
   on a Terrorist Attack Is *Jahil*" 31

3 The Engineer: "A Virgin in Paradise Is Like a Little Girl" 45

4 Shari'a Judge: "Women Lack Two Things: Intelligence and Religion" 53

5 The Adolescent Terrorist: "You Go to Jail, You Can Study for
   Matriculation Exams, You Get Special Considerations If
   You're in Jail" 59

6 Brother and Sister, Suicide Bombers 73

7 Special Bonuses for Each and Every *Shaheed* 81

8 Terrorist to Her Dispatcher: "Why Did You Betray Me? You
   Know I Love You" 89

9 Clerics on Women in Terrorism: "What Will She Get in Paradise,
   a Couple of Virgins?" 99

10 Salima, Mother of Seven: "My Husband Only Thinks about Himself,
    I Don't Love Him" 107

11 Nawal, Palestinian Knife Wielder: "Jail in Israel Is Better Than
   Hell at Home"   113

12 Women under Interrogation   117

13 How to Talk to Terrorists   125

14 Arab Lawyer: "Every Woman Involved in Terrorism Is a Romantic"   133

15 Nabil, Dispatcher of Terrorists: "A Pity I Sent Her to Blow
   Herself Up, She Could Have Given Birth to Three Men Like Me"   141

Afterword: Disrobe for a Terrorist Attack—Is the *Shaheeda* a Heroine?   165

Acknowledgments   181

Glossary   183

Selected Bibliography   187

Index   191

Foreword

A nat Berko has spent the past fifteen years in Israeli jails interviewing terrorists, giving her peerless authority on this subject among academic researchers, and no one has shown so great an ability as she to get interviewees to express themselves candidly. The results, published in a series of studies on personalities, circumstances, and motives, have opened a hitherto mysterious topic to public scrutiny.

After previous research focusing on male prisoners, Dr. Berko in this book turns her attention to women and children. The differences are profound, as one might expect, especially in Muslim society, where women are particularly disadvantaged. The strictures on sex that dominate much of a Muslim woman's life have deep implications for women's engagement in terrorism: Chapter 7 shows that women dream of "that thing" (i.e., sex) in paradise. Chapters 8 and 15 establish a pattern of women going on terrorist missions sometimes after having had sexual relations with their dispatchers. Chapter 11 demonstrates the remarkable fact that "a significant number [of Palestinian women] preferred an Israeli jail to their own homes" because of maltreatment by relatives; indeed, some of them pretend to attack Israelis so as to go to jail and leave their miserable home lives. Chapter 14 points to the recurring opportunity for women to escape sexual dishonor through violence.

Dr. Berko, who works at the International Institute for Counter-Terrorism in Israel, provocatively asks, "Is a woman who carried out a suicide bombing attack a smart bomb or a stupid bomb?" In other words, do these women know what they are doing, and are they effective? In reply to the first question, Berko distinguishes among a wide range of terrorists, from well-educated and hyperpolitical sophisticates to illiterate peasants. As for their efficacy, with the exception of those sophisticates, generally women do a poor job, killing themselves without doing serious damage to Israelis.

The book contains a wealth of information, much of it presented as raw data in the form of reports on conversations. Others can benefit from Dr. Berko's valuable work to draw their own conclusions. Some of the major themes that emerge from the pages ahead include:

- The utility of women in terrorism (due to their raising fewer suspicions than men) contrasts with their poor performance (due to their being less ideological).
- Tension is apparent between admiration for a woman who forgoes her life and suspicion that her self-sacrifice involved some form of shame, anger, or guilt. As a Palestinian journalist put it, when a woman carries out a terrorist attack, others joke that "she blew up masturbating. . . . She didn't get enough sex. . . . She wasn't satisfied."
- In some cases, desperate circumstances impel women to desperate actions in the hope of ending their wretched existences. As one accomplice to a suicide bombing put it, "Those girls don't think they will go to jail, they think they will die. They think death is better than living the way they do."
- They want to go to jail to solve personal or family problems. Reading court records reveals that many females in prison tried to escape forced marriages or were accused of improper behavior or beaten at home. They tried to stab soldiers, waved knives in the air, or threw acid in the general direction of an Israeli soldier at a roadblock. Being sent to jail in Israel served for them as a safe haven.
- Terrorists see Israelis as less than human, but after spending time in Israeli jails, where prisoners (as one put it) "give respect and are respected," their perceptions often change, at least during the time of their detention: "The Jews take better care of me than us [Arabs]."
- To a surprising extent, women engage in violence to associate closely with men to whom they are physically attracted. As a defense lawyer put it, "I never met a single woman who was motivated by ideology . . . every woman involved in terrorism is a romantic."
- For these reasons, Dr. Berko finds that a "significant number" of female prisoners prefer remaining in an Israeli jail to returning to their own homes. As one put it, "I would rather be in jail, they help me here."
- Female prisoners generally come from broken families or families lacking a strong, protective male.
- The whole notion of women waging war and going to prison upsets Palestinian concepts of order. In the illustrative words of the deputy head of Hamas, "If a woman is in jail for a long time she will become a man" (meaning she gets wrong-headed ideas of independence).
- Accordingly, Palestinians keep their distance from female security prisoners: "She's a heroine, but I would never let my son or brother marry a woman like that."

In passing, Dr. Berko also reveals much about the daily circumstances of female security prisoners in Israeli jails. Because they are part of a support network with other imprisoned women, many are unrealistically optimistic about how they will be recognized by their communities after their release.

Anat Berko's sensitive treatment of a repugnant topic brings the mentality and social universe of Israel's female enemies to light, and the insights she gleans will profit all engaged in counterterrorism concerning Muslim women.

Daniel Pipes (DanielPipes.org) is president of the Middle East Forum.

Preface

We'll be good together . . . One of my girlfriends will let me use her apartment so that we can be together . . . Bring condoms. You have some, right?" That was the message received by a sixteen-year-old Israeli boy, tempted by promises of sexual adventures into meeting a girl he didn't know, victim of a plot to kill him.

"Do you have a girlfriend? . . . Are you going to tell your friends about us? . . . We have to . . . Are you younger than I am? . . . Do you want to have sex??? I want to, but I don't want to get pregnant . . ."

Sixteen-year-old Yair had a secret he didn't tell anyone. He thought he had met a girl older than himself who wanted to enter into a sexual relationship. Houda even made sure to ask, "What if your mother sees the condoms and finds out about us?"

"Don't worry," he said, "she won't."

Houda manipulated Yair, weaving her web around him until he was trapped in a classic male adolescent fantasy. Their chats grew longer and more frequent, and his desire to meet her increased daily. Finally he went to the designated meeting place, where not only Houda was waiting for him, but her friends as well, and they killed him in cold blood.

The Houda I visited in jail hadn't changed. Using guile, ingenuity, and cruelty she established her control over the other security prisoners until she became their spokeswoman and unchallenged leader. Even after she was moved to a different wing because of her negative influence on the other prisoners, her shadow still hovered and threatened them. Any prisoner who dared to stand up to her or who made her angry risked having boiling margarine mixed with sugar thrown in her face and being scarred for life. There are prisoners who will remember Houda forever.

For the most part, women in Palestinian society are pawns in men's hands, passive during the stages of planning and carrying out terrorist attacks. They do not become terrorists as the next step in a life of crime, as opposed to some of the men. The examination of trial transcripts and discussions I held with Palestinian intellectuals made me suspect that the women sent on suicide bombing missions were often sexually exploited: "You're going to die anyway, so what difference does it make . . . ?"

Carrying out a terrorist attack is supposed to upgrade the status of the terrorist's family, but the benefits received by the families of female suicide bombers do not equal those received by the families of male suicide bombers. The families of female suicide bombers are discriminated against because of the circumstances under which women become terrorists, usually different from the men's. What motivates a woman to become a terrorist? What terrible thing did she do, or what terrible thing was done to her, that made her try to purify herself in such an awful way?

In many instances, women do not join a terrorist organization to carry out an attack. Rather, the organization seeks them out and recruits them close to the prospective date. The various organizations are in serious competition over the number of attacks, and they hold a kind of head count to compare results.

Some of the chapters of my first book, *The Path to Paradise*, about suicide bombing terrorism, were devoted to women. Since its publication I have focused on women and children and on the interaction between women terrorists and their dispatchers. My research indicates that women are simultaneously important and unimportant. This book examines the subject in depth and provides new insights and various ways of viewing the involvement of women and adolescents in the service of terrorism. To gain a broader knowledge of the issue I interviewed Muslim clerics, terrorists, dispatchers of female terrorists, lawyers, and senior members of the Muslim community, both inside and outside prisons. The book is also based on conversations with female terrorists themselves. I spent many days observing military terrorist trials and reading transcripts and indictments. For the past fifteen years I have met with security prisoners in Israeli jails, among them those who orchestrated and carried out murderous terrorist attacks against Israeli civilians. The most notable was Ahmed Yassin, the late founder and leader of the Hamas movement. In recent years I have focused on women and adolescents who participated in terrorist attacks.

Some of the names of the people and places in this book are fictitious, in part because of the extremely personal nature of the revelations of the people I interviewed. We shared a desire to deal with genuine issues without having them exposed to harm. What is written here is based on conversations held with people whom many consider impossible to understand. The special, close relationships I developed with them enabled me to document our meetings and try to understand their personalities and motives. I am certain that some of the events recounted in this book will open wounds for many Israelis.

Within the words I looked for answers to the questions that prompted me to conduct this study: Can a woman be "good" according to the criteria of Palestinian society and a terrorist at the same time? Is the involvement in terrorism a sign of Palestinian women's liberation, or is it another way of oppressing? Who are they, the Palestinian women who dared to leave their homes (in most cases without their fathers' permission), what made both them and Palestinian children join the terrorist machine? Can the human bombs of Islamic terrorism be stopped, and if so, how? Is a woman who carried out a suicide bombing a smart bomb or a stupid bomb?

Introduction: "Good Enough to Die, Not Good Enough to Marry"

She's been in prison for a week. Very sensitive because of the burns and scarring. She cries a lot. It hurts her to be like that. She cries and screams, but she doesn't curse. Twenty-one years old, from the Jabaliya refugee camp in the Gaza Strip, she is in bad shape. Her whole body is covered with burns, even her fingers. She cannot dress herself, so the women in her cell help. It is hard to talk to her; she is introverted and wounded by everything people say to her, as if they were laughing at her or looking at her in a way she didn't like . . ." That was Farah's description of Muneira, a would-be suicide bomber who was arrested at the Erez crossing in the northern Gaza Strip in 2005, on her way to Israel with an explosive device strapped under her clothing. When she was young a gas pipe in the house exploded, and the fire left her entire body scarred. According to the court transcript, she was raped twice, once when she was eleven, and again at sixteen.

Muneira was detained at the Erez crossing on her way to a suicide bombing attack at the Tel Hashomer Hospital in the Tel Aviv area. Her original target was the Soroka Hospital in Beersheba, where Israeli doctors had treated her burns after the fire. However, since many Arabs receive treatment in Soroka, her dispatchers decided it would be preferable to have her blow herself up in Tel Hashomer, where she would kill more Jews. Arriving at the Erez crossing, she was required to undress in front of the security cameras, and it was discovered that her underpants had been soaked with liquid explosive and were attached to electric wires and a detonator.

Muneira was one of the few would-be suicide bombing terrorists who spoke at their trials. When her punishment was being considered she said, "I received a terrible blow. Not one blow, many. I flunked out of university and my father always treated me badly; he used to hit me a lot and told me I would never get

1

married. He said I would be a cripple for life. I have third-degree burns from my neck to my knees, and psychologically I am also wounded. Now I am in jail, and the other girls don't like to see me like this, and they don't treat me well, and that upsets me a lot. My health is poor as well. I can't use my left hand or move the little finger of my right hand. I am sorry for what I did. The man who sent me exploited me—I was disappointed in love. I had a boyfriend in Gaza. I look at other women, at how healthy they are, and that influences my moods. I wanted to end my life. I wanted to blow up at the [Erez] crossing, and that meant ending my life. I ask the court not to give me a long sentence because I want to get treatment. I want a future, I want my life. Now there is the withdrawal from Gaza, things are better, and now there will be peace.[1] I regret what I did. I have already asked for medicine for my mental state. What I said on television was only because people were watching."

During the trial Muneira removed her militant mask that she had worn for the media and revealed herself as a terrified woman. Her family had looked for a way to get rid of her, and she found a way to do something that would change her situation, despite, and perhaps because of, her sense of inferiority.

I went to Muneira's cell to talk to her. On the way, Houda stopped me to tell me that "she won't talk to anyone, not even me. She can't say two words without crying, because she thinks everyone is talking about her or laughing about the way she looks. The girls try to talk to her and be gentle, but it's hard."

Muneira's case is also exceptional because her parents pushed her into trying to blow herself up, since "in any case," they said, "no one will marry you." They knew she was being fitted for an explosive belt in their house. During the trial her lawyer said that "the defendant suffered from extreme emotional disturbance and caused severe problems for her family, which led to the situation in which the tragedy noted in the indictment occurred. Both father and mother motivated their daughter to carry out a suicide bombing attack to remove themselves of the burden of their daughter. . . . Her parents' rejection worsened after she was burned in a fire in their home. . . . It is obvious that the people who sent her [on her terrorist mission] exploited her difficult situation, and actually, the defendant is a victim of both her family and her dispatchers."

I entered her cell in the morning as the prisoners were getting themselves ready for the strict daily prison routine. We greeted each other in Arabic, and she studied me carefully when she saw, to her amazement, that the other prisoners seemed quite friendly toward me. This was during my fifth year of visiting female security prisoners for my research. That made me an old acquaintance, someone from outside the prison whom they could talk to, and it meant a great deal to them, considering the circumstances of their imprisonment. I looked at Muneira and saw a nice-looking girl with light brown skin and straight hair. Her eyes were sad and expressed her emotional dissociation. It was clear that being in prison for the first time was a shock and that she was not yet used to her new surroundings.

Although her hair was covered with a *hijab* (head scarf worn by Muslim women) and she wore a *jilbab* (a loose traditional Arab dress), I could see the scars on her neck. They looked like the roots of a plant twisting around her neck and winding down to the palms of her hands, which were stiff and deformed, the result of the fire.

"Please, forgive me," she whispered without looking up, "I can't talk." Her eyes, her voice, her body language, seemed to beg for the earth to swallow her, not to be seen by anyone. She was withdrawn and presented a picture of distress. She had little contact with the other women prisoners beyond the help she needed to carry out simple, everyday actions. She was the last woman prisoner sentenced by the military court in Gaza before the disengagement in 2005, when the Jewish settlements were evacuated and the Israeli Defense Forces (IDF) pulled out. She refused to speak to her family and seemed very angry with them for the part they had played in the suicide bombing attack she had tried to carry out.

Deciding to do the attack was perhaps the first time Muneira had actively made a choice. Although it was made under pressure, it changed her position in both her family and society. Suicide bombers such as Muneira are handled by terrorist dispatchers who work on the bombers' urge to kill themselves by killing others as well. Altruistic suicide, as described by Durkheim,[2] is different from suicide caused by depression.

Can suicide bombers be motivated by altruism? In my opinion, they cannot. Suicide bombers usually act on impulse and the desire for immediate gratification, expecting sexual and material rewards immediately after the explosion. They have a strong need for recognition, if not during their lives, then at least after their deaths. The respect they will have as *shaheeds* will be reflected glory for their families. They imagine the songs that will be composed about them and the posters bearing their pictures that will be hung throughout the city.

In many instances, would-be suicide bombers describe a sensation of elation before they leave on their missions, the "groom syndrome." Youmana, a suicide bomber I interviewed, described the day she left to blow herself up as "the most beautiful day" of her life. During the month before the attack, she felt she was going to carry out the most important act of her life, delivering her family from the agony of the grave and providing a "get-into-paradise-free card" for seventy relatives, whom she was supposed to meet there.[3] Her desire to kill Jews was a secondary consideration. She was the only woman who told me about the link between the elation she felt before the attack and the supreme happiness of a bride on her wedding day. On the other hand, there were many women who told me it was the worst day of their lives, and they felt that from the moment they decided to blow themselves up they were falling into a bottomless pit. Remarks made by most of the women led me to the almost certain conclusion that from the day they started along the path to a suicide bombing attack, they were highly committed and expected to succeed.

Would-be female suicide bombers are frightened women who are first and foremost victims of Palestinian society. The victim then becomes the aggressor. The hypothesis is supported by studies[4] I carried out with Professor Edna Erez from Illinois University about the motivation of suicide bombers, especially women. There has been an increase in the number of women participating in terrorist attacks since 2000, when the Al-Aqsa *intifada* popular uprising began.

Many attacks in which women participated were precipitated by a specific situation of victimization. The turning point was Wafa Idris, the first female suicide bomber, a Red Crescent worker who was dispatched to blow herself up in a clothing store on Jaffa Road in Jerusalem on January 27, 2002. The explosive device was transported in an ambulance, and Wafa was wearing a Red Crescent uniform at the time. Her husband, who was also her cousin, had divorced her because she could not bear children. The divorce meant she could not start a new life, so she decided to become a suicide bomber and take the lives of others. A victim of her own sterility and a life without substance or hope, she became a role model and a symbol for other women in her situation. The Palestinian terrorist organizations were careful to turn her personal tragedy into a myth, fostering it as a model story and using it to recruit other women. For five straight months after Wafa blew herself up, women carried out suicide bombing attacks. So far, ten women have blown themselves up in terrorist attacks.

The first *shaheeda* to become a heroic victim in Islamic history was Sumayyah Um Ammar ibn Yasir,[5] considered one of the first martyrs for the sake of Allah and a role model for every *mujahed* (jihad fighter), according to the legacy of Muhammad and his path.[6] Sumayyah, her husband and son, and their heroism are described in the book by Muneir al-Ghadban.[7] They were among the first in Mecca to accept Islam and as a result were tortured by Abu Jahl, the prophet Muhammad's enemy. He had them dressed in iron armor and left in the sun to die. Muhammad saw their suffering and told them not to worry because they were on their way to paradise, and that "the breezes of paradise already blow in your hearts and extinguish your agony." His words soothed them, and Sumayyah did not break under torture or renounce her belief, becoming the first *shaheeda* in Islam. According to the story, Abu Jahl stabbed her in her genitals and killed her. Sumayyah was the mother of Ammar, who fought at the side of Muhammad and also erected the first mosque.

The use of women in terrorism is not unique to the Israeli-Palestinian conflict, and radical organizations regard female bombers as the ultimate weapon. A large number of women have been active in the terrorist Tamil Tigers in Sri Lanka, the Kurdish PKK, and Chechnya. Their total number reaches about 30 percent of the various organizations. Al-Qaeda also recruits women for suicide bombing missions in Iraq. At the beginning of 2008 it sent two women with Down syndrome to carry out attacks, detonating their explosive belts by remote control. Hamas has threatened to flood Israel with female suicide bombers, and Al-Qaeda has made similar threats toward the West. Sometimes women are raped and then forced to blow themselves up to expunge the shame.[8]

Orchestrating a suicide bombing attack is not an entirely male province. Sometimes there is a female involved in the recruiting process. She is generally an older woman whose role is to keep up the morale and strengthen the will of the would-be suicide bomber. Sometimes she hides with the male terrorists in a safe house or helps them recruit women for attacks. On many occasions, since she is older, men and women regard her as a reliable mother figure, someone who can be trusted. She strengthens the resolve of the would-be suicide bomber to blow herself up by expressing sympathy and providing moral support. One prisoner told me that when she was in the safe house, "there was an old woman who took care of me, like a mother. She didn't let me talk to anyone, not even to my own mother."

Farhana Ali,[9] a terrorism analyst, has studied the possible reasons for a rise in the use of female suicide bombers in Iraq. She notes the desire for revenge felt by a mother whose son had been killed. In Saddam Hussein's Iraq during the war with Iran from 1980 to 1988, women were trained to fight and defend themselves. Many women who lost their husbands in the war felt the need to protect their families from foreign soldiers and demonstrate their nationalist feelings. Ali noted that social pressures had turned some Muslim women in the conflict areas into terrorists. Iraqi women whose modesty had been defiled in one way or another turned to suicide bombing terrorism. In Shi'ite circles the women were exposed to the anti-Sunni and anti-American sermons of an Iranian *imama* (female preacher). The propaganda was usually effective with women who harbored feelings of guilt or embarrassment. My research has shown many similarities between what happened in Iraq and what put Palestinian women into their impossible situation. The Palestinian terrorist organizations value such women, but they are not part of a women's liberation agenda. The organizations have a well-defined gender hierarchy; women do not fill key roles and are often oppressed by the men. They are trained differently and assigned different functions. They are considered weak and in need of male protection. Women bombers have advantages, especially the relative ease with which they pass through security checks and the relatively low level of suspicion they arouse. Sometimes they are teamed with children for camouflage and to make them look decent and innocent. Israeli Knesset member Avi Dichter, former head of the Israel Security Agency and minister of the interior, called them the "soft and easy bomb" (personal communication, 2010).

Arab society is ambivalent regarding the place of women in the struggle. On the one hand, they have more value than men because of their particular capabilities, and on the other, their motives are suspect. There is concern that perhaps they have a need to cleanse themselves of some bad or improper act. There is also the fear that carrying out military actions might give them ideas above what is considered their station. Al-Qaeda women resented it when Ayman al-Zawahiri, bin Laden's second in command, said that women supported Al-Qaeda fighters on the Internet but were not themselves fighters in the organization. He added that the role of women was to care for the families of Al-Qaeda fighters. He made the statement following women's demands for military ranks and formal recognition, a demand that was not honored.[10] I heard a similar opinion voiced by Abu Tir, deputy head of the de facto Hamas administration, whom I interviewed in 2007, who said that "I would not want someone from [my] family to marry [such a woman] because she would be the master of the house."

In addition, the nature of the terrorist activities undertaken by women and the reasons they undertake them are strongly criticized. Concerning Houda, who enticed an Israeli teenager to his death, an Arab intellectual told me that "she was looking for sex; it all began with an erotic conversation and in the end she said, this is my chance to do it. She was having sex with men in the Palestinian Authority in Ramallah. Her father was old and powerless. Her mother was the dominant figure at home, which is why she went out of control. In Arab society, because of the pressure the girls are under, it explodes, and that was why she engaged in sexual relations. It's like letting a bird out of the cage. She brought [the victim] to Jerusalem and took [killed] him." Other people I interviewed told me the same thing.

Marwan, a Palestinian journalist, told me how Palestinian society views such women. "There are," he said, "girls who turn to attacks after they have been sexually exploited; they stab policemen. The fifteen-year-old sister of a woman I know went to the Old City in Jerusalem, waved a knife in the face of a border policeman and was detained. The Department of Welfare got involved, and it turned out that her father had had sex with her, as had some of her brothers and uncles, and she wanted to escape. . . . For example, Wafa Idris was divorced, and every woman who has been thrown out by her husband bears the stigma of *sharmouta* [whore]. Divorce is a curse; being divorced is like being a whore, *metalaka* [divorcee]. People ask, 'Who is that girl,' and get told 'Shut up, she's divorced . . .' These are women who rebelled, who didn't agree to stay within bounds, who didn't automatically assume that there was something wrong with being a woman, that it's her fault if she is sterile because the male is a symbol of potency. In Nablus they tell a joke about relations between the sexes: Someone asks, 'Why did you divorce her?' and the other answers, 'Because she didn't scream with pleasure when we had sex.' The bottom line is that the woman has to obey the man in everything, including the sounds she makes, so that the man will think what he is doing is good. If she doesn't, he has to find someone else, someone who knows how to appreciate him."

Marwan seems amused and angry at the same time. He is a liberal, but he admits that sometimes the inflexible dictates and concepts of society create tension concerning the woman's place in marriage. "You want to know what woman is a terrorist? I'll tell you. The woman who rebelled, crossed the lines, hung around with men, couldn't be controlled. Arab men don't like that kind of woman, they will call her a *shaheeda*, but subconsciously, they will call her a *sharmouta* . . .

"There's this joke you hear every time a woman carries out a terrorist attack: 'She blew up masturbating . . . She didn't get enough sex . . . She wasn't satisfied.' A lot of young Arab girls are victims of sexual assault, one way or another. Mostly during the first years of adolescence, thirteen to seventeen. I don't know a single girl who hasn't experienced it. They stay at home and there are always male neighbors, and if there is a chance to do something, they take it. In a car, an abandoned building, when their parents leave the house or in a girlfriend's house. They tell their parents, 'I'm going to visit a girlfriend,' and there were a couple of cases where girls were caught in the act. Most of the fights between *hamoulas* [extended families] are over things like that but you never hear the real reason; all of a sudden they start shooting at each other. After a suicide bombing attack they say she was a heroine, but in secret or over coffee in a café they say, 'She was a bad woman and had problems.' Everyone knows and no one says anything; it's a conspiracy of silence. It's amazing."

The Israeli legal system is part of the conspiracy of silence. An attorney told me that if a female terrorist admits to a crime, the indictment and sentence will not mention what she did before the attack. Sometimes the indictment will be worded discreetly so as not to embarrass her or her family. Ignoring the circumstances is bad when it comes to prevention: if more were known about what happened beforehand, the stories might deter other women from carrying out terrorist attacks, which bring neither honor nor glory.

Marwan continued, saying, "If a man rapes or gets raped, it isn't important. A woman has to be obedient, in society and at home; people will say, what was she thinking, she left home without permission to carry out an attack? She must have met men who enlisted her where they were hiding, and bad things happened [i.e., sexual relations] . . . and people build on their fantasies. There are things a woman is forbidden to do, only a man is allowed to do them, like smoking. A woman is only allowed to smoke a hookah. A woman who smokes cigarettes is imitating a man, and that makes her a whore, because smoking cigarettes is a male prerogative. Girls who smoke *nargilas* will only pass them to other girls, because no man is allowed to take it from the mouth of a woman." I wrote a note for myself: "In the eyes of Muslim society, a female terrorist is like a woman who smokes, she does something not appropriate for women, imitates male behavior, and is considered wanton."

"A woman who winds up in jail," said Marwan, "regardless, her status is inferior. She is not the ideal woman. She is a woman serving a jail sentence. As to what goes on in jail, people's imaginations know no bounds. I don't think anyone would want to marry such a woman. She is not normative; she is deviant, atypical and crossed all the lines. In a macho society she is a woman who has taken a step in the direction of being a man, a woman who lost her femininity in a society ruled by men. They say she is a heroine; for the sake of national honor they praise her, say she participated in the struggle and was a patriot, but she's not a woman an

Arab man wants to marry. They will ask what made her do it, how did she leave the house, go around with an operative from some terrorist organization; that's not something positive. A woman who carries out a suicide bombing attack has meetings her family knows nothing about, rides in cars with men. A lot of men are involved in it. An Arab man begins to think, 'What do I need a woman like that for?' The overwhelming majority of Arab men will not want a woman like that. Obviously, in public no one will criticize her. They will always say that she was a fine person and participated in the struggle and a heroine, but with all due respect, that's not her role in life. That's not the woman the Arab man is looking for; she's a problematic woman. The atmosphere in jail is not one of respect; being in jail does not add respect; jail is jail!"

As Marwan's remarks reflect, the concepts of femininity and masculinity, like the traditional roles of men and women, are preserved and sanctified in Palestinian society. In Palestinian society in general, not only in the terrorist organizations, the more militant roles are reserved for the men. Are similar qualities required of a male suicide bomber, or is he also just a piece of disposable equipment? If so, for the sake of a suicide bombing attack, can a mere woman suffice? The Palestinian women I interviewed did not feel that the terrorist organizations that recruited them genuinely empowered them. Women in the organizations usually do not wear uniforms during training but remain in their traditional dress, which covers their bodies and limits their movements. A woman at a shooting range wears a *hijab*, *jilbab*, and gloves. If she can barely move, how can she fire a weapon?

Regarding the relative marginality of women in the Israeli-Palestinian conflict, Marwan said that in his opinion, women don't count, even if they consider themselves leaders: "There are no women leaders in an Israeli jail today. [All the female prisoners mentioned in this book were released in 2011 after the Hamas released the kidnapped Israeli soldier Gilad Shalit. When Hamas negotiated with Israel about the prisoners list, it didn't even know how many women were in jail, and it forgot to put their names on the list, in spite of the fact that the deal said all female prisoners would be released.] Most people don't even know their names, not even Houda's. Most people don't know who she is. She was a problem before; then she met a boy on the Internet. The trouble she made in jail only hurt her. I don't see a typical Arab boy going to live with a girl like that. People know more about the men; what they did is more widely recognized. That's the man's job, and here and there you have the exceptional case of a woman. It's not the general rule because the girls are guarded and women understand that it's not their role. It's hard to get into Israel, so there are logistical reasons for recruiting women and children."

As far as I could determine, Houda did not have sexual relations with the Israeli boy she killed, but for Marwan it was a matter of fact that she did. Rumors are extremely powerful in Arab society, and a rumor can be the basis for an "honor killing," murdering a woman to preserve the honor of the family. Young male security prisoners complained that they were recruited for terrorist attacks with the threat of "If you don't, we'll say your sister hangs out with men."

In general, female members of terrorist organizations hide their activities from their families. Organizations that accept women do not have to humiliate them, but sometimes the women are sexually harassed and respond passively. In Iraq there were reports that rape was used to coerce men and women into participating in terrorist attacks lest their shame be publicly revealed. The terrorist organization serves as a kind of surrogate family and increases the sense of belonging. One would-be female suicide bomber told me that she met boys when she was in training, and "they treated me like their sister."

Some of the women are required to have sexual relations with men before an attack. Their prospective certain deaths serve as a kind of moral justification. The men say, "What difference does it make, in any case you're going to blow up." There were terrorist operatives who told me that a woman just disrupts the agenda. Ahmed Yassin, Hamas founder killed by the IDF in 2004, told me when I interviewed him in jail in 1996 that "there is no need for them, there are many men to do the work."

The female terrorists have neither the need nor the desire to imitate the behavior of Arab men. Their very presence spurs the men to action, their presence and the way they challenge and defy the men verbally, something Arab men are not used to. During the *jahilia* (the period of ignorance before Islam), bare-breasted women were used to inflame fighters before they left for battle.

Nabil was a terrorist dispatcher who sent Darin, a female suicide bomber, to blow herself up at an IDF roadblock in 2002. He told me that he did not want to accept Darin, who said she wanted to become a *shaheeda*, but that she pressured him. He said, "The story of Darin is important. She took a knife and called me every day and said, 'I'm watching television and I want to kill. I want to feel I did something for the Palestinian struggle.'" A similar story is that of Ikhlas, the terrorist who escorted the female suicide bomber to the Sbarro restaurant in Jerusalem in 2001. Before that she had detonated a bomb in a supermarket, but there were no casualties. After her "unsuccessful" attempt, she called Abdallah, her dispatcher, and warned him that if he didn't send her on a "serious attack to kill Jews," she would go to a different dispatcher. She asked, "What kind of man are you?"

The women who want to participate in terrorist activities find a way to join the struggle, sometimes even as human shields for wanted terrorists leaving a mosque. In one case in the Gaza Strip, terrorists hid in a group of women who were wearing *hijabs* and *jilbabs*, and some even wore female clothing themselves. The women were middle-aged, and thus it was not considered inappropriate for men to be so physically close to them.

Women's involvement in the terrorist organizations in general, and in attacks in particular, is seen to help raise awareness about the Palestinian cause. Their involvement is widely covered by the media and drives public opinion. The media still relate to women terrorists and especially to Muslim women terrorists as exceptional, strange creatures and report the issue at length. Arab women are viewed by their society as submissive, obedient, and passive. Superficially it might seem that female terrorists are feminists, standard-bearers in the struggle to raise their inferior status. However, both Arab-Palestinian society and the terrorist organizations make it only too clear that even if women do participate in the struggle against Israel, they will never achieve equality. Every time a woman sets foot outside the family unit and enters the public arena, she is doing something irregular. Her most important roles remain first of all bearing children, preferably male, obedience, and serving her husband and family members. One mother whose daughter blew herself up said she would have been happy if her son had done it, that would have been normal, but her daughter should have gotten married and had children, not become a *shaheeda*.[11] The authority and strict, well-defined boundaries of the patriarchal family have been weakened by satellite television, the Internet, and cellular phones. Nevertheless, Palestinian men still find it hard to accept that women can perform deeds that are regarded as masculine.

As far as Palestinian men are concerned, a woman in a situation perceived as military or a woman in jail is a change in the world order. The media, especially the Internet, are a link to the outside world for a girl who should be staying at home. In certain cases it is the way women cope with the deaths of their fathers or with other family problems, an attempt to find support without the severe judgment of the people around them. Many women are recruited for terrorist activities through romantic chats on the Internet. The conversations of innocent women, who have had no experience in relationships with men, are exploited and later used for terrorist objectives and sometimes to satisfy the terrorists' sexual needs.

A Palestinian woman does everything she can to be accepted and esteemed by her *hamoula*. The interrelationships of its members are vital in everything, from safeguarding the security of the household, to economic issues, to eventually finding partners for the children. The *hamoula* functions as a patriarchal cooperative with a clearly established built-in hierarchy with women and children at the bottom, and the general good is more important than the individual good. The honor of the family, the *hamoula*, is a function of the behavior of the women, especially when it comes to modesty. During my research I often heard it said that "a girl must not make a mistake the whole family will pay for." A woman can only lose her honor, *a'rd*, she can never extend or regain it. It is a function of her sexual behavior (or lack of it), as opposed to the man's honor, *sharaf*, which can grow throughout his life. Sometimes, behind the façade of family love is a great deal of anger, distress, score settling, control, and exploitation (even sexual), all connected to the issue of family honor. What seems like a warm, loving family can be a hornet's nest of anger and accounts to be settled, situations that remain unchanged even in old age.

The loss of family honor demands that the shame be removed by killing the woman. The late Naziq al-Malaika, an Iraqi poet and feminist, wrote a poem entitled "Erase the Shame":[12] "Not a smile, no joy, not a glance / But a dagger waits for us in the hand of our fathers and brothers . . ." Any reference to a woman's body, wrapped as it is in clothing that covers it entirely, is forbidden. Only the woman's hands and face can be exposed, although sometimes even they are covered. Sensual and sexual references to women's bodies are expressed in the dream of the women in paradise—the eternal virgins.

Sheikh Ahmed Yassin told me that "Allah, who created both man and woman, created them with different potentials. A woman has fewer abilities, but she has the special ability of being able to give birth. . . . Islam believes in justice, not equality."[13] He believed that the woman's main role was bearing children; otherwise, Allah would not have created her with the "special potential." Abu Tir (deputy head of the Hamas administration) said much the same: "I am against women going out and blowing themselves up, it's a line that shouldn't be crossed. . . . A woman's place is in the home, at school, in the hospital, in doing social things. . . . I agree that she can be a 'doctor,' like you, and work at a university. It was like that in the past as well; women used to help the wounded, bandage them and give them water, that's the woman's role. I would not send a woman to blow herself up, I wouldn't agree to that. . . . I wouldn't even let my daughter go to a demonstration." The same was true when Ikhlas, who abetted the suicide bombing attack at the Sbarro restaurant, asked Abdallah to let her volunteer for a suicide bombing attack when they met in Jenin. He told her that they had enough men to carry out the attack and didn't need her. So while there are definite advantages to having a woman carry out an attack, using one is an affront to Arab masculinity. It induces men to enlist in the struggle and even to become suicide bombers, on the grounds that "if even women can blow themselves up and in that way contribute to the struggle with Israel, then we men certainly can."

Rasha, accused of attempting to carry out a suicide bombing attack, asked the court to grant her leniency because, she said, "I live in a refugee camp, a small refugee camp, and we have needs. My mother and I live alone and there is no one to take care of me. When someone asks me for something, whether a commander or a wanted man, I don't know whether to say yes or no, because there is no one who will protect me. When I was a young girl they exploited the fact that I live alone with my mother. . . . I talked to Daoud [a local terrorist operative] . . . and asked him to keep the people harassing me away, because he has influence." Rasha, having no father, asked for protection and in return had to participate in a terrorist attack.

Today women fill a variety of roles in anti-Israel terrorism. They serve as scouts, human shields, and couriers, accompany operatives to terrorist attacks, help launder money, and carry out suicide bombing attacks. As of June 2012, Palestinian women had carried out ten suicide bombing attacks and were involved in others as escorts and abettors.

Muslim women are guided and defined by a wide variety of religious prohibitions, the secrecy in which they lead their lives, and the traditional society that pressures them into bearing children and serving their families. Their place in the terrorist organizations is determined and defined by the same set of rules, which relegates them to the sidelines in secondary roles. The automatic reaction of Palestinian society and its clerics is that women have no place in "military activity" and that if, by chance, a woman should find herself in such a situation, she may very well pay the price of being stigmatized and marginalized in the society from which she came as "a woman who is no good and even a whore."[14]

NOTES

1. Despite expectations for peace and security, since Israel's unilateral disengagement from the Gaza Strip in August 2005, rockets and mortar shells have continued to be launched into Israeli territory from the Gaza Strip by Hamas, which controls the strip, and the other terrorist organizations (2010), although fewer than before Operation Cast Lead (December 27, 2008–January 17, 2009). In most instances, they are launched from within densely populated civilian areas, and in some cases from what are now the ruins of abandoned Israeli settlements. Also, since the "Arab Spring"/revolution in Egypt, there are also terror activities and missile launches by Palestinian terror organizations from the Sinai area of Egypt.

2. Emile Durkheim, *Suicide: A Study in Sociology* (1897; repr., New York: Free Press, 1997).

3. According to Muslim belief, a *shaheed* spares his or her family from the torments of the grave and assures seventy of them a place in paradise.

4. Anat Berko and Edna Erez, "Martyrs or Murderers? Victimizers or Victims? The Voices of Would-Be Palestinian Female Suicide Bombers," in *In the Name of the Cause: Female Militancy and Terrorism in Context*, ed. Cindy Ness (New York: Taylor and Francis, 2008).

5. Muneir Muhammad al-Ghadban, *Al Manhaj-ul-Harki Le Seerat-un-Nabawiyyah* (Jordan: Zarqa, 1983), 59.

6. Muneir al-Ghadban, in Reuven Berko, "The Islamic Operational Code Emerging from the Teaching of Sheikh Muneir al-Ghadban as a Guide for Islamic Fundamental Movements" (PhD thesis, University of Haifa, 2011).

7. Al-Ghadban, *Al Manhaj-ul-Harki*. Muneir al-Ghadban was born in Damascus in 1942 and became a leader of the Muslim Brotherhood in Syria. He won the Sharia' prize at Damascus University in 1967 and holds a doctorate from Al-Qur'an Al-Karim University in Sudan. He worked as a researcher for the World Center for Young Muslims writing religious propaganda and books in various fields, among them the political importance of Islam and the laws of the prophet Muhammad.

8. Phyllis Chesler, "Raping Women as a Terrorist Recruiting Tool," available at http://www.phyllis-chesler.com/417/raping-women-as-a-terrorist-recruiting-tool.

9. Farhana Ali, *US/Iraq: Suicide Bombing by Women Play Larger Role* (Oxford Analytica, 2008).

10. Associated Press, "Al-Qaida's Stance on Women Sparks Extremist Debate," *USA Today*, May 31, 2008.

11. Barbara Victor, *Army of Roses: Inside the World of Palestinian Women Suicide Bombers* (New York: Rodale, 2003).

12. "Women in Iraq: Between Conservativeness and Revolutionism," in *Women in the Middle East: Between Tradition and Change* (in Hebrew), ed. Ofra Bengio (Tel Aviv: Dayan Center for Middle Eastern and African Studies, Tel Aviv University, 2004), 134.

13. A. Berko, *The Path to Paradise: The Inner World of Suicide Bombers and Their Dispatchers*, trans. Elizabeth Yuval (Westport, CT: Praeger, 2007).

14. Anat Berko and Edna Erez, "Gender, Palestinian Women and Terrorism: Women's Liberation or Oppression?" *Studies in Conflict & Terrorism* 30 (6): 493–519.

1

❧❧❧❀❧❧❧

"Just As Long As the Girl Doesn't Make a Mistake"

When I entered the security wing after an absence of several months, the women gave me a warm welcome. Two in traditional Arab dress were playing backgammon but stopped when they saw me. One smiled and asked if I remembered our conversation some months previous. I smiled back and said, "How could I forget the taste of the juice you gave me?" Her face shone with joy. She asked me if I would say a few words to Abir, a security prisoner who had asked to talk to me on June 25, 2006, the day Israeli soldier Gilad Shalit was abducted by Hamas and taken deep into the Gaza Strip.[1] I said yes, I would.

Abir's cell was very crowded. She came to the small grille in the door so that we could talk. I said, "I thought they had already released you . . ." She shook her head, smiled, and said, "In another few months, with the help of Allah." I said good-bye and left her, but not before she had made me promise to visit her again.

I remembered my first visit with her, on the day of the Shalit abduction. I had come to interview ordinary female felons, not security prisoners, but some had been transferred to this prison after a violent disagreement had broken out between the women in their former jail. As I walked into the main prison yard, they shouted, "*Doctora* Anat!" from the other side of the fence. I walked over to them. Abir was wearing a brown *jilbab* and smiling from ear to ear. Across from the exercise yard was a flagpole with an Israeli flag waving in the breeze, and I wondered whether they resented it. I told them why I was there, and they were surprised to learn that I also spoke to regular criminal prisoners. I put my hand through the fence to shake hands with them, each one in turn, thinking privately that no man could do the same.

Abir waved to me with the embroidery she was working on. I admired it and told her she should frame it. She said, "I'll make you one just like it. Come on in,

15

you know we won't do anything bad to you, you've sat and eaten with us before."
I accepted her invitation, knowing it was important to them. The abduction of
an Israeli soldier had raised both hopes and questions regarding their own fates.
Abir said, "On Arab TV they said that maybe the soldier wasn't abducted, maybe
he ran away. Israel has been in the Gaza Strip for sixty years. I know every inch of
Gaza; where could someone hide him?" (Note: In point of fact, Israel was in Gaza
for thirty-eight years, having withdrawn the year before this conversation took
place, and Gaza was under Egyptian control before that.) I said, "We all know
that Israeli news and Arab news are two different things," and Abir and her two
cell mates laughed.

Abir said, "Not long ago a boy was abducted in Nablus, and then they let him
go." I asked whether she meant the boy with American citizenship. She nodded,
and I said, "No one wanted trouble with the Americans, not the Palestinians and
not the Israelis." They laughed again, and the atmosphere lightened.

One of the prisoners said, "You know, before I went to prison I thought all
the Jews were monsters. The TV kept saying how bad they were, but now I see
that all people are the same. I made a mistake. Ask them to let you come into our
cell, we want to talk to you."

After a while I did go into their cell, which was clean and tidy, and they gave
me fruit juice to drink. We sat together on one of the beds. Abir told me that her
brother died as a *shaheed* in a suicide bombing attack and that her fiancé, who
had been on Israel's wanted list, was killed in an assault by an Israeli helicopter. A
female cousin carried out a suicide bombing attack in 2002, and a male cousin also
died a *shaheed*. I asked the women whether they thought that people on the outside
respected them. Abir said, "People on the outside don't think of us as heroines;
they don't think about us at all. There are people who say that a girl is not a man
and shouldn't do things like that. They respect a girl for it, but it won't be easy for
her to find a husband. The women in the man's family won't respect a girl who
was in jail, but the men are respected. A girl who has been in jail is like a man, and
other women are afraid of her. The old women in the family are afraid of women
who were in jail because when they were young, the only time they left their homes
was to go to their husband's house or to the hospital. There are families that don't
let the girls go out of the house at all."

Abir began a romantic relationship with Nabil, the dispatcher who sent
her brother on a suicide bombing mission in Tel Aviv (see chapter 15), when
he came to her parents' house to pay a condolence call. She said that now that
both of them were in jail, they were going to get married. It is common for the
dispatcher who sends a suicide bomber to his death to visit the parents' house to
console and congratulate them. He often uses the situation to enlist other family
members for attacks. Not wanting to waste time, he exploits the mourning, anger,
and desire for revenge against Israel to seek a candidate for the next attack. I asked
her whether it upset her to be romantically involved with the man who had sent

her brother to his death. She said, "My brother wanted to go and blow himself up, it wasn't that Nabil wanted to send him. It doesn't bother me. If Nabil hadn't sent him, someone else would have." Her brother was apparently easy to recruit and fit the profile of a potential suicide bomber: an introverted young man on the fringes of society whose masculine identity was not well defined, with low self-esteem and in search of recognition, if not in life, then at least in death. Some time later, Abir and her cell mates were returned to the security-prisoner jail they had come from.

A few days later I asked to speak to Jemilla, about whom I had heard from several sources. She was the girl who had not spoken when she was supposed to testify in court. When a terrorist operative asked her to carry out a suicide bombing attack, she said, "No way, I'm not going to blow myself up. I like being alive." In prison she slowly achieved status among the security prisoners. She belonged to the "secular" Fatah wing, whose spokeswoman was Houda. After a power struggle between them that led to repeated violations of prison discipline, Houda was removed from the wing, and Jemilla inherited the status of leader.

A thin girl came into the room dressed in low-slung, well-worn jeans, an orange-and-black-striped cotton knit shirt, and flip-flop sandals with gold sequins pasted on them. She had wavy, shoulder-length hair and no head scarf. Her face was not made up. She had thin eyebrows and large eyes that reflected optimism and curiosity. I imagined she was about seventeen years old and was surprised to learn she was twenty-five. She smiled and said in fluent Hebrew, "Everyone thinks I'm younger than I am." She looked Western, fragile, but she broadcast self-confidence and power. According to her indictment, she was "bloodthirsty, devilish, methodical, and intent on murder and destruction."

She said, "I've seen you here many times." "Yes," I said, "and I've heard a lot about you. Now that you're the leader in this wing, I've come to talk to you to find out more." Jemilla was overjoyed. I could see she needed reinforcement and formal recognition of her position—it would be hard to take Houda's place. If Houda had not been removed from the wing, they would have had a violent power struggle. Like a beehive, there was room for only one queen.

I offered Jemilla the mineral water I had brought with me and joked that coffee would be better. She immediately called to one of the women, and a few minutes later a tray was brought in with two small glasses of coffee laced with cardamom and a plate of tiny cookies. I took a sip and said, "It not only smells good, it tastes good, but no cookies for me, I'm on a diet." Jemilla laughed. *"L'chaim"* [to life!/Cheers!], I said, raising my glass, and she smiled and sipped her coffee. The atmosphere was friendly and open, and Jemilla began to talk:

"I was born in Tulkarm and I'm twenty-five. I have a brother who is twenty-three. I studied sociology at An-Najah University in Nablus for two and a half years. My mother is a housewife and my father worked in a bakery in Israel until the *intifada*. Now he sells cheese in the West Bank. I didn't lack for anything; I'm the only girl in the family and I have everything. My father studied medicine in Greece but had to come home before he finished because his father died and he was the oldest son. He didn't want a large family, only a few children he could give everything to. Why have a lot of children and not be able to give them anything? So he said, 'Two children and that's enough, and I can give them everything they want.'" It was the first time I had ever heard anyone say such a thing about a Palestinian family. The general opinion is that the more children there are, the better, both for the sake of the *hamoula* and as a weapon in the demographic war with Israel.

Jemilla shifted on her chair to find a more comfortable position and said, "I have been here in prison for five years and I miss my family. Only my mother visits me, and I miss her the most. I haven't seen her for a month. Every time she comes, she cries and complains, 'Why did you do it, what need did it fill?' She says, 'You didn't like the life we had.'" I saw that Jemilla was looking for words in Hebrew and couldn't find them. I hold her she could speak Arabic because I understood a little, my parents came from Iraq. That made her curious, and she asked whether I had ever been there, whether my parents had gone back to visit. I told her no, never, and that surprised her. She said, "Now that there is no Saddam Hussein, maybe you could visit." She was even more surprised to learn that Jewish refugees from Iraq could not visit, even if they had been born there. The magnificent Iraqi Jewish community, which had existed since 586 BC, had been persecuted, expelled, and completely destroyed.

Jemilla continued: "My real name is like a prayer to Allah. I am not religious, I belonged to the Popular Front for the Liberation of Palestine [PFLP] even before I was sent here. I like the way they think. There is democracy for women in the Popular Front. In the [Palestinian Authority–administered] territories it is hard for women to do things, but the Popular Front respects women and thinks a woman is like a man, that she can do what she thinks; they don't treat women like furniture," she said, and pointed to the chair she was sitting on. She used that simile often.

Her Hebrew being what it was, when she said "a woman is like a man" (*ish* in Hebrew), she pronounced it like the word for fire (*esh*), and I could not help but think that a female terrorist is like fire; people keep away from it for fear of being burned. The "liberality" of the secular Popular Front was another way of attracting girls to the organization. The organization's proclaimed equality tempted women who were happy to join an organization that accepted them and seemed not to treat them as inferior. Jemilla became excited as she continued, and she explained her feminist perspective: "There are places where they treat women like furniture, and that's bad. We are also human; we think and we feel. I have everything, I don't lack for anything, and if I study and can work, I'm like a man—what makes me less than a man?" She shook her head, and I could tell that she spent a lot of time thinking about gender equality and that entering the world of terrorism satisfied her demand for some kind of recognition. "Why can a man do what he wants to and I can't? If we make the same mistake, he will be forgiven, and I will have to spend the rest of my life worrying about what I did . . ."

She talked about the kinds of mistakes women are liable to make—forbidden romantic alliances and sexual relations before marriage. She was far more ready than the other female terrorists to talk about such issues. Many of the Arab women prisoners I spoke to, both terrorists and ordinary criminals, used the word "mistake" to refer to premarital sex: "Just as long as the girl doesn't make a mistake," because the entire family would pay for it.

Jemilla continued, saying, "I already wanted to belong to the organization, the Popular Front, when I was in my first year at the university in Nablus. I liked the way they thought, not just the way they related to women, and I joined. My parents didn't know. They said, 'As long as you don't go near anything dangerous you can do as you please.'" I asked what she meant by "going near," and she said, "Something that would bring me here. My parents didn't care what I wore, but they didn't want me to get into trouble. My mother always wears a kerchief and a *jilbab*, but I wear jeans. My mother says, 'For Allah be religious, so that Allah will not be angry with you,' but my father says, 'Do what you like and when you grow up, think about it.' In most families it is the opposite, it is the mother who says do what you like and the father who uses force and says, 'Do what I tell you.'" Jemilla smiled and said that the girls in prison didn't believe her father was such a liberal; they had lived their entire lives in the shadows of their fathers' threats.

"Before I went to the university," she said, "I sat with my father every night and he said that he was familiar with university life, that I would have friends. He said, 'I want you to tell me everything you want and I'll help you, and don't worry, I don't care about other people who will say things about you, but just tell me if you have any problems.' I think about it all the time, about the first time I lied to my father about involvement in a terrorist attack, and that's what brought me here, to jail."

During the interviews I discovered that many of the women involved in terrorism had lost their fathers or had weak fathers. The absence of a father makes a girl easy prey for terrorist organization recruiters. Jemilla's father, according to the criteria of Arab society, was weak and did not raise his daughter properly. In Arab society, removing a father's protection from a girl is a terrible violation of the strict rules of accepted behavior and is liable to lead to a campaign of revenge against dispatchers, recruiters, and family members. Sometimes, to prevent the family of a female terrorist from taking revenge, the woman must sign a kind of contract stating that she herself approached the organization of her own free will and asked to carry out a terrorist attack.

Jemilla said, "At first my family was angry with me. To this day my brother won't talk to me. All the other girls in the family have to do what their parents want them to, but I do as I please. My uncles used to say to my father, 'Enough.

She needs to be like other women; she shouldn't wear what she wants to and do what she likes.' One of my uncles has one daughter and five sons, and she isn't allowed to dress the way she wants to or do what she wants to. She keeps telling me how lucky I am. My uncles complain to my mother about me. When I was first sent to jail my father was very angry and said it was entirely his fault, and that he was sorry he let me do what I pleased. He said he should have listened to my uncles, who told him I had to be kept within limits."

The intervention of her uncles, her father's brothers, in her life was not something unusual. In Western families it would be unacceptable, because the Western nuclear family is an autonomous unit, and any and all intervention is considered a violation of privacy. In Middle Eastern (Arab) families, however, the father's brothers, especially his big brother, intervene in the lives of their relatives. I remember how my father used to speak about his nieces and nephews regarding their success at school or their behavior, and I remember him taking his sister to task. That was how it was in Iraq, and for him that was how it was in Israel. Jemilla's father, like my father's sister, did not regard the intervention as an invasion of privacy. The opposite was true; it was regarded as a sign of closeness and showed that Jemilla's uncles cared about them.

Before her incarceration, Jemilla rented an apartment with two other girls in Nablus. One came from Jordan and the other from Saudi Arabia, but they both had grandparents in the Palestinian Authority–administered territories. Three Muslim Arab girls lived with no male supervision in one apartment. I asked her how the people around her received the news. She said, "It upset the older women. They said, 'It's not good for girls to live alone without a man, and it's frightening. Don't go anywhere except to the university! Your girlfriends can come to the apartment, but not boys.'"

Thus on the one hand, most older women object to the relative freedom the girls have, and on the other, there are also older women in the terrorist chain, mother figures who encourage the desire of the potential suicide bombers to blow themselves up. One Iraqi woman, about fifty-five years old, said she had recruited eighty female suicide bombers, some of whom had been raped to ensure they carried out their attacks. The recruitment process was carried out in the woman's own house from among the friends who came to visit her daughters.[2]

Older Muslim women treat young girls very strictly if they think the girls have rebelled against societal conventions. In their own youth they suffered from discrimination but internalized it, and in effect they use the same patriarchal methods and conventions to oppress young women and girls. They are the women who hold little girls down to have their clitorises excised. In Chechnya, older women participated in recruiting and escorting female suicide bombers to their targets. Many of the terrorists were regularly drugged, and some were even abducted and forced to carry out suicide bombing attacks. However, that is not the situation among Palestinian terrorists.

I kept asking Jemilla, either directly or indirectly, why she was in jail. Eventually she told me: "I escorted a *shaheed* to an attack in a market in Israel. Three people were killed. I accompanied him so that no one would suspect him. He was eighteen, a child, small. He wanted to do it because he was thinking about paradise; he thought he would go to paradise. When I talked to him about his mother and his brothers, and about his life, I asked him, 'Why are you doing this? What are you thinking?' We left Nablus on our way to the attack and he told me that there was a war and that the country was ours, and that he wanted to help and thought this was the only way he could do it. He thought he would meet girls in heaven. Paradise in Islam is better [than in other religions], because that's what Allah decided, but I don't believe it. I believe in paradise, but I also believe in life. I can do anything I want to while I'm still alive, but when I'm dead I won't be able to do anything. When they asked me why I didn't become a suicide bomber, I said that I think about paradise, but Allah gave me life. Why should I die?" It was Jemilla who chose the location for the attack. After she had looked at several places, she chose a market in the center of Israel not only as a suitable place for a suicide bombing attack, but as the place from which she could escape unharmed.

She was clearly flattered by my interest in her. All of a sudden, she said, "Do you think there is one mother who would agree to have her son die? None of the parents or brothers wants someone in their family to die. When I talked to the suicide bomber I escorted about his mother and father, I said, 'Maybe you change your mind? Maybe you don't do it? Don't you have a life?' He said, 'Maybe, if I had met you first I would have thought twice.' And then he started crying. They didn't let him talk to his mother. Our representatives [the Popular Front] told him it was forbidden. When we were on our way to the attack, he asked me to let him call his mother, and I agreed. She could tell from his voice that something was wrong and asked him what it was. He said nothing was wrong. She said, 'Come home!' I told him, 'If you want to go back, let's go back,' but he said, 'No, I don't want to.' His dispatchers didn't want him to talk to his mother so that he wouldn't change his mind."

It was obvious to Jemilla that talking to him about his family, and especially the conversation he had with his mother, had shaken him, and that his desire to blow himself up was shaky. His dispatchers knew talking to his mother was liable to make him change his mind and had specifically instructed Jemilla not to let him talk to her. For a terrorist, the mother figure is very important, and there is often a symbiotic relationship between a child or adult and his mother. Before he is married, she is the only woman that he is permitted to hug and kiss. Sometimes he pities his mother's vulnerability, and sometimes he witnesses his father's cruelty toward her, including polygamous unions. The word *umi* (my mother) had an enormous emotional importance throughout many of the conversations I had with terrorists. I heard about one case in which Israeli soldiers rushed the house of a terrorist who agreed to surrender only after his mother had asked for a megaphone and called to him. "*Ya ebni* [my son]," she said, the way a mother calls her child into the house when he is playing outside. Having heard his mother's appeal, he left the house with his hands raised, wearing only underpants to show he wasn't wearing an explosive belt, without a single shot having been fired.

Jemilla continued, saying, "The suicide bomber I escorted held my hand and gave me a ring so that I would remember him." I asked her where it was and was surprised to hear that she didn't know, she couldn't remember where she had put it. That reminded me of a conversation I once had with the late Sheikh Ahmed Yassin, the founder and head of Hamas, who had a great deal of praise for the *shaheeds* but could not remember the name of even one. That was in 1996, when the number of suicide bombing attacks was small compared to what Israel suffered during the second *intifada*. Then Jemilla said, "I heard the explosion but I didn't feel anything, just that I had succeeded." She stopped for a minute and frowned, and then she said, "I did what I wanted to. The Popular Front treated me well the whole time. There are girls who go to attacks because their families aren't nice to them, but I miss my old life. If I could go back in time maybe I wouldn't do it, not because I don't think it's the right thing to do, but because I see my mother and hear my father on a radio program about prisoners, and it hurts me every time. I believe there is a war and that both sides have people who have to do something. I think that for our side it is the only thing we can do because we don't have weapons." Jemilla never expressed regret for the deaths of innocent shoppers who had gone to the market. She also seemed quite satisfied that the boy had blown himself up. As far as she was concerned, she had carried out her mission. She also had no regret that the boy himself had died, an eighteen-year-old who wanted to talk to his mother.

She said, "I don't look for [Jewish] children to kill, but just watch television, see what happens in Gaza and the territories every day. The parents of those who die aren't in pain? They are in great pain! Look at what's going on, we don't have a home and we don't have children and we don't have anything. That hurts. I think about children, I'm not married and I don't have children, but I think about my brother's children [Note: Her brother was unmarried at the time.], about my uncle's children. Don't they want them to be like all the other children in the world who have everything? They do, believe me, they all do!" She repeated what I had heard many times from women in jail who were not mothers: "Why should your children have everything and ours have nothing?" Jemilla expressed a longing for the motherhood she did not and likely would never have—she was serving three consecutive life terms. Talking about family and children makes female terrorists very angry. On the other hand, there were male security prisoners who were gentle, and in general they did not want to appear as child killers. When Arab men kill women and children, it makes them seem less masculine, but when Arab women, whose biological clocks are ticking, kill women and children, they seem to feel that if they can't have children, then no one else should, either.

Palestinian men found a way to explain the contradiction between killing Is-raeli civilians and the claim that they were not child killers, and to neutralize their feelings of guilt. They say, "Every Israeli child will be an Israeli soldier, so we want to kill them while they are still young." Jemilla sipped her coffee and continued. "We think that something will happen because of Gilad Shalit. We think they will release us, the security prisoners. I don't think I will be here forever. From the day I got here I never thought I would spend the rest of my life here, because if I did I couldn't survive. I want to study here and not feel that I am in jail but that it's like I'm outside, because I can do almost everything I want. When I get up in the morning I tell myself that I wear what I want to, and sometimes I put on makeup. The girls say, 'Are you going to a party or something?' Every day when I get up it's like a party, because I think, maybe today they'll release me . . ."

Jemilla's hope of early release is not uncommon. Security prisoners, especially the women, feel they will stay in jail for a while and then be part of the exchange deal for the abducted Israeli soldier. They think the women security prisoners and minors will be let out first. There is some justification for this expectation: after Gilad Shalit's abduction his captors apparently demanded that all the female prisoners and minors be released from Israeli jails in return for handing over the Israeli soldier. Then, as in every Eastern bazaar, they began to raise the price and demanded hundreds of prisoners. In September 2009, twenty-one women were freed in return for a one-minute video, a sign of life.

She continued her story: "I had a boyfriend I wanted to marry, I met him in the organization. He loved me, but at first I didn't like him. Later, when I was in jail, I agreed to marry him. So far my family hasn't agreed because we are both in jail . . . My mother says, 'You are my only daughter, I want you to have a big wedding, but here in jail I can't arrange it.' My mother says it is a disgrace to tell my father I want to get married. My father says maybe I'll be released and he won't be. I was sentenced to three terms of life imprisonment, and so was he. He was involved in the attack." Jemilla's is not the first instance of a romantic attachment between two terrorists. The closeness between them is necessary for planning and carrying out the attack, but it is a chicken-and-egg question: which came first, the need for an intimate relationship to ensure the success of the attack, or the rela-tionship as a result of the planning the attack? What the West views as ordinary, legitimate relations between men and women are forbidden and dishonorable in traditional Arab eyes.

Jemilla's mother told her that she was ashamed to tell Jemilla's father that their daughter wanted to get married. She said the initiative should not come from the girl, but from the boy, who has to ask the father for her hand in marriage. The girl should speak to her mother, who would then speak to the father. When I asked her how she imagined her husband, she said, "He should let me do what I want to and not treat me the way other husbands treat their wives. I want him to be like my father, an understanding person . . . No one ever ruled me. All I had was a little brother, and I told him what to do. But when he grew up and I told him to do something, he would say to me, 'You do it!' I don't know him very well [the boy who wanted to marry her]. I have his picture, he is tallish and he has blue eyes. He is very handsome. When we were on the outside he did everything I wanted. He wanted me to be happy and satisfied all the time. We went out in Nablus to a place called Arouf. We sat there and drank and talked. I don't care what people say, not all men think the same thing about women." Jemilla's description of a relationship with a man is considered liberal and unacceptable in Arab society.

Jemilla seemed like a liberated woman who could say and feel whatever she liked, so I asked her directly, "Are you the spokeswoman for the girls here instead of Houda?" Jemilla hesitated before answering, still afraid that somehow Houda would settle accounts with her, and finally she said, "She belongs to Fatah and I belong to the Popular Front. She controlled the girls and didn't want them to talk, not even one word. It was hard all the time. She wanted us to do what she wanted, and my whole life I never did what other people wanted. She would get angry with me and say, 'Do what I want!' All you had to do was wear a tight shirt and she would say, 'You can't do that! You're a security prisoner!' If I'm a security prisoner it means I have to stop living? She wore tight shirts, so what, she could and we couldn't? She had rights, but she wouldn't let us have any. Someone came to visit me and I wanted to go [to the visiting room] and she said, 'If you go, don't come back.' Once five of us didn't go into the yard for exercise because we fought with Houda. She didn't want us in this wing because we were independent. She kept saying, 'This is my wing!' She thought that if I went with the girls who brought the prisoners their food I would be considered the leader, and she was afraid [of losing status]. I went to the visiting room and she yelled at me and wanted to hit me, but one of the guards kept her away. After that, they separated us because she threatened that the girls would spill hot water on me, and maybe hot oil."

Even though she was in solitary confinement, Houda continued to control the Fatah Tanzim wing by remote control. She even sent a note to her deputy authorizing the women to talk to me; otherwise, none of them would have said a word.

Jemilla continued, "They separated us for four days. I went back to my cell with the girls, and they took her and some others to a different jail. I don't like the way she acts. Everyone can do what they want. I don't like fights, not even with Houda. I'm not that kind of person. Maybe she thinks about what she did. She is definitely angry with me, since because of me they took her out of jail [i.e., moved her to a different jail].

"Everything about prison life annoys me. I miss my old life. I want to be outside, and I dream about it. I don't dream at night. At night I sleep like the dead; I always have. It is harder for women to be in jail than for men. The men want to carry out attacks, they make the decision and do it. There are girls who didn't make that decision. They only wanted to get away from their families. They were unlucky—people didn't treat them nicely, didn't respect them, maybe they were beaten at home. That is why some of the girls carried out attacks. Their mother and father and brothers beat them; maybe they made a mistake like improper sexual conduct. The father yells at the mother and calls her names, and the mother wants to do the same, so she takes it out on the girl. Who can she yell at? Her husband? He's Allah at home! So she yells at her daughter and calls her names, and the daughter runs away from home and carries out terrorist attacks. Maybe she doesn't say she is unhappy at home. Maybe she can't get along with the people she knows because she knows her own mind, what she wants to do. It's unacceptable, you understand, and not all parents will agree. Those girls don't think they will go to jail, they think they will die. They think death is better than living the way they do."

Jemilla was giving a direct, clear description of the situation of many women prisoners. According to what she said, many of the women who participated in terrorist attacks had not made a choice but found themselves involved because of the difficult circumstances in which they lived. She said, emotionally, "I tell such girls, if my life is hard and there is nothing in my life, I keep trying. It is better to try, it is better than dying. I try to do something all the time, even in jail, that's what I tell them. I am happy [*mabsouta*] not because I am the girls' representative, but because I can do something for them, make them think a different way. Their lives are good, and if there is something bad, it has to be changed."

Despite her dominant position and her role as wing representative, she hesitated to say she had replaced Houda. It was important for her to show me that she was prompted by a genuine, sincere desire to help the other girls. "Now," she said, "the girls are learning Hebrew and English and once a week we have a meeting. I sit with them and we talk about our dreams, our thoughts, and what we want to do when we get out of jail. I want to be a social worker. I like that kind of work. I want to be a good mother. At the meetings everyone says who she wants to marry when she gets out. Now no one wants to go back to jail. If my life is hard, I can change it. You try once, twice, and in the end you succeed. There are girls who prefer to be in jail than to be with their families or girls who want to stay in jail because a boy made fun of them [had sexual relations with them], and they ran away from the family. There are also girls who did attacks of their own free will. Most of the girls went to university. There are maybe five who ran away from home, but the others went to university and had good lives and carried out attacks because they wanted to. We don't just have no freedom in our families, we don't have freedom anywhere in society."

Jemilla was describing the desire for the normative life of a woman in her society. She wanted to have children and work in a profession perceived as feminine. In her opinion, it was better for a woman to die doing what she thought was right, even in a suicide bombing attack, than to live a life of oppression and humiliation. She spoke of free will and free choice, concepts that are basically foreign to women in Palestinian Arab society.

She looked at me for a long time and then turned the conversation to paradise and the meaning of life. She asked whether I believed in heaven and about the meaning of life in this world as compared to the next. I gave her the standard answer I always gave would-be suicide bombers: "We live here and now and have to do the best we can. In any case, it is more important for me to hear what you have to say . . ." What is absurd is that even in paradise there is no gender equality. The *shaheed* gets seventy-two virgins, while the *shaheeda* doesn't get seventy-two males, although both men and women told me that in paradise she [the *shaheeda*] would be a virgin.

Jemilla continued her discourse: "There are girls who believe that they will get what they want in paradise. Do you believe in Allah? How do you know he exists?" Many times in the course of our conversation, she tried to draw me into theoretical discussions as a kind of intellectual game. I avoided her question as delicately as possible, and she continued: "Maybe right now my life is better than in paradise. I have never seen it. There are boys there and boys here. There is water there and water here, and vegetables here as well, and honey, and sex. Someday the women prisoners will get married and have sex, once, twice. If they don't marry in this life, they will have boyfriends and they will be killed if they have sexual relations. Believe me, Arab women have sex, but they will never say they aren't virgins. It's not a problem. They will have the operation to restore the hymen. Those who have the operation live the way they want to, and then they have the operation . . ."

Members of the Egyptian parliament banned the import of a Chinese appliance that makes it possible for a woman to fake losing her hymen. It releases a red liquid that the woman can claim is blood the morning after her wedding night, because in some cases the husband's family expects to see the blood-stained sheet. The proposition to import the appliance raised a storm and led to claims that it encouraged promiscuity, which is punishable by death under the Shari'a [Islamic religious law]. So there is opposition even if it is a question of saving lives, because it would mean men would lose control over the sexual conduct of women, and as a function of that, their honor would be severely tarnished.[3]

Tikva, a prison officer who worked with security prisoners for many years, often told me about female security prisoners who asked for help in reconstructing their hymens, describing the operation as a life-saving medical process. She continued, saying, "No family is proud of having a daughter in jail, but if it's a son, they feel like a family of fighters. The men know that women in prison are exposed to male guards and what happens next, and they prefer to keep them at home. The family also knows that in a certain sense there is more freedom in jail than at home. At home they can force a girl to cover her head, but in jail she can wear jeans and a belly shirt if she wants to, and expose as much of herself as she likes. Men regard women prisoners as a burden because of the need to preserve their honor. No one, not even the most enlightened family, likes the idea of having a female member in jail. A woman's place is at home. Just joining one of the organizations means she is defying the men at home. Sometimes women prisoners are rude because, paradoxically, they have more freedom in jail than at home and can speak their minds. Women who cannot leave their parents' or husband's house can walk around the prison yard without asking permission; they can watch television and wear what they like. Women in jail are also more extreme and cruel to one another. There were cases where a woman was punished by having her sit on a hotplate . . ."

Jemilla said, "If I want to have sex, that's my decision, I'm not underage. I don't have to tell my father . . ." It seemed important to her to be very clear about sexual issues to show me that she was liberated and not afraid of anyone. In both style and content, her speech was provocative and different from all the other women I interviewed in jail. Even Houda did not allow herself to do more than hint at sex. Jemilla straightened her shoulders and said, "So far I haven't had sex because I haven't met a man I want. I haven't found the right boy, someone I can have sex with, my one and only." She spoke excitedly, and I could see she enjoyed expressing herself so freely, much more freely than the average Arab woman. I did not think she spoke that way to her friends. If she had, she would have had a reputation for being cheap and easy.

I had almost finished talking to her when she asked me shyly, "How is my Hebrew?" She told me that she spent many hours reading the Hebrew newspaper to improve her knowledge of the language. I smiled and said, "I wish my Arabic were as good as your Hebrew." That made her happy, and she said, "Before I went to jail I didn't know anything about Israeli society, but today I understand. At first I hated all Israelis, but now I see that they are people like us; they think, they have feelings. There is life here between the Israelis and the prisoners. They give respect and are respected."

I left Jemilla's cell and walked toward the wing where the Hamas and Palestinian Islamic Jihad prisoners were held. Samira, who had been wing spokeswoman for a long time, was my host and asked for me to be brought coffee. When the other prisoner had left to make it and before I even had a chance to sit down, Samira said, "Not one of us carried out an attack for the Palestinian people, that's just bullshit [*kharta*]!"

Samira sat on a white plastic chair next to a little round table. The table held materials for the small decorations the security prisoners made: sequins, beads, glue. She offered me the chair next to hers and began to talk as she carefully cut out pieces of paper. The prison yard had a net roof, and birds flew in and out. The women prisoners came closer when they saw me sitting next to the Hamas and Palestinian Islamic Jihad spokeswoman. At the time bitter battles were taking place between Hamas and Fatah. Hamas was killing Fatah activists in the cruelest ways, throwing them off roofs, shooting their kneecaps, dragging their bodies through the streets. When the fighting was over, Hamas emerged as the power controlling the Gaza Strip. "Here in the wing, what happens between Hamas and the Palestinian Authority doesn't affect us," said Samira, and began talking about other things.

"We believe," she said, "in fate, and this is the fate Allah gave us. At first our parents are angry [with us], then they come and visit, and that gives us strength. It's hardest here for those who have children." There was a booklet on the table with examples of arts-and-crafts projects. Samira waved a little bag of beads and sequins and said, "You see this? The families bring them for the girls." She shifted gears and began talking politics. "All of the decisions made by the government of Israel are really made in the United States. They decide everything in the White House, and everything comes to Israel from there. Now the United States has problems in Iraq. They went in there and said the Iraqis want democracy, which is very strange. It was the same when there were elections in the Palestinian Authority: the Palestinian people voted for Hamas and all of a sudden they say it isn't democracy."

Samira had raised a very problematic issue. The American-led West regards democracy as the only form of government that will lead to progress and modernization in the Muslim world. However, as Middle East expert Guy Bechor has noted, Islamization is as intense a process as democratization, and in several instances democracy has brought radical Islamists into power, such as Hamas in the Gaza Strip and Hezbollah in Lebanon. The same fear exists regarding the January–February 2011 revolution in Egypt, that is, that the Muslim Brotherhood will take over the country and institute an Islamic regime ruled by the Shari'a regime, along the lines of Iran, but in a Sunnah version. Samira continued and talked about "a television program you have to watch; it is called *Coffee and Cards*. The people there, fortune-tellers, knew what would happen before America went into Iraq and even about what would happen between Hamas and Fatah." She said that they could read the future in coffee grounds and had predicted the second Lebanon war between Israel and Hezbollah in 2006, and the Hamas-Fatah bloodbath.

She asked me whether I believed you could tell the future from coffee grounds. I said I knew about it and I even had an aunt who was supposed to have such powers, but I evaded answering directly. Samira was amazed that there were Jews who believed in fortune-telling. She continued, saying, "The war between the Israelis and Palestinians will never end. Even in 1995 there was the Oslo peace [She wasn't accurate; the Oslo Accords were signed in 1993.], but there was no peace between the two sides. There were attacks by Palestinians against Israeli civilians, and there were the targeted killings of Palestinians by Israel. In my opinion, if Israel agreed with the Hamas government and let them take care of things, they would make peace better than the Palestinian Authority. Hamas is ready for a *hudna* [temporary cease fire of unspecified duration] for fifteen years, because they agree that you are there, that the State of Israel exists. Hamas is better than Fatah when it comes to controlling the situation; it has a lot of power. Islam also has a lot of power. Who says that fifteen-year *hudna* means recognition of the State of Israel? If you and I fight and I say, 'Let's stop for two days,' that doesn't mean I recognize you."

It was obvious Samira, like the other prisoners in the wing, completely identified with Hamas. And it was also clear that Samira, like Hamas, had no intention of accepting Israel even though she held Israeli citizenship and was born and had grown up in Israel. Some time after I spoke to her, a *tahadiya* [lull in the fighting] went into effect between Israel and Hamas, regularly broken by rocket and mortar shell attacks from the Gaza Strip targeting Israeli civilians. It seemed that Hamas wanted an Israeli reaction as proof that Hamas continued to exist, breathe, and kick. Israel reacted at the end of 2008 with Operation Cast Lead.

NOTES

1. On October 18, 2011, Gilad Shalit was finally liberated by Hamas, in exchange for 1,027 Palestinian terrorists imprisoned in Israeli jails. Twenty-seven female security prisoners were released, including Houda, who was deported to the Gaza Strip. She refused to go, fearing Hamas would retaliate for the physical and mental anguish she had caused female Hamas and Palestinian Islamic Jihad prisoners while in jail. In the end, she was deported to Turkey and will probably reappear.

Hamas was of the opinion that all the female security prisoners would be released but erred in preparing the list, and a few remain in jail. No mistakes were made in the names of a thousand male prisoners, but the women were considered marginal, and the Hamas leaders did not even know all the names of the women prisoners.

Israel rejoiced modestly at Gilad Shalit's return, their hearts wrenched by his pallor and obvious signs of malnutrition, while the Palestinians indulged in an orgy of receptions, parties, and ceremonies held for well-fed, well-treated murderers.

The State of Israel made it clear that supreme efforts would be made to achieve the return of every soldier beyond the borders of the country. Despite the heavy price involved, the Israeli public overwhelmingly supported the exchange.

2. Qassim Abdul-Zahra and Brian Murphy, "Iraq Arrests Female Suicide Bomber Recruiter," *Huffington Post*, February 3, 2009, http://www.huffingtonpost .com/2009/02/03/iraq-arrests-female-suici_n_163505.html.

3. Joseph Freeman, "Fake Hymen Kit May Be Banned," *Huffington Post*, October 5, 2009, http://www.huffingtonpost.com/2009/10/05/egypt-fake-hymen-kit-may- _n_309737.html.

2

⚜

Hamas Deputy Prime Minister: "Whoever Sends a Woman on a Terrorist Attack Is *Jahil*"

After the Israeli soldier Gilad Shalit was abducted in June 2006, Israel arrested members of the Palestinian parliament and Hamas administration in response. Among the detainees was Sheikh Muhammad Abu Tir, deputy head of the Hamas administration, called by Hamas its "deputy prime minister." In January 2007 I went to the jail where he was being held to interview him, the first of several meetings.

I waited for him in the warden's office in the security wing of a maximum-security prison in the center of Israel. The sheikh walked in and smiled, a way of signaling that he agreed to talk. When I introduced myself, he put his right hand over his heart and nodded; we did not shake hands. He simply sat down facing me. Like ultra-Orthodox Judaism, Islam does not permit a Muslim man's hand to touch a woman unless the man and woman are married. He shook hands with the warden and said a few words to him in Arabic. Most of the time we were alone during our conversations and spoke a mixture of Hebrew and Arabic. His beard was white, and his eyes were inquisitive. I could see the remains of henna on his beard, the red henna of celebration in honor of Hamas's having won the Palestinian Authority elections. He was wearing a brown prison overall and slippers without socks despite the mid-January cold. One of the prison staff offered to bring us something to drink. He asked for mint tea, and I asked for coffee. I poured mineral water into plastic cups for both of us and made sure to refill his cup every time he took a sip. Every now and then, members of the prison staff entered the office; he smiled at them and they exchanged a few words; he was obviously on very good terms with them. He appeared flattered by my interest in him, the interest of the "doctor." Throughout the interview he addressed me as "*Doctora*" and never called me by name. I used the polite form of address and called him "*sheikh*." To break

31

the ice, I told him that all the members of my family were Jewish refugees from Iraq, that my father and mother had been born in Baghdad and that the Arabic I knew from home was "Jewish Arabic," the language of Babylonian Judaism, which has slowly died out since the expulsion of the Jews from Iraq that followed the founding of the State of Israel.

We spoke freely, and the sheikh told me about himself. "I am fifty-six years old," he said. "I live in Sur Baher in East Jerusalem, and I have a problem with my Israeli identity card. They took it away from me . . ." Sheikh Abu Tir, deputy head of the de facto Hamas administration, actually complained that his Israeli identity card had been taken from him. He could not vote in Knesset elections, but the ID card brought him and his family the same benefits every Israeli citizen received, including social security benefits and medical insurance. There was an irony and absurdity to his complaint: a member of the Hamas administration, which not only calls for the annihilation of the State of Israel but does its best to bring it about, was upset because the State of Israel had taken away his access to health insurance.

He continued: "I have five daughters and two sons. My oldest daughter made me a grandfather, and I have three granddaughters and one grandson. If a man is in jail, after a year his wife can ask the Shari'a court for a divorce. He doesn't have to give her one, but the court can decide otherwise." We talked about the fact that in Islam, as opposed to Judaism, a woman can receive a divorce without her husband's consent. Abu Tir laughed and said he knew a famous divorce rejectionist who had gone to jail because he refused to release his wife.

"I married three women," he said, "but I only lived with one at a time. When I had two wives, the first and the second, it was all right when I was at home, but when I went to jail they fought."

"What did they fight about?" I asked.

"I wasn't there to take pictures," he said. He continued, saying, "My first wife is fifty years old, the second is thirty-four, and the third is thirty-three."

I couldn't help laughing. "Tell me, each one of your wives is younger than the last?" He said, "It's just by chance, people like me . . ."

"People or women?" I asked.

He seemed amused by our conversation, although perhaps a little embarrassed as well. On the one hand, his masculinity was being noted, but on the other, he did not want to present himself as a womanizer.

"No," he said, "I talk to men, not women. I have greater love and respect for women than what you think. I have great respect for my ex-wife. Our house has two floors; my first wife lives on the ground floor with the children, and I live on the second floor [with the third wife], and there are no arguments. The children sleep with their mother but the house is open to them, the second floor as well. I eat with their mother [wife number one], and my third wife comes downstairs, and we sit and talk. My second wife went back to her father's house with my daughter after the Shari'a court granted her a divorce on the grounds that I was in jail all the time. Sometimes my daughter comes and sleeps with her sisters. There is respect. A lot of my family is in jail, but the children love each other and get along well. If my second wife remarries, I will take my daughter to live with me. That's the way it is usually done. When I was outside, my daughter was with me and not with her mother. She only visited her mother." One can assume that his second wife will never remarry because she doesn't want to lose her daughter.

I asked him about the involvement of women in terrorism. He said that as far as he was concerned, the participation of women in the *muqawamah* (struggle) was unacceptable. "According to our religion, a woman is respected. She is my wife, my sister, my daughter, and we respect her so that she will grow up and be a support for the next generation. She is a wife, a sister, she is everything, and we will respect her, respect her, respect her." Several times during our conversation he said, "You know, you grew up in an Iraq house, you were brought up in those values."

He continued, saying, "It is forbidden for a girl to live outside the house, especially to live in jail. Even if we send her to study at a university we don't feel good about it. The university is there to teach her how to help society, and the work of students is not to detonate bombs. I have a daughter who is studying at the university, but I don't let her meet [people] outside. I don't even let her participate in a march or go to a demonstration. My son would never marry one of those girls who got out of jail. People know it's hard for women to be in jail. If a woman is in jail for a long time, she will become a man. When a woman is released from jail, her ideas and her personality change, and she thinks she is a leader, a heroine because she was in jail. She is a heroine, but a woman has to stay a woman and preserve her femininity. What is it worth if she never has children and a home, never gets married? She has more freedom in jail than at home. But at home there is a family atmosphere, respect, a father, a mother, a brother. There are accounts that have to be settled at home that don't have to be settled in jail."

Abu Tir claimed, in effect, that there was something wrong with the ethical-moral system of a woman who was in jail and that a woman who lived with relatively more freedom than she had at home would have too good an opinion of herself and dare to undermine the man's position. She would subvert the social order of the patriarchal family. As opposed to a man for whom terrorism reinforced his masculine image, a terrorist woman would not be considered feminine, obedient, or caring about what people think, because in jail there was no one from her family to control her thoughts and actions. She would be a woman who wanted control, who wanted to make decisions, who was independent, and who did not realize her ultimate purpose: getting married and having children, preferably boys. In fact, the security prisoners had more freedom in jail than at home; there were those who said it openly. In jail they wore what they wanted and met with whom they wanted, no one hit them or harmed them (unless there were physical conflicts between the prisoners or they were particularly vulnerable), and they no longer served other people, only themselves. It is true that in jail they acted as a group, not as individuals, as opposed to criminal prisoners. After longer or shorter periods, they had a need to be like one another and to dress the same way, in traditional Arab dress, to emphasize their group identity and belonging. They feel personally special, but they don't want to be conspicuous. They aspire to be absorbed into the group because it gives them a sense of belonging, status, protection, and power, and the ability to identify with what is going on outside the jail walls. It is a different type of behavior from that of the criminal female Arab prisoners, who serve their time with Jewish prisoners, share cells, and sometimes enter into lesbian relationships with them. In the female security wing, the women spoke and acted as they pleased and were not forced to accept the authority of their fathers or "big brother," but they definitely accepted the authority of the group they belonged to, and especially the authority of the all-powerful wing spokeswoman.

I thought perhaps Abu Tir had nothing else to say. He looked at me for a while, deciding whether or not to say what he wanted to most, and finally he spoke: "*Doctora*, I'm against all this suicide bombing from beginning to end. After he blows himself up the person will be naked. I can't find any logic in that. I don't want to see naked people." He seemed genuinely distressed about naked male suicide bombers, to say nothing of female suicide bombers. Nevertheless, I asked him why no one issued a *fatwa* forbidding suicide bombing attacks. He evaded my question and said, "I am against it. The reason for it is the occupation. If the occupation ends, there will be no more problems, no more war."

I asked, "What is the occupation? [The Israeli cities of] Acre, Haifa and Jaffa are the occupation?" He said, "Between '48 and '67 there was a *hudna*. We are asking for a *hudna* in the territories [which were occupied by Israel] after '67. Give us the West Bank and Gaza and there will be a *hudna*. These times are not good. How can we tell our people that we don't want Haifa and Jaffa? It's hard to accept. If we had a country without a fence . . . The situation is complex, and neither I nor other people can solve the problem, only if the Messiah and the Mahdi ["the guided one," the Muslim messiah] come."

Ultimately, Hamas demands all the territory of the State of Israel. They might agree to a *hudna*, but it will last only until they feel strong enough to attack. Their stated goal is the total destruction of Israel. Sheikh Abu Tir did not hide his feelings. He was not referring to the territories conquered by Israel in 1967 (Jerusalem, previously governed by Jordan, and the Gaza Strip, Egypt's responsibility). That has been made very clear by the thousands of rockets and mortar shells fired at the kibbutzim and cities in the western Negev from the Gaza Strip, from which Israel unilaterally withdrew in August 2005. It is possible that a *fatwa* against terrorist attacks in general and suicide bombing attacks in particular issued by a senior religious personality might make a change, as I heard more both from Muslim clerics and from terrorists. I asked him what he thought about children taking part in terrorism, a situation that worsened during Operation Cast Lead, in which children were openly used as human shields.

He answered, "I don't like the sight of blood when people get killed. I can't stand it. If the occupation ends, I will be against children going to war. It isn't logical, it doesn't make any sense. A child doesn't know what war is, his mind is too immature." Another sheikh I interviewed said something similar about children and terrorism but added that children kill themselves without killing Jews because their minds are too immature. Sheikh Yassin also told me that children did not know what they were doing.

I looked him straight in the eye and asked, "Would you send your own children to fight in a *jihad*?" He seemed surprised.

"My own children?"

"Yes, your own children."

"I never have and I never will. I believe in soldier versus soldier, army versus army, that's what I believe. I don't like it when Qassams [homemade Hamas rockets] are fired at Israel . . . The occupation started this war . . . During the last war [i.e., the second *intifada*] five hundred people were killed in the Gaza Strip, true or false?"

I asked him what he thought about the sixty-eight-year-old woman from Beit Hanoun (in the northern Gaza Strip) who blew herself up at a roadblock near Jabaliya—was she thinking about her children, her grandchildren?

He said, "Her children were pleased [*mabsoutin*], they were so pleased," and began to laugh. A suicide bombing attack carried out by a grandmother seemed like a joke to him. I tried to ask him as delicately as possible about the sexual exploitation of women involved in terrorism. I said, "Men strap an explosive belt to a woman's body, and sometimes people say the woman was with the man before the explosion." He obviously understood what I meant, and said, "I have heard about it." He looked at me for a long time and said, "I am a father and you are a mother. I don't think there is a father alive who would let that happen to his daughter, no matter how hard the situation was." His implication was that he did not justify the participation of women in terrorism, and he made similar comments several times during the interview.

He said, "When I was a member of the Palestinian parliament, [the Israelis] knew me. At the roadblock [at the border between Jerusalem and the Palestinian Authority] they let me wait, not for an hour, not for two or three hours, but for four hours, deliberately! No respect, the roadblocks destroyed people's self-respect. Go to the roadblocks and see how the soldiers behave." I could understand his pain and how sensitive an issue it was for him. I also did not mention that the roadblocks had been erected to protect Israelis from terrorist attacks.

Abu Tir returned to the subject of women and his daughters. "My daughter is at the university. Women should busy themselves with education. I respect and trust my daughters. I ask their teachers at the university about them, and I ask their friends. My daughter comes to visit me here in jail and I ask, and she answers, 'Daddy, I don't go [to demonstrations].' We have love and understanding, and we don't lie to each other.

"I'm not against her going to school, I'm against her going to jail. It's painful. They say there is an exchange with Gilad Shalit. First they'll release the women, right? It's hard for us that the women are in jail. I'm against a girl leaving her home or the university and going to jail. And not just jail, I'm against her blowing herself up as well," he said. I asked him what his position was on women who escorted suicide bombers to attacks, which happened quite frequently, and without hesitation he said, "That's not their job. A woman should study, work in a hospital, a school, and not do something that will put her in jail. Whoever sends a woman on a terrorist attack is *jahil* [ignorant, untutored, someone from before Islam]. I can send my son, my brother, someone who understands and accepts what it means to be a *shaheed*, but I would never send my daughter or my sister.

"Why did Sharon [Ariel Sharon, former Israeli prime minister] kill Sheikh Yassin [Hamas founder and leader]? And was happy about it? Who goes to blow himself up? Men from Hamas go. There are people who are educated and have degrees and finished university. Their souls tell them to, they believe in it . . . They will solve the problem of the occupation and there won't be a situation like the one there is now . . . Gaza is a prison. It's more than the occupation. There is a blockade of Gaza, the crossings are in the hands of the Israelis, everything goes the way they want it. Even the sea is closed—it's a prison . . ." However, the Gaza Strip, which was formerly Egyptian territory, shares a border with Egypt, a sister Arab country, yet almost all the humanitarian assistance received by the Gazans flows in through its border crossings with Israel.

I asked him about the relations between Sunnis and Shi'ites. I asked him why they were killing each other. [The Palestinians are Sunnis.] He said, "It's depressing to see what's going on in Iraq between Sunnis and Shi'ites. Both sides belong to Islam, and I'm against what's happening there. No one will profit from the war, not the Sunnis and not the Shi'ites. Everyone is under the American occupation. I don't like to think a Sunni would kill a Shi'ite."

I asked, "How would you react if your daughter told you she wanted to marry a Shi'ite?" The question seemed to shake him. Suddenly it was no longer a question of the same religion. "No! That is unacceptable. We haven't come to that. Here there aren't Sunnis and Shi'ites. There are Sunnis and there are no Shi'ites here. Sunnis and Shi'ites aren't going to get married. That isn't going to happen."

"But Ismail Haniya [head of Hamas administration, and a Sunni] went to Shi'ite Iran," I said. "Why shouldn't he go to Iran?" said Abu Tir. "Iran opened the door to him. If America or Europe opens its door, Haniya will go there, and if they close the door, he won't. There are men in Lebanon, America, who married Shi'ite women. There was one, Muhammad Salah, he is in America being investigated about terrorism-funding money. His wife is Shi'ite but she converted and became a Sunni, it's a change in the way she thinks." (In a previous conversation, another sheikh told me that it would be better for his son to marry a Christian or Jewish girl than a Shi'ite because the Shi'ites know the truth and have strayed from it.) Throughout my research, especially when I spoke to young terrorists, I found that more Sunnis converted to Shi'a than the other way around because of their admiration for Iran and Hezbollah leader Hassan Nasrallah.

I asked Abu Tir about paradise. He said, "Paradise is a different world. Now is our first world, but there is a different world. If a person behaves well, as [Islam] wants, he goes to paradise. If a person drinks wine and plays cards and kills people, how can he go to paradise? How can he be honest? An honest man believes in everything that comes from Allah. When the Torah came, it was light. If the Jews don't do what is written in the Torah, they are not Jews and lie to Allah. The same is true for Muslims. If a Muslim doesn't believe what it says in the Qur'an, he isn't a Muslim, he is fooling Allah, he is lying. Drinking wine is forbidden. The Qur'an tells me not to kill and not to steal, and I don't kill and I don't steal." I heard similar claims from Hamas leader Ahmed Yassin, who said that the Jews did not obey the precepts of the Torah and, therefore, as far as he was concerned, they were not Jews, and for that reason they were punished and Allah took from them the right to be a people with its own country.

I thought about Abu Tir's interpretation of the Qur'an, according to which a Muslim was forbidden to kill: he did not consider killing a Jew, Christian, or any non-Muslim as killing. Perhaps the way Hamas operatives killed Fatah activists in the Gaza Strip was also not considered killing.

He continued his description of paradise. "In paradise," he said, "there are not only *houris* [virgins], but a *shaheed's* brothers and family. Everyone is clean [i.e., there are no excretory functions and the women do not menstruate]. No one is against anyone else; everyone is clean inside and looks at Allah. The *shaheed* won't only be with the *houris*, he will be with the prophet Muhammad, the righteous, the other *shaheeds*, and with honest, wise men. It's true there are people who think they will have girls, but it's more than that. Faith is the greatest thing. Why am I in jail and not with my wife and children? Is there something greater than that? What am I paying for with my time? In paradise there aren't just virgins, there is a different world. You like to visit the zoo in Tel Aviv or go to a park. There are trees there, everything is green, there is water. You will look around you and be pleased. In paradise there is more than that, there are no dirty people there. People don't use the toilet. Only someone who is clean can enter paradise. Every Muslim believes in Allah and the prophets. Abraham said, 'I am a Muslim,' Yitzhak and Ya'akov said, 'I am a Muslim.' In the Qur'an chapter Bani Isra'il [which deals with the Jews], according to history and logic, the Israelites' country was only in Judea and Samaria [the West Bank], and not Haifa and Acre. If the Jews believe in the Torah, they should go to the West Bank and leave Haifa, Acre, and Jaffa . . . If the Messiah comes, the one our religion calls *Masih ad-Dajjal* [the false Messiah], the Mahdi will come and the Messiah, the son of Mary, and stop the wars. Allah says that, not I."

His analogy between experiencing paradise and visiting the zoo was amusing, but I did not dwell on it. Perhaps he was only referring to the beauty of nature. What was interesting was his complete ignorance of Jewish history as it appears in the Torah, which divided the Land of Israel into the provinces of the twelve tribes over an area that covered all of the State of Israel with the exception of the Gaza Strip. Haifa and Acre were divided between the tribes of Asher and half of the tribe of Menashe. The other half was settled east of the Jordan River.

I asked him which religion was closer to Islam, Christianity or Judaism. He said, "As far as religion is concerned, Judaism. The Jews don't say that man is the son of Allah. The Christians say that Issa [Jesus] is the son of Allah, but the Jews don't. So the Jewish religion is closer to Islam."

We talked about the Christian displacement from Bethlehem. In the past, it was a Christian city, but over the years the Christians left, in many cases fleeing for their lives after Muslims attacked them and molested their women. Abu Tir blamed the Israeli occupation, although today Bethlehem is under Palestinian Authority control. "Hamas," he said, "respects the Christians, more than Fatah."[1]

I asked him about the unique status of the mother figure in Islam, and like Ahmed Yassin he said, "The mother is more than a wife. It's the same with you [the Jews] in the Torah, it's holy. Allah said, 'First pray to Allah and then to your parents, mother and father.' A man asked the prophet Muhammad, 'Who should I pray to more, my mother or my father?' Muhammad answered, 'Your mother, your mother, your mother, and then to your father.' Woman has respect, but your mother carried you in her womb for nine months and it was hard for her. All of a sudden a little boy turns into a man. I don't believe a family should take their mother and father to an old age home. Children view their mother and father differently. The father is strong, the mother knows how to take care of the children, and the grandparents are wise. Even old people can bring up children better than the father. The mother is most important, then the father . . ." Yet when a man and woman divorce, if he remarries he brings up the first wife's children.

He invited me to visit him once he was released and to bring my mother and children. He said I had nothing to fear, and asked me to tell my mother that I had met him. I wanted to get the conversation back on track and talk about women and children. We agreed that parents do not want their children to die, not even as *shaheeds*. "That's right," he said. "I agree with you that no one wants to let his children blow themselves up. People who do that [blow themselves up] don't ask their mother and father.

"I like it when girls engage in sport. They can play ping-pong and jump rope, but only at home. They can play catch with other girls, but at home. I tell girls not to go to demonstrations. I don't want them to leave the house at all.

"A girl who gets out of jail thinks she is a leader [*za'im*], stronger and more angry than the *shabab* [a group of friends, usually young, and exclusively male]. There is no decision in principle in the Islamic movement about girls being involved in attack, and so only a few have been." Thus what seemed to bother him was that Palestinian women who served time in jail got ideas about their own importance or, worse, might take control of their own lives after they were released. That might question the social order and was absolutely unacceptable. It was forbidden for a woman to think she deserved something because she was in jail, despite the fact that she participated in the Palestinian war effort.

Regarding Houda, Abu Tir continued, saying sarcastically, "Well done, Houda, good for you!" Seriously, he said, "I believe in good manners and not things like that. The *watan* [nation, homeland] is something sacred, and a person stooped to sex? What, sex? What kind of nation is that? Who is she trying to fool? The nation wants people with honor and not people who talk about sex, smoke hashish, and steal cars. That's not honor for a great nation." Like others, he believed Houda tempted the boy to satisfy her sexual needs and not to kill him. Even if that was not the case, and as far as he was concerned, there was no justification for a woman to tempt a man with sexual promises, not even as part of the "struggle."

I told him about cases where women had carried out suicide bombing attacks because they had committed acts considered immoral by society. He mentioned Rim Riyashi, the first Hamas female suicide bomber, mother of two small children, who blew herself up at the Erez crossing in 2004, and there were rumors that she was romantically involved with someone from Hamas. He said, "I don't know that she had a boyfriend, or that she blew herself up because she did something forbidden [*haram*]. How can I know what is true, one way or another? So people say that, but not me, I refuse, but I did hear people talk about it. I don't know what was going on in her family, only Allah knows. Only Allah and the neighbors know. Forty days later her husband remarried. According to the Muslim religion, a man is not allowed to be without a woman even for one night. In religion, you don't look for reasons, you accept it the way it is. A man whose wife dies, even from an illness, has to marry again. For the woman it's different. If her husband dies and she is pregnant, she has to wait for four months and ten days to know if the child was fathered by her dead husband or her new husband . . . I am against sending women on suicide bombings. Who will raise the children? A man can't raise children. A child feels better around its mother." He ignored the woman's fate, ignored the issue of sending children to carry out attacks. Other sheikhs told me at length that it was ineffectual to send children on attacks and a waste of the "resource," but never was one word of sympathy spoken for the child as a person or victim.

I met Abu Tir for the second time on June 5, 2007, the fortieth anniversary of the Six-Day War. He came toward me, his right hand over his heart, and greeted me. I could see he was happy to see me again. "I told you I would come visit you again," I said with a smile. "Yes, Dr. Anat, welcome!" We sat on opposite sides of the table, and I said all I could offer him was mineral water, which I poured into two glasses. He called out to have coffee brought, and said, "It is an honor for me to offer you coffee." Within minutes, two steaming cups of coffee redolent with cardamom were brought. I sipped and said, "The best coffee in the world." He smiled broadly. The coffee was very good and reminded me of my parents' house and how my mother prepared it the way she had learned in Iraq.

The traces of the red henna I had seen on his beard during our previous interview had disappeared, and his beard seemed whiter than before. After we had spoken for a few minutes, he said he wanted to have a member of the Hamas parliament join us because his Hebrew was better. He said, "He studied at the Hebrew University in Jerusalem and he knows Hebrew very well. Don't worry, I will still speak freely." Ahmed Atoun entered the office and greeted me but did not shake my hand. He was short with a smoothly shaven, round face. He tried to turn the conversation to politics. I explained that I had not come to talk politics, that we would not resolve the conflict, and that the sheikh knew I had come to talk about something else. Abu Tir nodded his agreement. I poured water for Ahmed Atoun, and we continued our discussion.

Abu Tir began by talking about Hamas. He said, "I was second in command in the 'reform,' or 'change.'" There was something amusing about his looking for another name for Hamas. Ahmed Atoun, whose Hebrew really was quite fluent, said, "The Islamic organizations made no overall decision that women would participate in attack. The Islam movement does not intend to involve women; we respect them. They take girls from weak families. There are a lot of weak families. Ismail Haniya is not prepared to send women on attacks, Abu Tir is not prepared, nor would I send my own son to blow himself up. I want to see my children grow up, all parents want that. We want to live with a little respect . . . It is worse to have a woman blow herself up than a child. We have a saying, that a girl is like a diamond. You don't put a diamond out in the street, you hide it from the neighbors. Someone wants to destroy my honor, to steal my diamond. It's disgusting to send girls [to suicide bombing attacks]."

Abu Tir added, "There is pressure on us—we are under the occupation, we feel an injustice has been committed. No one tells his mother and father that he is going to do it [participate in suicide bombing attack]. Girls are the red line [out of bounds] as far as I'm concerned, and [sending them to blow themselves up] is a blow to my honor and soul . . . Anyone who sends a girl has no shame, he's sick."

Ahmed Atoun told me about a reality television show in Lebanon called *Academic Star*. It destroys, he said, the boundaries the traditional family tries to impose on its children. It was not the first time I had heard the program referred to by Palestinians as having a negative influence on youth, that it undermined and weakened the taboos of Arab society and promoted ideas considered liberal.

Atoun said, "Girls are forbidden to enter Internet chat groups with boys. They are also not allowed to wear Western-style clothing. It's wrong. It's more sensitive if a woman carries out an attack than a child, because the daughter is the family's honor. And there is something else about a girl. It's a matter of my honor as a man: an insult to the honor of a woman means an insult to the honor of a man."

I asked them what they thought about the relations between Sunnis and Shi'ites and about mixed marriages. Ahmed Atoun said, "In our religion, a man may marry a Christian woman or a Jewish woman, but a Jewish man may not marry a Muslim woman. It's against our religion." He refused to relate to the Sunni-Shi'ite issue, saying there were no Shi'ites in the Palestinian Authority or the Gaza Strip.

Abu Tir was willing to answer. He said, "The Shi'ites don't see eye to eye with us. Iran wants us to be more Shi'ite, but according to our understanding, we are loyal to Sunnah, that's an absolute for us. We won't convert to Shi'a. If a person converts to Shi'a he is not a true believer; he has some personal advantage in mind. If the situation between Hamas and Fatah were not so bad, Haniya would never have turned to Iran. Nasrallah wants the whole world to convert to Shi'a, but we would never do that. That will never happen, we will never exchange Sunnah for Shi'a, because it is our religion. We know that there is a difference between personal advantages [*maslakha*] and honor."

He changed the topic: "You think Iraq has a problem, Sunnis and Shi'ites killing each other? That's not the problem. The problem in Iraq is that the Americans are killing people. Their occupation is responsible for the whole mess. Those of us here have the Palestinian Authority and Hamas, and Hamas won the elections. The Palestinian Authority is responsible for the mess here. There are people in the government in Israel, in Europe, in the West, Britain and America, who don't want us to succeed. We are not radicals, we are not like Al-Qaeda, we are in the middle . . . Al-Qaeda in the territories makes things worse. I believe that Al-Qaeda does a great deal of damage to us all over the world. Because of their attacks, the whole world is against the Muslims." Abu Tir's approach to terrorism was, as before, completely practical, and he made no mention at all of the many victims of Al-Qaeda's murderous attacks.

After my interview with Abu Tir and Ahmed Atoun, I went to meet Naif Rajoub, a former minister in Haniya's administration. He was wearing light-colored, ironed clothing, and I wondered why he did not have to wear an ordinary prison uniform like the rest of the prisoners, including Abu Tir. He had a brown beard, and he appeared suspicious and guarded. I smiled and said, "I heard your brother was an important man in the Palestinian Authority, so is that what it's like in your family, everyone in a different organization?"

"No," he said firmly, "I'm not in any movement. I am in the administration but I am independent." He told me that he had a doctorate in Shari'a, was forty-nine years old, married, and the father of eight children, four boys and four girls. His family lives in a village near Hebron.

"I heard that people from the Hebron area are hardheaded and stubborn," I said, trying to lighten the atmosphere. He nodded and said, "There is a story about a man who wanted to drive a nail into a tree and the nail wouldn't go in, so he looked at the other side and saw the head of a man from Hebron," and we both laughed.

He was in jail for the fifth time. In 1992 he was one of the Hamas operatives deported to Lebanon, on the orders of the late prime minister Yitzhak Rabin, after the murder of the border policeman Nissim Toledano. He said, "In Lebanon we were on the border at Marj al-Zuhour, near Gabel al-Sheikh [Mt. Hermon]. First we lived in tents, and then we returned to the territories. The Israelis took us during the winter, and it was very cold and it snowed. We suffered during that period. There were religious Lebanese who brought us food and blankets and helped us. [I asked him whether they were from Hezbollah, because it was well known that Hezbollah trained the Hamas deportees.] I don't know if they were from Hezbollah. We learned how to cope with the cold and difficult conditions."

From his expression I could see that the deportation to Lebanon was a watershed because of the inconvenience involved and because of the connections formed with Hezbollah, although he never admitted they existed. However, those connections were manifested in a deal that took place about two years after the second Lebanon war, when Hezbollah gave Israel the bodies of two soldiers who had been abducted and murdered before the beginning of the war, Eldad Regev and Ehud Goldwasser. In return, Israel released security prisoners, including the Lebanese murderer Samir Kuntar, who in 1979 murdered Israeli Daniel Haran before the eyes of his four-year-old daughter, Ainat, after which he smashed her head with the butt of his rifle. Ainat's two-year old sister, Yael, was smothered as her mother kept her from crying and revealing their hiding place. Deporting Hamas prisoners to Lebanon led to the creation of a strategic bond and Hamas's imitation of Hezbollah's modus operandi in its campaign against Israel. What seemed like punishment and banishment was later revealed as the ideological union of two terrorist organizations whose goal has always been the annihilation of the State of Israel. The relations between the Sunni Hamas and Shi'ite Hezbollah grew closer every day, and Hamas follows Hezbollah's actions and the way it negotiates with Israel.

I had asked Abu Tir earlier whether he would approve of his son's marrying a woman who had participated in a terrorist attack and been arrested. He was appalled. "Our women don't do such things. That's man's work!" When I asked about his son, he evaded the question, saying, "My children are still very young." I said, "What about your brother?" He answered, somewhat reluctantly, "There is no problem if he loves her. My sister was in jail for a year and a half when she was thirty-five. Today she is fifty-two and unmarried. She has never married." I asked why not, and he said, "She says she didn't want to." I thought the truth was probably that no one wanted to marry her because she had been in jail and a terrorist, meaning that she had had relations with men and become a morally stigmatized woman (or perhaps she was stigmatized because of something in her past). I often heard the same sort of double-standard, double-talk answer: "She's a heroine, but I would never let my son or brother marry a woman like that."

I asked him what was waiting for the *shaheeds* in paradise. He said, "In paradise everything is good, everything is sweet. Whatever is sweet in this life is sweeter there. Food, drink, clothing, houses, river, flowers, honey, intoxicating liquor, intoxicating liquor [he said that twice], milk, even cream [here he laughed]. Anything someone can think of, anything he wants."

"How many women wait for you in paradise?" I asked. He laughed and said, "Seventy-two, a total of seventy-two. If someone deserves two, he will get them. If he deserves more, he will get a hundred if he deserves them."

"And what waits for a woman?" "If she goes to paradise she will be the most beautiful woman and she will marry men in paradise. In paradise there is no pregnancy or children . . . people see Allah and sit with him."

NOTE

1. Hamas, in the guise of "masked Islamic militants," has systematically attacked Christian institutions, including a school run by nuns and the YMCA library.

3

The Engineer: "A Virgin in Paradise
Is Like a Little Girl"

One winter day I arrived at the women security prisoners' wing in the middle of their exercise period. I stood on the sidelines and watched. Some of the prisoners walked back and forth across the small yard for exercise, holding hands. Others stood in small groups, laughing and talking excitedly, enjoying what little sun there was. There was a great deal of noise. I had been coming for four straight years, and they were used to me. They didn't pay much attention to me, even though I hadn't been there for several months. Looking around the yard, I saw a woman holding a baby dressed in a pink overall, waving at me and smiling. I knew who she was, although I had never met her.

Samira, the prison wing spokeswoman, came over and hugged me and kissed me on both cheeks in the Eastern fashion. "How are you?" she asked, smiling. "It's been a long time since I've seen you." "You look wonderful," I told her, "a *jilbab* with flowers really becomes you."

"Yes," she said, happy to be complimented, "I love this dress." Smiling, she said, "You know, we have a new baby in the wing, one you don't know." Children were our connection as women. During my visits to prisons I also got to know the inmates' babies, some of whom joined us and slept in my arms. "I know," I said, "I saw her in the yard. I want to meet Sabiha, the mother, and to see her sweet new baby."

Sabiha had been arrested a few months before. The newspapers called her "the engineer," because she was an explosives expert and had been involved in various terrorist attacks, perhaps as the female counterpart of Yahiya Ayash, also known as "the engineer" (killed by an exploding cell phone in 1996, an attack orchestrated by the IDF). Sabiha was married and two months pregnant at the time of her arrest. She gave birth to her son in jail and he was still with her, because according to

Israeli law, borrowed from the British, women prisoners could raise their children in jail until the age of two.

Sabiha came into the room where I was sitting with Samira. She seemed surprised to see us together, surprised to see us sitting close to each other and chatting freely, two women from two different worlds. She smiled at me and sat down. Samira helped with the translation. The Jewish-Iraqi-Arabic dialect I had learned at home was insufficient for exact translation. Sabiha was pretty and smiled all the time. She wore a black *jilbab*, and her face was partially covered by a white *hijab*, clasped at the throat with a pin. Her smile revealed her dimples. She projected calm and acceptance, and it was hard for me to see her as "the engineer," whose horrible exploits as a terrorist I had learned about from the media. She gestured with her hands a lot as she spoke, acting out the things she wanted to say. She did it all the time.

Sabiha was the middle child of nine siblings. She had been a student in the Islamic studies department in Gaza, and her husband, who was a cousin, worked in construction. He was also involved in terrorist activities and after his release from jail was deported to the Gaza Strip. She and her husband lived in Tulkarm, a city on the West Bank. She described imprisonment as the worst experience of her life. She had been convicted of preparing explosive belts and bombs. Being pregnant hadn't stopped her. Not only did she prepare explosives, she taught others how to as well.

"I didn't have problems at home. I went from home to school, from school to home. The Jews didn't let me be happy. I was only married for three months and then they came and took me. I called my son 'Innocent,' because I am innocent." I said I was surprised a married woman had been recruited. She ignored the remark, saying nothing. I asked her if she were religious, and she answered immediately and resentfully, "All Muslims are religious." Sabiha said, "I have worn a *hijab* since the ninth grade, all the girls in my family wear them, all Gaza wears a *hijab*. It is both our duty and our desire." At the time I interviewed her, the women in the Gaza Strip could still wear Western clothing, but later, in 2009, Hamas intensified its policy of Islamization and forced women to wear a *hijab* in the streets, and women who refused were publicly denounced and punished.

Sabiha explained that to reach paradise it was very important to follow the precepts of Islam. I asked her what was special about the Islamic paradise, and she became emotional: "Muslims have to believe in paradise. The things that are there are things no one's ear has ever heard and no one's eye has ever seen. First of all, Allah promised paradise to just people and true believers. In paradise women sit under Allah's seat of honor." (The expression she used, "seat of honor," appears in Judaism as the seat of God in heaven under which are the souls of men, and it existed before creation.) Talking about paradise affected her deeply. She said, "The best part of paradise is that you can see Allah and the prophet Muhammad [*rasul*]. Only *shaheeds* get eternal virgins, we women don't get anything. An old woman will become young again, and all the women who were married when they were alive become virgins again, and each one can choose the husband she wants. If a woman was a true believer, and just and good, then her own husband chooses her. If the women who reach paradise don't want the husbands they had because their husbands were bad and evil, the bad husbands go to hell. The woman can choose one husband and she will be a virgin again. That is the power of Allah, to make women virgins forever."

Virginity is of supreme importance in Arab society, to women but especially to men. Sabiha was obsessed with the story of the virgins in paradise because virginity is literally a matter of life and death in her world. The prisoner who told me that an operation to restore a woman's hymen would save her life was only stating a fact. Sabiha continued spinning her theories of paradise. "Neither men nor women go to the toilet. They have no excretions. There is no urine, no feces. There are no prayers in paradise . . . Whoever prays to Allah goes to paradise, and whoever doesn't goes to hell. Women don't menstruate. I don't mean postadolescent virgins, but virgins who don't have monthly periods, like little girls, the way an old woman becomes young again." It was the first time I heard that the virgins in paradise were not simply women who did not menstruate, but immature little girls. Sabiha made it clear that she did not mean young women, but virgins like little girls. The more excited she became, the more she waved her hands. "There are no children in paradise, no old people, no retarded people, only young boys and girls. I hope Allah sends me there and lets me in. In our religion, Muslims say that this life is a prison for the true believer and paradise for the person who doesn't believe. We suffer in the prison, and the evil we have in this world is because we believe that in the end something good is waiting for us in paradise."

Several months later I visited the jail again. As soon as I entered, Samira came to greet me, holding Sabiha's son, Bassam, now a year and two months old, in her arms. Without a word she gave him to me to hold. "See how big he is now?"

"Big and so sweet," I said. I stroked his black curls and chubby cheeks. "And you are so well dressed," I told him. He was wearing a white undershirt and brown jeans with a belt. Samira took him back, and we went to the second floor of the women's wing, where the Hamas and the Palestinian Islamic Jihad prisoners were housed. I wanted to talk to Rania, who had been apprehended with a woman relative on their way to a suicide bombing attack. Rania was special because at the time she was not only pregnant but already had eight children and was a grandmother as well. I stood with Samira outside the door to her cell, and green-eyed Rania looked at me through the grille. She told Samira she didn't want to talk to anyone, that the newspapers had printed lies about her. Muneira's face appeared next to hers. She laughed and said hello, and she seemed to be in a better mood than the last time I saw her, and she even said she felt better. In the end, Rania agreed to talk to me. It was hot, so we went to a room with air conditioning: Rania, Samira with Bassam on her lap, Sabiha, and I.

There was a large aquarium, and Bassam reached out, trying to catch the fish through the glass. "Look how much he's grown!" I said to Sabiha. She loved being complimented and said to him, "Say '*Allahu akbar*' [Allah is most great]." Bassam remained silent and kept watching the fish.

I had not brought my usual bottle of mineral water, so Samira asked one of the other prisoners to bring us juice, and I poured the juice into plastic cups. Rania had fair skin, but she was pale as well. She was wearing a brown *jilbab* with large buttons, which covered her completely. Her head was covered by a fringed white scarf decorated with small white plastic beads.

I asked, "Are you all right? You look very pale," and gave her a cup of juice. She looked around suspiciously and said, "I'm tired. I'm pregnant. I wish I could get out of jail and be with my children. I'm thirty-seven-and-a-half years old. Why did the newspapers write I was thirty-nine and make me older, why did they lie? They write about me a lot and I don't like it, it upsets me. I have eight children, six boys and two girls. The oldest is nineteen and the youngest is four and a half, and maybe this time I'm having twins." I felt that she was slowly relaxing. She smiled and continued talking about herself. "I live in Gaza, in Shuja'iyya. My family has always lived there. We are not refugees. I finished high school but I didn't take the matriculation exams because I got married when I was seventeen and eight months. My husband agreed to let me take the exams, but people said, 'What do you need a matriculation certificate for? Let your children take the exams.'" Palestinian women often marry before they graduate high school, and their husbands or families sometimes demand they drop out of school, because in any case they will stay at home and take care of children. Rania was not a refugee. She came from an old, established Gaza neighborhood but nevertheless was involved in an attempted suicide bombing attack with her niece, her brother's daughter.

She started crying bitterly. She was worried about what would happen to her daughters in her absence. "One of my daughters is fourteen years old. What will she do without me? I care about my children, they're my children, that's all I care about!" Samira nodded in agreement. "It's a good thing I'm not a mother," she said, "because if I were it would break my heart to go to jail." Rania continued, "The articles in the paper have a bad influence on me. Everyone says I'm in my ninth month, and I'm not. [She was in her second month.] They said I wanted to carry out an attack and kill myself and the baby in my stomach." Suddenly she said, "I like you—you speak from your heart. There are men and leaders who do what they want. I hate blood, and when I see a bleeding child I send him to his father to get bandaged." Rania was particularly upset by the media reports of her age and the state of her pregnancy. She felt that reporting she wanted to carry out a suicide bombing attack in her ninth month made her seem like a baby killer. Beyond their age, women prisoners also worry a great deal about whether their husbands will take a second wife.

Other women came in, and Samira laughed and said, "Tell her about your mother-in-law." The other women laughed and nodded as well. Rania, laughing and crying at the same time, said, "Maybe my husband will get married. If Allah has written that he will, then let him. [Islam] allows him to, so let him do it. I am his only wife now and I hope it stays that way! It will be terrible if he takes another wife. He is a good person, good, good. If my mother-in-law tells him to get married, he will." All the women laughed: misery loves company. Rania said, "My mother-in-law says, 'The food is no good, there isn't enough salt.' When I become a mother-in-law, all I ask of Allah is that they live in their own house." Wives know the power of the husband's mother over him and the nature of the relations between mother and son regardless of his age or marital status. In Arab society in particular, the mother has tremendous influence over her son. His wife's influence is negligible in comparison. Apparently, Rania did not get along well with her mother-in-law, who came to their house to sleep over and examine how she took care of her house and husband. I got the feeling that the mother-in-law was trying to sabotage Rania's relations with her husband. Maybe for her it was reason enough to carry out a suicide bombing attack.

The idea that her husband might take another wife worried her. "If my husband marries again, I will cry a little and be sad, but it comes from Allah. I am a religious woman and I believe in Allah. I became religious when I was seventeen, before I got married. My parents have always prayed to Allah, ever since we were little. If we take the correct path, we will go to paradise and see the prophet Muhammad. I will be in charge of the virgins in paradise for my husband's sake. I will be their princess. I will be superior to them, and they will be inferior to me. I will be most important for my husband, more important than they. Even if a virgin marries in paradise, she never has children. A woman will be a virgin and will not menstruate or urinate. Allah said that there are things in paradise that the eye cannot see and the ear cannot hear, and I absolutely believe that."

I was fascinated by her theories of the female hierarchy in paradise. A female would-be suicide bomber believed that she would be in charge of the virgins, and the question is why they would need someone in charge of them. It was Rania, pregnant with her eighth child, who wanted more than anyone to believe that there were no children in paradise. Perhaps she felt that finally, after so many births, she would be able to rest. Many women told me that women did not bear children in paradise, despite the fact that the male *shaheeds* would have children. It was paradoxical that men were encouraged by believing they would father children in paradise even if they blew themselves up before they had the chance, and the women rebelled against their traditional role and hoped not to bear children.

I met Rania a few months later, late in her pregnancy. Her face was calmer and more relaxed. She held my hand, and it seemed she had adjusted to prison life, and in the near future she would give birth. It was sad that the baby would begin life in jail.

Self-portrait of a female suicide bomber.

After Rania I went to speak to Suad, the niece with whom she had been recruited for the attack. She sat opposite me, her face expressionless, giving away nothing. Her head was covered by a blue and white flowered *hijab*, and she wore a black dress decorated with asymmetric white patches. She was shod in plastic sandals instead of shoes. She seemed not to have fully internalized what had happened and that she was in jail. She was thirty years old, the mother of four, and she had accompanied her aunt on an attempted suicide bombing attack. Like many of the women terrorists I interviewed, she bit her nails nervously, and when I asked, she said she had always bitten them. She was too depressed to cry. She began to speak, hesitant at first and then gaining confidence. "I was happy. I had a good life. Financially we were okay. We come from Shuja'iyya in the Gaza Strip, we are not refugees . . . The woman is the most important person in the home, and the man works outside. The man eats and sleeps, and the woman takes care of the children. She is everything for the family. If my husband wants to marry another woman, so it is written, if I am in jail or not."

The fear lest the husband rush to marry another woman was great among the women prisoners. The woman in jail cannot voice her opposition, and the man's decision to marry is perceived as reasonable and logical, even to members of her family. Suad told me about a wanted terrorist who incriminated a woman "who didn't want to marry him." Women are used as a lever to induce both men and women to act. Sometimes threats are used, and sometimes rumors are started to pressure a brother into protecting his sister's reputation by participating in terrorist attacks.

"In any case, things are better for women here than in Saudi Arabia. Here a woman can choose a few things, like who she wants to marry, work, studies, although yes, there are cases in which she is forced to marry." I asked her what she thought about paradise. All of a sudden she laughed and seemed to wake up. "There is no hatred, no bad things, and there are only Muslims. In paradise the woman is the princess of the *houris* [the "seventy-two black-eyed virgins"]. The Prophet Muhammad is there, and all the other prophets. I don't know if there are any children. I heard that anyone who lost a child [miscarried] will find the child in paradise. I lost two children. I was carrying twins and miscarried in my sixth month. We had moved to a new house and I worked very hard. I don't think about it. I believe that I will see them in paradise. There is a river of milk in paradise. Things are real. You don't get tired, you don't work, no one gets sick, life is completely different. I don't know if my husband will be in paradise . . . From the religious point of view, a woman is not allowed to be a *shaheeda*, because a woman's body is not like a man's. It is forbidden [*haram*] for men to see a woman's body, even after it blows up." It was ironic that a woman who planned to become a suicide bomber was now justifying the fact that it was forbidden. Suad was weak and easily influenced, and it was not by chance that she had been recruited.

Samira changed the topic to Gilad Shalit and Alan Johnston, the BBC correspondent who had also been abducted. Johnston was released after three months, but as of this writing Hamas was still holding the Israeli soldier captive. At the time of our conversation, however, Samira was of the opinion that neither would be released unless the Muslim prisoners in Israeli and British jails were released as well. Although she belonged to Hamas, she said that "no one is happy about what is happening in the Gaza Strip [the brutal murders of Fatah members by Hamas operatives after Hamas took over the Gaza Strip]. People say that Hamas will ensure security, but I don't believe a Muslim has the desire or strength to kill other Muslims because he cares about their safety. If they cared about their security, they would think about what they were doing before they did it." Suad listened to Samira, and her thoughts seemed to be wandering.

A woman named Layla came into the room, very pretty, carefully made up and wearing a pink *hijab*. She took out a picture of a baby girl and told me unhappily that her husband had married another woman and that it was a picture of his new daughter. It was important for me to know that the baby had been named after her. She had obviously thought her husband would wait for her to get out of jail and would not take another wife. Mother of four, Layla had escorted a suicide bomber to an attack in Jerusalem on Mother's Day in 2002, both of them carrying flowers for camouflage. She wore daring Western clothes even though she belonged to Hamas. Who orchestrated the suicide bombing attack? None other than Nabil, the Casanova whose name came up quite frequently when women were implicated in terrorist attacks. He had a way with women and exploited it.

There were many women in jail around whom he had spun his terrorist web. They became his puppets, and he knew which strings to pull.

Layla told me her story without my having to ask. "My husband married again, and I asked for her to be a mother to my children. It was very painful, but what could I do?" Then she showed me her daughter's high-school diploma and said, "She got sixty-six in English," but what really bothered her was her husband's remarriage. "I know, Rim Riyashi's [a Hamas suicide bomber who blew herself up in 2004] husband married again, too. If only Gilad Shalit could go to his mother and I could go to my children. There is talk about releasing the women, adolescents, and people whose health is bad."

The night before our meeting, the battles between Fatah and Hamas began in the Gaza Strip, and Layla wanted to talk about it. "People who kill each other are not Muslims. Allah doesn't allow it. He doesn't allow one Muslim to kill another—that is forbidden. In the religion of the Prophet it says that anyone who kills and is killed goes to hell." Samira broke in, saying, "In Iraq you have the Shi'ite organizations on one side and the Sunnis and Kurds on the other, but in the Gaza Strip everyone is a Sunni." That is, she understood Muslims from different sects killing one another, but it was hard for her to accept war between Sunnis, which was the situation in the Gaza Strip. To this day there is a rift between Hamas and Fatah. Hamas has established what is virtually an Islamic emirate in the Gaza Strip, and Fatah controls the more secular Palestinian Authority in the West Bank, the two parts of the "Palestinian Authority" that have no good relationship and no territorial contiguity.

In September 2009, Rania and Suad were among the prisoners who were released in exchange for the brief video of Gilad Shalit.

4

Shari'a Judge: "Women Lack Two Things: Intelligence and Religion"

My husband and I were sitting in the car in the gas station at the entrance of the Israeli-Arab city of Umm el-Fahm, waiting for Sheikh Ziyad Asaliya, who was supposed to meet us and take us to his house. Umm el-Fahm had recently been declared a city, but its residents still referred to it as a village. The sheikh was a *cadi*, a judge in the local Shari'a court, he lectured in the Islamic College of Baka al-Gharbia, and he was writing his doctoral thesis for a university in Jordan.

My husband, Reuven, skilled in Arab customs of politeness, said, "I hope you realize you will have to sit in back and let him sit in front next to me, and that you will have to be sitting there when he arrives." I got out and moved to the back seat. It was not the time for feminism; it was more important to meet the sheikh on his terms. The gas station and the stores and auto-repair shops around it filled with people making noise, and the ground was littered with empty soft-drink cans, cigarette butts, and old tires.

The sheikh called to say he would be there in about five minutes, which turned into twenty-five. Middle Eastern societies work on their own clock, and time is an approximation. He finally arrived, wearing a gray vest over a checked shirt, and greeted us with a smile. He got into the car, and we started up the hill toward his house. "This is Jerusalem Street. Maybe in twenty years it will reach my house, when the city becomes part of the Palestinian Authority," he said and laughed. He spoke Hebrew fluently. He knew that many Israelis think Umm el-Fahm should be transferred to the Palestinian Authority in a land swap, while the local Arab residents, who harbor no illusions about life under the Palestinian Authority, object strongly. Many Jewish Israelis regard it as a city hostile to the State of Israel and as a stronghold of Islamism.

His large villa, faced with stone, was situated atop a hill on the West Bank border, its windows facing untamed green scenery. We went into the living room and Souhila, his wife, rushed to bring a small electric space heater, which she placed near our feet. She was well educated and courteous and wore a long black skirt and dark sweater, her head covered by a light pink scarf. She participated in the conversation and was firm in her objection to things that displeased her. She was retired, having taught English in the local school, and now she devoted all her time and energy to her family. She poured coffee and gave me the first cup, saying "Ladies first, even though you sit on the left-hand side." The sheikh explained that the prophet Muhammad said *tyamanu*, things should always be done from the right: you enter a house with your right foot, eat with your right hand. I was familiar with the custom, which was prevalent among some of the Jews who lived in the Arab countries.

The sheikh said, "In the Arab world there are people with brains, with potential. The problem is the leadership. There is no leadership. There is no democracy in the Arab countries." Souhila broke in, saying, "All Islam is democracy; it was the first democracy!" There were many times during the conversation when Souhila disagreed. For example, when we asked the sheikh for his interpretation of Muhammad's slaughter of the Jewish tribes at Khybar, she did not accept his explanation and gave one of her own. He said that "the Jews betrayed the prophet, so he exiled and slaughtered them. So it is written." It was important for her that Muhammad be seen as a positive, moderate figure. Throughout the conversation, I sensed her pain and solidarity with her Palestinian brothers on the other side of the border, on the other side of the fence around her yard.

"What is the difference between a *shaheeda* and a female Israeli soldier?" she asked defiantly. I said that a *shaheeda* was sent to kill Israeli civilians and be killed, while a female soldier, regardless of nationality, was expected to return alive from a mission. Without hesitation, Reuven continued, "The difference is enormous. Soldiers fight terrorists and defend the country. The State of Israel must ensure that its soldiers return safely, while for a *shaheeda*, only death can ensure the success of her mission, her death and the deaths of Israeli civilians."

Souhila said, "The *shaheeda* feels pain and wants to make her people rise up and take action." Then she smiled at Reuven and said, "Why shouldn't a Palestinian from the Palestinian Authority come here to Israel and build a house, and you could build one in Nablus?"

I had heard that often; it was a challenge to the Jewish identity of the State of Israel. The truth is that many Arabs from the Palestinian Authority–administered territory and even from Jordan have come to Israel via family connections through marriage to Arab Israelis. Some live in Israel illegally. However, it is out of the question for any Jew to live in Nablus or in almost any Arab country today from whence they have been driven.

The Jewish settlements in the Palestinian Authority–administered territory are perceived by the Palestinians and some Israelis as alien and illegitimate. Anti-Israel terrorism does not stop at the Green Line (the border between Israel and the neighboring Arab states), and Palestinian terrorist organizations carry out attacks on Jewish settlers, such as the one on a school bus in November 2000, drive-by shootings at Israeli vehicles on West Bank roads, such as the one that killed Rabbi Meir Hai in December 2009, and the slaughter of the Fogel family in 2011, when the parents and their three children (ages eleven, four, and four months) were murdered in their beds.

I wanted to talk to the sheikh about the inclusion of Palestinian women in terrorism, but Souhila kept getting away from the subject. We took a break, and she brought us homemade cheese (*labaneh*) and olive oil, and pita breads she had baked herself. Then she went to make lunch for the family. I went into the kitchen and asked her what she was cooking. She said *maqluba*, which is a chicken, rice, and eggplant casserole. I told her I always wanted to learn how to make it but never found anyone to teach me. For the next half hour she showed me how to prepare this dish and waited while I took notes. When we returned to the living room, she no longer interrupted her husband, and I could ask the questions I wanted.

I asked him about the involvement of women in terrorism. He said, "When it comes to religious law, Islam does not distinguish between men and women except in two areas. The prophet Muhammad asked women to give charity, because women lack two things: intelligence and religion. People who read that think women are discriminated against, but that isn't the case. A Muslim has to pray five times a day; even if he is paralyzed, he prays with his neck and eyes. A menstruating woman is allowed not to pray, or to fast, or to circumambulate the Kaaba (the sacred stone at Mecca) seven times. But a man must do it. Therefore, women lack religion."

He continued: "Women don't have intelligence. That is, they do have intelligence, but sometimes they are ruled by their emotions. For that reason Islam has no female judges, despite the fact that the Hanafi School of Islamic law says that women can be appointed judges, but they are limited in the punishments they can hand down and are not allowed to order corporeal punishments such as execution or cutting off the hand of a thief. In Egypt a woman judge was appointed, and the population objected. Why? Because they said that Allah gave the woman other roles. In the wars of the prophet Muhammad, women went after the men and brought them aid and support, intelligence information, but they didn't fight. If a woman blows herself up all her flesh will be seen, and that leads to a very difficult situation. When does Islam permit suicide? There are schools of thought that say, 'It is absolutely forbidden,' and there are those that say, 'It is permitted.' Every school has its own authorities and references."

Like all the Muslim men I interviewed about female suicide bombers, the sheikh had great difficulty in relating to their bodies. I told him that many times after a suicide bombing attack, the intimate areas of the woman's body were exposed, and I asked him whether that was a difficulty for him. It was clearly hard for him to deal with the question, and he was unable to answer. I could see it was a problem not often discussed. A woman who blows herself up is perceived as an exhibitionist. Even the most revered *shaheeda* is considered by some as carrying out a striptease in the middle of the city. The boldness of such women grows in stages: first they stop wearing traditional Muslim clothing, then they wear tight pants and shirts, maybe even with a plunging neckline, and finally their naked, bloody body parts are exposed and come into contact with those of infidels.

The sheikh continued, more comfortable speaking about men. "There is a firm, accepted Islamic rule which states that a *shaheed* is someone who died in glorifying the name of Allah. The head of the Islamic state, the Caliph [Muhammad's replacement], makes the rules. He decides if there will be peace or war. The Caliph decides there will be a war against the Jews or Christians to glorify the name of Allah, and whoever dies is a *shaheed*, but if Ziyad Asaliya [the sheikh himself] decides on jihad, then there is no *shaheed*." That is, the decision to wage jihad is the exclusive province of the religious ruler, the Caliph, and only those who die in jihad can be considered *shaheeds*.

"Woman is forbidden to physically fight in war. She has duties in Islam, such as medicine, intelligence, food, logistics. And one of her most important tasks is to bear children. That is the objective of marriage, to bring up children and to take care of all the needs of the home." The relative advantages women have, especially in intelligence work, are exploited more and more today in fundamentalist terrorism. The Iranians[1] recruited Shi'ite women in Iraq as spies, training them in Tehran and sending them back to their own country.

The sheikh continued. "If a woman leaves her home because [her relatives] are infidels, then she is allowed to leave her father's house without an escort. There is a religious law governing it: 'When the need is critical, forbidden things are permitted.'" Thus, a woman may leave the house to carry out an attack or may be taken from her parents' house. As it is permitted to leave the house of infidels, she may also leave without a related male escort to carry out a suicide bombing attack.

He continued, "There are *fatwas* stating she may participate in war if there are no men to protect the women and children, for example, in a little village where all the men have left for war and only the women remain. If enemy soldiers enter the village and there are no men, just women and children and old people, then it is the women's duty to fight. If there are men, women can help them to the best of their ability."

I wanted to get back to the topic he kept avoiding. "What about women who blow themselves up and parts of their body are visible, is that permissible?" He thought for a while. "That's a problem. That's nakedness, lewdness. The body of a woman is *a'wra* [the shame of a woman's genitalia]. There are *fatwas* stating that a woman's voice is lewdness. According to Islamic rules, only a woman's face and hands may be seen, the rest is forbidden. Period. If necessary, it is possible to waive the rule, but the question is how you define 'necessary.' A woman must defend herself and her honor. Individuals aren't supposed to issue *fatwas*; a forum of clerics issues them. For example, if it is a question of health, professionals are invited to issue the *fatwa*.

"The question is whether a cleric can say everything he thinks. There is a story about a doctor who answered a student at Al-Yarmukh University in Jordan. The student said to the doctor, 'Oh, sheikh, I have a question for you, but before I ask you, I asked another sheikh who gave me the following answer . . .' So the doctor said, 'There are three types of sheikhs: the first, who is appointed by Allah, the second, who is appointed by time because he is old, and the third, who is appointed by the rulers or the Devil, since they are both the same. Most of the sheikhs nowadays belong to the third category.'"

He seemed pleased with himself and his story. I asked him about relations between Sunnis and Shi'ites, especially the war in Iraq and the increasing power of Shi'ite Iran. He was upset by the choice of topic. He seemed to harbor a lot of anger toward the Shi'ites. "The Iranian dream," he said, "is to establish the Islamic Republic as a Shi'ite country. The Arabs and Persians hate each other, hatred born of the Shi'ite sense of humiliation. The Shi'ites want to establish a Shi'ite republic. They changed the name to the Islamic Republic." It is apparently a case of Persian Shi'a versus Arab Sunnah. He explained that Arabs have always felt it was more noble and preferable to be an Arab, because the prophet Muhammad was an Arab, and for that reason, the Iranians feel inferior.

We thanked the sheikh and said good-bye. Souhila asked us to stay for lunch, but we declined. They had been wonderful hosts, and we could still smell the aroma of the chicken as we walked to the door. Things the sheikh told me were reinforced by Sunni clerics whom I interviewed for my research. Riyad, an Israeli Arab who pleads cases in the Shari'a court, told me that women are forbidden to wear clothing that exposes their bodies. "Even if it means killing a thousand infidels, it is forbidden for a woman to expose herself to escort a suicide bomber. That is against Islamic law." Sheikh Ziyad mentioned the problematic nature of women dressing in Western clothes to take part in attacks, usually to obviate suspicion. I also heard it said that makeup is forbidden, but it is ignored if it is not obvious. Riyad echoed what the sheikh had said: "Wearing skimpy or tight clothing makes the soldiers see such a woman as a regular girl, and no cleric would allow that."

Each Muslim sect has its own religious council that provides the terrorist organizations with solutions for the problems raised by modern jihad. I often found different and sometimes opposing opinions, depending on the ideological needs of the organization. Riyad summed up, saying that anyone who sacrifices his life as a *shaheed* does not want to make the smallest mistake (i.e., does not want to compromise any aspect of his duties as a devout Muslim).

NOTE

1. "Iran Recruiting Female Spies in Iraq: Report," *Iran Focus: News & Analysis*, http://www.iranfocus.com:80/modules/news/article.php?storyid=9763.

5

※◎◇※

The Adolescent Terrorist: "You Go to Jail, You Can Study for Matriculation Exams, You Get Special Considerations If You're in Jail"

From the trial transcript of an adolescent who turned himself in and admitted to having thrown a Molotov cocktail at an IDF soldier:

Attorney:	What grade are you in?
Defendant:	The twelfth grade.
Attorney:	What is your average?
Defendant:	Fifty [the lowest possible passing mark].
Attorney:	Why did you turn yourself in?
Defendant:	I had a problem in school, they expelled me, I didn't know what to do and I was afraid of my father. I thought about going someplace else, but I didn't have any money. So I decided to surrender.
Attorney:	What does your father do for a living?
Defendant:	He's a doctor.
Attorney:	Can't you take the tests in your village?
Defendant:	No, I'm not a good student.
Attorney:	Where did you want to take the matriculation exams?
Defendant:	In [Israeli] jail.
Attorney:	In your confession you said you turned yourself in because your friends at school recommended it, because people told you the Shabak [Israel Security Agency] mentioned your name and were looking for you.
Defendant:	No one told me anything like that. I only said that because I wanted to get arrested.

Attorney:	You confessed to throwing Molotov cocktails and stones.
Defendant:	I admitted it, but I never did anything like that. I only said I did to get arrested.
Attorney:	If your father knew you threw Molotov cocktails and stones, what would he do?
Defendant:	He would punish me.

I spoke to Monir, a Muslim sheikh, about sending adolescents on terrorist missions, a subject he found painful. "Children do things because of peer pressure, and it's hard for their mothers to influence them. The mother says, 'If I touch him while his friends are watching, he'll never live it down. They will call him a coward.'"

Amjad, an Israeli-Arab lawyer who got his degree in London, once represented an Arab minor accused of security-related crimes. I interviewed him to learn about young offenders. He said, "After I defended him and he was convicted, he studied for the Jordanian matriculation exams in jail, and he asked me for books. He later told me he had passed the exams and could start living. It is easier to pass them in [the Israeli] jail. If you deserve eighty, you will get ten or twenty extra points because you take them in jail and not in school.

"The boys want to show they are heroes. They throw Molotov cocktails. They don't want to hurt anyone, they just want to have it reported on TV or the radio. They want the publicity, that's what's important. I am familiar with a case where an adolescent boy involved in security crimes boasted he had thrown a Molotov cocktail, and a friend said he hadn't heard anything about it. So he threw another Molotov cocktail at Israelis, just to have people talk about it. The whole thing is organized, they don't do it alone. They are pressured to do something, to throw something, it's like a dirty game.

"The people who dispatch children use them as cannon fodder. It is easier for children to fight the Israeli army. The people who incite them want the army to shoot at them so they have something to tell the media. When I was studying in London I was surprised by how much influence the Palestinians had with the media. They learned it from the Jews. In Europe the Palestinians are stronger in the media than the Jews, despite the fact that the Jews control the media.[1] The Palestinians hold demonstrations in London every Saturday, and there are always lots of children in attendance. They tell the children they will go to paradise. I don't pray, but if someone in the Palestinian Authority–administered territories prays and the sheikh tells him he will go to paradise, he believes the sheikh. They have a special way of influencing children, primarily through stories about the pleasures of paradise. I don't need it. We live in paradise already, and I don't know what happens afterwards, after you die."

His description of recruiting young men through manipulation is connected to the adolescent need to show manliness, especially under peer pressure. Often it is a question of adolescents whose sexual identity is not yet fixed and who have to represent themselves as excessively macho. At the same time, they also have to satisfy their parents' desire for good grades in school.

I asked Amjad what he thought about the suicide bombing attack carried out by the sixty-eight-year-old grandmother. He was very angry that a woman that age had been dispatched to blow herself up. "Why did they look for an old woman? Because it would be easier for her to carry out the attack. A justification can always be found if a sheikh brainwashes her. There are people who take the sheikh's word as holy. They most likely told her she would go to paradise and become young again. It is not clear whether she had a history [some kind of moral stigma]. Maybe she worked for Israeli intelligence and wanted to atone for it, because if you carry out a suicide bombing attack you are clean again, you become a *shaheeda*. Maybe someone in her family was killed, her husband or a son, and she wanted revenge. Islam forbids women to fight in a jihad. They aren't even allowed out of the house. Men are also forbidden to commit suicide. I heard about a twenty-year-old girl who slept with someone, so they told her, 'Go cleanse yourself.' So she blew herself up. They find a reason for a woman to do it, so she does it."

Terrorist operatives also use children to recruit their peers for attacks. I wanted to meet Hassan, a boy who, when he was in the tenth grade, recruited two of his schoolmates as suicide bombers. One of them was his cousin. It was hard to understand how a fifteen-year-old would invest all his energy in finding children who would blow themselves up, and not just children, but relatives, friends, people he grew up with. Was he without feelings, without a conscience? Was he unaware of the consequences? Those were the questions I wanted to ask him. The thought of sending friends to their death, to say nothing of killing innocent victims, should have been enough to stop him.

I said, "Good morning" in Arabic and gestured with my hand, inviting him to sit down. It was a sunny winter morning, but the sun's rays didn't penetrate the cell. He looked at me with the curiosity of a child, as if to say, who are you and why are you interested in me? He had only been transferred to the adult wing from the juveniles a few days previous to that. Arrested at the age of fifteen and four months, he was now eighteen, and the date of his release was still far in the future. He was tall and brown-eyed and looked younger than his eighteen years, an adolescent for whom time had stopped when he was sent to jail. He had applied a liberal quantity of gel to his hair, with one lone curl standing up in the center of his head, something which had obviously taken a long time to fashion. He was neat and clean, wearing a sweatshirt and jeans, with a large watch on one wrist and a macramé bracelet of colored threads on the other. He was calm and eager to talk, to tell me about himself, and maybe even to justify his actions. He had no trouble expressing himself. Jabbar, a good friend he had recruited, blew himself up in a suicide bombing attack, but Jamil, another boy, was arrested with the explosive belt still strapped to his body and was also in jail. Hassan did not seem particularly bothered by either.

Throughout our conversation he repeatedly referred to the deeds of a would-be suicide bomber as "*nazal amaliyyah*," "leaving for an action." On one occasion I asked Abu Tawfiq, a well-educated Arab I interviewed, why young people did not speak of *istishhad* (self-sacrifice, the death of a martyr for the sake of Allah), but rather as "leaving for an action." He told me that the source of the expression was from Jordan, "those who sent their souls out," and that they "left" (*nazal*) Jordan through the Jordan River to carry out attacks in Israel.

Hassan was an adolescent, not yet in his final form as a man, and intelligent, and it was not by chance that he recruited suicide bombers for wanted terrorists who had set him up to take the fall. He was charismatic and, despite the hardships he had experienced, knew how to value life and did not yield to the entreaties of the dispatchers to carry out a bombing himself. He was born in Nablus (a city in Samaria under PA control). His father was a tailor, and his mother worked in an upholstery shop to support the children. The father was an alcoholic who beat the mother, and they divorced when Hassan was three and his brother was a baby. The children were raised by their mother, and their father returned to his parents' house, where he lived until he remarried. Most of the time his father was dysfunctional, and after the divorce, while he did maintain relations with his children, he did not support them financially. His mother was imprisoned for thirteen months, but Hassan could not tell me whether there was a connection with his terrorist activities. Of his parents he said, "When my mother went to jail I was totally destroyed; I didn't know what to do. She is my mother. She got married when she was seventeen, and I was born when she was eighteen. They forced her to marry my father against her will. He was her brother's friend. Everyone knows she didn't want to marry him. When she was twenty-one they divorced. She didn't remarry even though there were a lot of men who came and asked for her hand, because she wanted to raise us. If she got married again, they would have told her to bring the children [to their father or his family]. She didn't want that. We were her life. My father could keep me until I was eighteen and then I could say if I wanted to live with him or my mother. She is smarter than he is. She finished the eleventh grade, and my father only went to school for two or three years.

"My father's sister opposed the wedding. She gave my mother an amulet to make him divorce her. He used to hit my mother all the time and get drunk, my mother told me that. Once I went into the *boidem* [he used the Yiddish expression for "attic"] and found two amulets. One was a folded square of paper with my name and my brother's on it, and one belonged to my mother, but with no names. It just said 'Hate her.'" Hassan was convinced that his mother's hard life was the result of a secret charm his aunt had worked on her. He was obviously very attached to his mother and had great respect for her and her abilities, far more than for his father, although he described their divorce as a difficult period in his life. And with no father figure in his life, he searched for charismatic males with whom to identify.

"I love my mother more than my father," he said. "I haven't done anything with my life, and at fifteen I went to jail . . . My parents' divorce was the worst thing that ever happened to me, and a friend of mine carried out a suicide bombing attack and that was why I went to jail, and because of other bad things that happened to me." The friend he was referring to was one of the young men he recruited for an attack, something I discovered only toward the end of our conversations. It wasn't the first time that people who had been involved in or even responsible for dispatching suicide bombers distanced themselves from the event or from taking responsibility for the deaths of their friends, and asked innocently "why it happened."

I asked him why the most industrious child in class had sent his friends to carry out suicide bombing attacks. I knew he was considered an excellent student, and excellent students are usually not easy to manipulate. He said, "I never thought about jail. Wanted men came to me and said, 'We want people who are ready for *istishhad*.' They suggested that I kill myself [in a suicide bombing], that I be the first one, but I refused. I didn't want to leave my mother, and I was afraid of the act itself. Someone who blows himself up winds up in a thousand pieces, it's scary just to think about it. So they said, 'Okay, look for young people who are willing to commit suicide.' They wanted me to recruit potential suicide bombers. They convinced us by saying, 'You are only children! Whatever you do, no one will do anything to you because you're underage. You won't spend more than two and a half years in jail.' At that time we were supposed to take external matriculation exams and everyone was afraid they would fail, and they said, 'Let's go to jail, you go to jail, you can study for your exams, you get special considerations if you are in jail.' I don't know, they were older than we were, and they convinced us. Back then, if you told me to rob someone's house, I would have, but it's scary to kill yourself."

Hassan's story revealed several factors that made him and his friends choose terrorism. The Palestinian educational system indoctrinates children to hate Israel and in many instances inculcates the desire for martyrdom. Israel does not appear on the map, and the Holocaust is not part of the curriculum. In addition, for a variety of security reasons, classes are canceled and high-school students find themselves with time on their hands and bored. They leave the school premises, walk around town, and meet wanted terrorists who seduce them into carrying out terrorist attacks. The wanted men, older professional terrorists, convince them that their young age will keep them from doing hard time. In addition, the boys feel they are respected as men. They are also interested in the relaxed conditions of Israeli jails, which make it convenient for them to study for their Jordanian matriculation exams, as noted above.

Hassan kept his mother in the dark. "I didn't tell her anything," he said. "She knew I threw stones, and she beat me because of that. The wanted men talked to my friends and me. Our financial situation was difficult, and they said, 'If you go to jail, you will get 1,800 shekels [less than $500 at the current rate of exchange] a month for your mothers.' [The Palestinian Prisoner's Club took care of payments to the family until Hamas took over and the Palestinian Authority ran out of money.] My mother cries at home all the time because she can't visit me in jail, because she was in jail herself. [Former prisoners are not allowed to visit jails.] My father comes to visit because he was never in jail, and that makes me feel calmer." Obviously, parents do not want their children to commit suicide or be involved in attacks. Most of them try to protect their children from being exploited by terrorist operatives. Hassan never wanted to be a suicide bomber, and as a former dispatcher of suicide bombers told me, "Everyone has his own role to play." Hassan, an intelligent, charismatic leader, helped recruit his underage friends for suicide missions.

Hassan told me how he recruited them: "My life was always hard. I was never happy. I told Jabbar, a friend of mine, to carry out an attack, and he said, 'I'm going.' Then later the wanted men said they wanted to meet me in the town square in Nablus, and they took Jabbar, and he said, 'I need Hassan, so that he and I can go home together.' At the same time I was drinking tea in the Balata refugee camp, in the home of one of the wanted men. They said, 'Why did he leave [to carry out a bombing] and you didn't?' They tried to pressure me, but I refused. They tried even harder. '*Istishhad* and the virgins are waiting for you in paradise. If you commit suicide you go to paradise and you will be with Allah, think about it!' But I told them, 'No way!' I didn't say, 'In jail, whoever fasts and prays will also go to paradise.'

"Jabbar had problems with his parents. He was young and didn't know what he was doing, and when he came home late at night his parents would beat him. He smoked and made trouble, all kinds of stupid things. His parents didn't know he was going to *istishhad*, only I knew, but I didn't know the exact day or time. The day he disappeared and his parents started looking for him, I knew he would carry out an attack, and then I started thinking. Before the attack he didn't tell me anything. His parents asked me about him, and I told them I didn't know. Men from his family suspected me. They took me and beat me and asked me where he was. Only then did I tell them he went to carry out an attack." Hassan began snickering without sorrow or regret for having sent his friend to die or for the victims of the attack. He laughed because he felt like a big shot, because he hadn't said anything to anyone until men from Jabbar's family beat him, and then he told them he had recruited Jabbar for a suicide bombing attack.

"I was stubborn, and I don't like being stubborn. Maybe I hoped one of them would catch up with him and bring him back before he blew himself up. His older brother went to the Israeli army liaison unit and told them that Jabbar was going to carry out an attack. His family wanted them to catch him so that he wouldn't do anything, and bring him home. The liaison unit talked to the army, and two hours later Jabbar died at the Qalqilya roadblock [between the Palestinian Authority and Israeli territory]. I don't know if he blew himself up or if the soldiers shot him. He died and an IDF soldier was wounded, but not seriously." Many times the terrorist's family gives the IDF information to save the life of a family member, as in this case.

Jabbar's brother-in-law blamed Hassan for his death and threatened to kill him, and a feud began between the families. Hassan was afraid, because when Jabbar had merely disappeared, he had been beaten, so what would happen when they found out Jabbar was dead? They would blame him and kill him.

However, in the meantime Hassan continued locating potential suicide bombers and recruiting them. One of his friends was arrested, and the rest waited to go to jail to study at their ease for Jordanian matriculation exams. "Mahmoud talked about us when he was interrogated. He incriminated us and we were waiting to be arrested. But no one came to arrest us, so we said, we'll bring another [suicide bomber] and then the Israelis won't have a choice, they'll have to arrest us and we'll take the exams in jail. Jamil was a couple of months older than I, we weren't in the same class. The wanted men came to me again and said, 'We need another suicide bomber.' We were only kids, we didn't understand, and we brought them Jamil. I met him at a friend's house and I asked the friend to bring him, and I asked him if he wanted *istishhad*."

I had met Jamil three years earlier, in jail. He told me with great pride that he had been caught with an explosive belt at one of the roadblocks and that he was the man among his scared friends because he wasn't afraid to blow himself up.

Hassan continued, saying, "Everyone had problems. The wanted men talked to Jamil and at first he said he only wanted to go to jail to study for exams. Then they talked to him alone and convinced him to blow himself up. My friends didn't ask me why I didn't go. My mother didn't know what was going on, and she only found out after I was arrested. The wanted men told me that they would give me money for every one [potential suicide bomber] I brought them, but I never received anything!" He felt he had been cheated. He was a skilled recruiter who carried out his part of the unholy bargain and located many children for suicide bombing attacks, and nevertheless the terrorists cheated him and never paid what they promised. He summed up emotionally, "They laugh at children, they fool them like they fooled us. It was obvious they fooled us. They said two and a half years, no more, and I got sentenced to twenty years, and not one of them asks about me. They don't visit, they don't worry. I lost my parents, my mother and my family."

I asked him if he regretted his actions, and he said, "I'm sorry I lost a friend [Jabbar], and I have no connection with Jamil. I believe in paradise because it is written [in the Qur'an]. If it weren't written, I would doubt it. It'll be fun with the girls in paradise. The wanted men told me they would put me on posters and on television in paradise. They went around with us and we felt they respected us, because everyone looked at them." He described the admiration many Palestinian youths had for terrorists and how they viewed them as role models, which was leveraged into recruiting those youths for terrorist attacks.

I asked what he thought about women in terrorism, and he answered emotionally, "*Haram*, it is forbidden, they are girls. It is forbidden, and if a pregnant woman goes to jail or carries out an attack? That's wrong, it's wrong for girls to hang out with the *shabab*, the guys. A girl who carries out an attack is not a good girl. Outside [jail] female prisoners are respected while they are being punished."

Our conversation was over, and we shook hands to say good-bye. I felt that he would rather keep talking than go back to his cell, and to prolong the conversation he stood at the door and asked questions about my research. Afterward I complimented him on how clean and neat he was, including the hair gel. He came back into the room and shook my hand again, walked over to the door, turned around and came back to the table, and shook my hand yet again. It was hard for him to end the conversation. To me it seemed he was still an adolescent, and he certainly felt threatened and insecure after being transferred to the adult wing.

In the juvenile wing, I saw a group of adolescents telling jokes and laughing, forgetting where they were for the moment. I looked at the exercise yard in the middle of the wing and watched them play a kind of ball game. It was a combination of handball, volleyball, and dodgeball. It had its own rules, like the rest of the Middle East. The youths threw the ball as hard as they could at the arm of another player; they seemed to be enjoying themselves. Qatada, one of the wing inmates, had explained the rules to me. The game was strict and moved very quickly. The blows of the ball were hard, and the boys bent over, looking at each other and moving around the small yard as fast as they could. I couldn't help thinking that the yard and the game were a microcosm of our lives and the complexity we have to deal with.

I went over to talk to Qatada, a tall, black-haired boy who smiled all the time. He was wearing a blue T-shirt with something printed on it in English, jeans, and mountain-climbing shoes. His hair was done in spikes, and he explained how he used conditioner to fix them in place because he had no hair gel in jail. He learned Hebrew in jail, and we spoke a mixture of Hebrew and Arabic. He had the same name as a wanted terrorist who had been killed by the Israeli army, and I asked him whether they were from the same family. He laughed and said people were always asking him that, but that it was his first name, not his family name.

We sat down and began talking. "Soon I'll be eighteen and I'll be transferred to the adult jail. I asked to be in the same wing as my cousin. You know, it's always better to be with a relative. I am Qatada from the Taamra clan in Bethlehem [in the Palestinian Authority]. I have lived in Bethlehem for a long time. The Israeli army wants my father; he is on the wanted list. They told me my father was with the Palestinian Islamic Jihad, he was a famous terrorist. In 2006 Jews came and took me because one of my friends told the Shin Bet [Israel Security Agency] I had computer disks with classified information."

I poured cups of mineral water for both of us and said, "Let's toast '*L'chaim*' [for life]." "No," he said, "I see on television how you toast 'L'chaim' but I'm a Muslim and it's forbidden." Perhaps some Muslims believe that the pleasures of this life should be shunned in preparation for those of paradise and not to drink "for life."

"I was born in Bethlehem, and my sisters were born in Jerusalem. I was the only child born in Bethlehem. My father is forty-five years old. When I was about four, my father was exiled to Lebanon. They were there for a year and then they came back, and things were good. My sisters went to school and I started school early. I'm good when it comes to learning things. When I came home with good grades, my father gave me money. He used to encourage me to study. We are five boys and two girls. I'm the oldest. My father wants me to be a good boy and jail is not good. My father was in jail for eleven years. He had been sentenced to life but was released in the Jibril deal.[2] He said, 'Go to school and keep away from the Jews!' He saw me throw stones at soldiers, and he hit me and said, 'Don't do that, just go to school. You live for school.' He wanted me to be a dentist. He wanted to send me to Russia to study. I studied chemistry and physics, and the Jews arrested me."

His father wanted a better life for his son, different from his own. Qatada spoke of his father with open admiration, and the contradictory ideas he received confused him. On the one hand, his father was involved in attacks and spent many years in Israeli jails. On the other, his father hit him when he threw stones at Israeli soldiers. I was reminded of interviews I conducted with other terrorists, who refused to countenance the idea of their own children participating in terrorist attacks. There are enough children of other parents, they said, who can do the work.

I asked Qatada about relations between Muslims and Christians in Bethlehem, which in the past was a predominantly Christian city. "I heard," he said, "that there were problems with Christian girls in Bethlehem. It wasn't my father [who was involved], but other relatives from my family. In my family there is both Fatah and Palestinian Islamic Jihad. No Hamas. On Christmas everyone goes to the church to look at the girls, and they make a lot of trouble. I never saw it, but I heard they kidnapped girls and slapped their behinds. I guess the girls also wanted sex."

I said, "What would happen if boys acted that way with a Muslim girl?" He brought his head close to mine, opened his eyes wide, and said, emotionally, "War, war, war with weapons and a lot of trouble. Muslims would kill the girl. Many Christians left Bethlehem, but there are still some. The Christians in Bethlehem are weak. Whoever sexually harassed Christian girls is an animal." He knew about the stories of rape and sexual harassment that had led many Christian families to move away from the city.

I also asked Nabil, the dispatcher of suicide bombers whom I interviewed for my research, about the relations between Muslims and Christians. He told me that he personally had good relations with Christian Arabs and said angrily, "Suha Arafat [Yasser Arafat's widow] was Christian. She stole all the money that belonged to the Palestinian people, and she was hated because of the billions she stole and not because she was Christian." Nabil did not mention or did not know that she had converted to Islam before her marriage. He said that Christian Arabs were involved less in terrorist attacks because most of them had jobs and received recognition from the West through the Christian church. I asked him about what Qatada told me, about the rape of Christian girls and of the Christian families who moved away from Bethlehem, and he said, "The Christians are a minority in Palestinian society. If a Christian family is conservative, they would pursue the rapists, but the Christians do not relate to rape the way Muslims do. They don't kill, although there were Christian families that did. I know a boy in the village who killed his sister because she had relations with boys, not serious relations. They used to talk through the window. The Christian Arabs have blood feuds, but not like the Muslims. They are more influenced by Western ideas than Muslims. The Europeans and Americans help them. They have work—they don't work in Israel or the Palestinian Authority, but in Europe, America, and China. They send their parents money and their parents live well. You can tell by the house if someone is Muslim or Christian. Muslims are jealous of Christians. Why should the Christians live like that? But I don't blame them, I blame the Israeli occupation. If there were no occupation, my house would look like his. The Christians did not participate in the *intifada* uprising the way the Muslims did. You could count them on the fingers of one hand, because they have normal lives, different from ours, and they aren't willing to lose those lives. I heard about what happened in Bethlehem between Christians and Muslims when Christian girls were raped in Beit Jala [a Christian city near Bethlehem]. Rapists go to weak families. It doesn't have anything to do with religion."

Nabil verified what Qatada said about the incidents in the church in Bethlehem. After an increase in the number of cases of sexual harassment, a few families appealed to Feisal Husseini, an important Palestinian politician who died in 2001, and to a high-ranking figure in the Palestinian Authority to complain about their daughters' being attacked and about members of the Taamra tribe who were harassing and terrifying them. Many families not only left Bethlehem because of the situation, they moved abroad. Now the majority of Bethlehemites are Muslims from around Hebron, but the city used to be completely Christian. Nabil tried to shift the blame away from the Muslims, but it was clear that the rapists knew the girls were Christian and that a blood feud would not ensue, as it would had they attacked Muslim girls. Moreover, the Christian families were perceived as weak and unable to defend themselves. It is the same dynamic that makes them recruit members of weak families for suicide bombing attacks because they are easily exploited. That is especially true when it comes to women, because the general view is that there is no one who will protect them.

Qatada continued, saying, "My father said, 'Look, there are people who are big-time criminals, no one watched what they were doing and they got weapons . . .' My mother is forty and she stays at home. I love my mother best." He pulled at the black thong around his neck. On it there was a wooden pendant in the shape of the State of Israel, but without the name Israel on it, a map often seen in Palestinian ministry of education schools and textbooks. The children study from books that don't mention the State of Israel, and it doesn't appear on any map. I laughed and made a comment about the map, and he laughed as well, as though he had been caught doing something wrong, and said, "Okay, enough, there is no Palestine." He did not, however, take it off.

I asked him what he thought about sending women and children to participate in attacks, and he answered angrily. "Everyone in Gaza is crazy. Why give a boy an RPG? There are girls who might get hurt. A girl should carry out an attack? What's that supposed to mean? There are men, why should a girl put on an explosive belt? There are a lot of men for that."

I told him that I had met Sheikh Ahmed Yassin, the founder of Hamas, and that he too was against sending women on suicide bombing attacks. Qatada immediately said, "So why was one from Hamas?" He was familiar with current events and obviously he and his friends had discussed the issue. He continued, "She was a girl, why did they bring her? Why give a girl an explosive belt? Give it to her brother. Would you give it to my mother? There are young people who don't have much intelligence, they have problems at home, so they ask for a belt and go to the Hawara [the Israeli army roadblock near Nablus]. If someone's father beats him, he goes to a terrorist and says, 'Give me a belt, I want to sacrifice myself.' How can that be? There is a boy here in wing 2, he's fourteen years old. He said he had problems with his father, his father used to beat him, so he went to Hawara with a pipe bomb. Everyone here in the juvenile wing is underage, they aren't smart. A fourteen-year-old child who goes to *istishhad* is stupid. He's just a baby, he doesn't know the difference between right and wrong. They tell him there are girls in paradise and to take the money, and he says, 'Let's go, okay.'"

He began talking about paradise: "There are seventy-two black-eyed virgins in paradise. When I die, maybe I'll go to paradise, maybe to hell, to the fire and not to paradise, because I won't sacrifice myself. There is a paradise for every good man, for every *shaheed*. Seventy-two virgins for every man who was a hero in battle. Allah said, 'Sacrifice yourself.' All the prophets will be my friends. Paradise is full of golden palaces, and each one has a lot of land around it, and a river of milk and honey and alcohol. Every *shaheed* marries the girls, has a great life, and fathers children. Girls also go to paradise. If a girl wants me in paradise, she can join me and be more important than the seventy-two virgins, and she will be beautiful. I have been here in jail for eighteen months, ever since I was sixteen, and in fifteen days I will be eighteen and go to the adult wing. I will be released in fifty days."

I didn't understand why Qatada was so anxious to leave the juvenile wing and move in with adult felons. Perhaps to enhance his reputation outside of jail and to meet relatives in the adult wing? It was interesting that despite his enthusiastic descriptions of paradise, he didn't think he would go there. We had been talking for a long time, and I suggested coffee. He refused, saying, "Coffee is no good for your kidneys, but people here drink black coffee because they think it will make their mustaches black, and then people will think they're adults."

I asked him what the other inmates in the juvenile wing thought about the sixty-eight-year-old grandmother who carried out a suicide bombing attack. He laughed heartily and said, "The kids laughed that an old lady performed *istishhad*. She was seventy-six and blew herself up. Fatma, the daughter of the prophet, fought in jihad and did what Muhammad did, but she was younger." His reaction was the same as that of Abu Tir, deputy head of the de facto Hamas administration.

I asked him what else he could tell me about attacks in which children had been involved, and he said, "I heard they give a boy fifty shekels [about thirteen dollars] to carry out an attack in Israel. Why should I go kill myself? I want to live. Why doesn't he [the dispatcher] send his own son? Why does he want to send me instead? His son will travel, study, have money. My father told me, 'Be careful of what you say. Don't let anyone make a fool of you or send you to *istishhad.*' I'm eighteen years old, I have my whole life ahead of me."

Since 2009 there has been a military court to deal with underage offenders. In the past, minors were tried along with adult offenders, bringing impressionable youth into close contact with hardened terrorists. A woman judge has been appointed to preside over the trials of crimes committed by youths under the age of eighteen. She sits in a separate court when cases involving adults are not heard, and her attitude toward young offenders is often more personal and sympathetic than is generally the case with adult offenders.

Parents are allowed to be present in court and even in the investigation. On occasion, reports from social workers are presented to provide information about the minor's background.

I asked about prisoner relations in light of the violence and rivalry between Hamas and the Palestinian Authority. Our interview took place during the battles in which Hamas violently overthrew the Palestinian Authority and took over the Gaza Strip. He said things similar to the adult prisoners: "Their rivalry doesn't influence us, certainly not here in jail the way it does in Gaza. We are all brothers here, one family. There is no Fatah, Hamas, Palestinian Islamic Jihad here. We are all Palestinians; there is no division." What he said was true at the time, but later, because of the escalation in the internal Palestinian conflict, prisoners from the various organizations were strictly segregated. The situation became extreme during Operation Cast Lead, and the Fatah prisoners were so happy about Israel's direct attack on Hamas that some of them praised the Israeli army's actions to the guards.

Qatada, who like all Palestinians is a Sunni Muslim, spoke about his admiration for Shi'a. Many young people admired the Shi'ites, especially because the Shi'ite Hezbollah and Iran were so popular, and that worried the older Palestinians. "I surf the Jihad Web [a fundamentalist Islamic website]. I see what Shi'a is all about, and I want to know everything. Shi'a is pure, it's great, they have nice leaders. I look at it and my heart beats, I love, love Nasrallah and Khomeini, love them. I am a Sunni but I love Shi'a. I am not a Sunni, not a Shi'ite. I am only half religious, but my father and mother are religious. My father is a hero, but Khomeini, leader of the 1979 Islamic Revolution in Iran, is a hero. So are Ali and [his son] Hussein [important figures in Shi'ite Islam]."

The Sunnis feel encroached on by the Shi'ites, who are converting more and more Sunnis to their beliefs, especially in view of the Iranian threat and the war between Sunnis and Shi'ites in Iraq. Nasrallah has become a hero for the youth, both he and the Shi'a he represents. Qatada's eyes shone when he spoke about him.

Nasser, spokesman for one of the juvenile wings, was introduced to me by the wing commander. When Nasser smiled, two deep dimples appeared. Nasser extended his hand across the table and said, "I'll carry your bag." It was particularly heavy that day, full of papers and a large bottle of mineral water. He hung the bag over his shoulder, and we walked to the other wing together. Once we sat down he gave it back to me. He was proud of his courtesy and was extremely polite throughout.

Nasser's story was similar to Hassan's: "I was fourteen when I saw the older boys carrying weapons. That impressed me, and I myself asked why I couldn't be like them. I also like to carry a gun. Before I was sent to jail I admired them. We played with them and it was great fun. We liked them so much! We loved to get close to them, but we were afraid to, because we were underage and they had weapons. They kept saying they would give me money to buy cigarettes. There was a group of boys my age who worked with them, and they said they would give us money. They used to take the underage children with them as backup and convince the kids that if they were caught or if something happened, the older ones would be responsible. The men even used their money and told them that they should confess to things they hadn't done because underage children received more consideration from the Israelis. We didn't want to go to school, but our parents put pressure on us. We thought it would be better to be arrested and go to jail instead of school." Children are often exploited for criminal purposes, and there have been "honor killings" in which responsibility was assigned to an underage brother, who would receive a lighter sentence and thus save the father or older brother.

Nasser described the pride and sense of masculinity he felt in the company of wanted terrorists, but he also sounded bitter because he understood he had been exploited, like many others in the juvenile wing. He told me about a boy who had been beaten by his father because he got bad grades. The boy reacted by "taking two pipe bombs concealed in his toys and going to the roadblock to be rid of his father." Another boy, whose father gambled and was addicted to drugs, worked with wanted terrorists in return for money, and they "laughed at him." As to his own father, Nasser said, "My father knew I went around with the *shabab* [the guys] and he took a rubber hose and beat me with it. He beat me, but I continued going around with them. I did it more because he beat me and I wanted revenge for the beatings." Nasser wasn't the first inmate to tell me that he chose terrorism in revenge and to rebel against his parents. The wanted terrorists sent him to tell younger boys about paradise to recruit them for terrorist attacks. He said he didn't belong to any organization, but when he grew up he would join Fatah.

As to the involvement of women in terrorism, he said, "There were no girls with us. Girls shouldn't carry out actions. She's a girl, it doesn't matter what you say or how you explain it, she is still a girl going around among men. Terrorism is for men, not girls. A girl goes to jail, no one knows what she did, how she was arrested, how she was interrogated. Maybe there is something wrong with her and people will talk when she gets out. It's a defect. She won't find a husband, and she won't be respected. Go figure what happened when she was inside . . ."

NOTES

1. A common misconception, patently untrue.

2. In 1985, three Israeli soldiers held captive in Lebanon by the Popular Front for the Liberation of Palestine, headed by Ahmed Jibril, were exchanged for the release of 1,150 security prisoners in Israeli jails.

6

Brother and Sister, Suicide Bombers

A few months ago an Arab intellectual said of security prisoners, "When a woman goes to jail it is an affront to her honor, but a man is in jail because he is supposed to suffer. For a child, jail is a school."

Fawaz went to jail when he was sixteen. He was twenty-one when I met him. We sat in the cell where prisoners usually met with their lawyers. It was small and stifling, with two chairs, one on each side of a dilapidated Formica table. There were no pictures on the whitewashed walls, and the atmosphere was claustrophobic.

Fawaz was tall and looked younger than his twenty-one years, although he wore a small beard. He was relaxed, and his expression was open; he was not handcuffed. He spoke very quietly, as though to distance himself from his feelings. He was shy and introverted, and there was something childlike about him. He laughed and smiled a lot, although what we talked about wasn't funny. I had the feeling he enjoyed talking about his life, and he spoke willingly, needing to tell everything. Every time he said something about religion he opened his arms and said, "*Allahu akbar.*" He stuttered badly but couldn't tell me when it began. While he was still young he was forced to make choices that had an influence on the rest of his life. He had a need to satisfy his friends and dispatchers. Rejected and introverted, for him Hamas opened the door to social opportunities he hadn't had previously. He spoke freely and earnestly about the acceptance and sense of belonging they had given him.

When he was fifteen he was sent to carry out a suicide bombing attack on an Israeli bus, wearing an explosive belt. Apprehended by the Israeli security forces on the way, he pressed the detonator, but nothing happened. Stubbornly and with a great desire to carry out the mission, he fiddled with the wires, but the belt still did not explode. At his trial, a legal precedent was set regarding minors who try to carry out suicide bombing attacks. "When a minor acts as an adult, his status as a minor is not considered, and he is sentenced as an adult," said the judge. Until then, "minor" had been the magic word for lighter sentences, on the theory that minors did not think the way adults did. Fawaz was the first underage would-be suicide bomber who was caught red-handed. His age and young physical appearance were discussed during the trial, and he was described as a child with a peach-fuzz mustache, who had not yet begun shaving. He was thin and had a child's body.

One guard described him as a prisoner who was easy to deal with: "Although he belongs to Hamas he gets along well with everyone. He is industrious and works hard. The other prisoners don't take him seriously, they pity him. He is friends with everyone. He stutters. He speaks to me freely, and once I said, 'If you could turn the clock back, would you still want to blow yourself up?' He said, 'No, I never would.' His sister was also sentenced to jail." He told me that Fawaz's career as a terrorist began when he was twelve years old, when he joined Hamas and participated in religious studies. He threw stones at Israeli security forces, took part in demonstrations and marches, waved Hamas flags, and distributed flyers with picture of *shaheeds*.

The guard said he used to joke with Fawaz and say, "If there is a deal to release prisoners, I'll put your name at the top of the list," and all the other prisoners would laugh. When I asked the guard why he thought Fawaz had decided to carry out a suicide bombing attack, he said, "They exploited his weakness, his innocence, it wasn't because he wanted to. He wasn't smart, he wasn't developed. In my opinion he is weak, so they sent him on a joint Fatah-Hamas attack. His sister is nine years older. She started off in Fatah but changed to Hamas. Fawaz's dispatcher was a security prisoner, but he behaved like a felon."

I asked him what he meant, and he said, "Security prisoners don't usually interfere or shoot the breeze with the guards, for example. They don't talk about drugs. His dispatcher smoked grass and didn't even bother to hide it. The guards and security prisoners respect one another, and conversations with them are short and to the point." Once it was common to move from one terrorist organization to another, even between Fatah and Hamas. During the period Fawaz was active, the Palestinian Authority and Hamas still had reasonable relations and planned and carried out a number of joint attacks. Today they are bitter rivals, and joint attacks are out of the question. Fawaz began as a child, graduating from throwing stones, to throwing Molotov cocktails, to carrying out a bombing attack. For women it is usually a single act, and the path to it is not as well defined and clear.

Fawaz said that he wanted to kill Israeli soldiers and police, but not civilians. When I asked how he reconciled his refusal to kill civilians with the Qassam rockets fired by Hamas at Israeli towns and villages in the western Negev, he simply didn't answer. Many male terrorists I interviewed claimed they didn't want to kill Israeli civilians. Most of the women, on the other hand, told me enthusiastically that they preferred killing civilians, including children. The women's participation in attacks meant that they might never marry and fulfill themselves as mothers, and their anger was clear. "Why should your children have everything and ours have nothing?"

Fawaz told me how he became a terrorist: "My parents didn't know, they only found out later, and they were angry with me. I was recruited by a twenty-one-year-old guy from Tulkarm; he was later killed by the Israeli army. He suggested I carry out an attack after members of his family were killed. He used to sell baked goods near my school. I told him I would think about it for a day, and afterward I told him okay, and then I left for the attack and put on the explosive belt. He said, 'Get ready, and if you have a problem we'll take you.' I waited for two days. I was stressed because I was going to blow myself up. I was afraid I wouldn't go or that they would catch me. I said good-bye to my friends at school, just the way I always did, and no one knew. At school they talked to us about the *shuhada'a* . . . My parents didn't know I was going. I sent them a letter telling them that I was going to become a *shaheed* and that they shouldn't be angry and that they should just think I had gone and wasn't coming back. I had my picture taken with a gun and a Qur'an, and I felt I was a man and not weak; I felt I had power. It was a very strong feeling. When I went I felt brave and not afraid of anything. I didn't think about anything."

Throughout his speech he kept smiling, a contrast to what he was talking about. He described the events as occurring in the far-distant past and not relevant to his life, and he answered every question without hesitation. He enjoyed our talk and was enthusiastic to continue: "They took me to an abandoned house in Tulkarm two days before the attack. I was supposed to leave at noon, but it was postponed to the evening. All that time the Israeli police and the Shin Bet and my parents were looking for me. My parents only knew about it after I had left. They looked for me at home and found the letter, and they were very angry and started looking for me. I lived with my parents and my brothers and sisters. I went from home to school and from there to the coffeehouse to help my father in the family business. I also went to the mosque to pray. I come from a religious family—my sisters wear the *hijab* and I pray. One of my sisters is in jail. She was sent to jail two months after me. I visited her a month ago. It's hard when your sister is in jail. They accused her of wanting to sacrifice herself, but she didn't want to do anything. She has a twelve-year-old daughter. She was framed. My sister is divorced, so my mother is bringing up her child. After my sister's husband divorced her, he remarried and divorced twice more, and now he is married to someone else."

Two days after he was recruited, he was on his way to the attack. "I went to Kfar Saba [a city inside Israel] by taxi. I felt I would just press a button and go to paradise. I believe that black-eyed virgins are waiting for me there. I am certain paradise is better than the life in this world. I have never been involved with a woman. I was little and I didn't know about that kind of thing. The virgins in paradise and good things were waiting for me, things I can't describe. What's up there is a thousand times better than what there is here. Even today I believe in paradise, certain of it, until I die." He hinted he was a virgin and that he was going to realize his sexual fantasies in paradise.

All the would-be *shaheeds* I spoke to described paradise in similar terms. As far as they were concerned, beyond meeting Allah, the prophet Muhammad, and other *shaheeds*, paradise was a place for the pleasures of the flesh. There were eternal virgins with transparent white skin, and there were no physiological needs. There was food, rivers of honey and alcohol. Fawaz added it would be a place where sexually inexperienced adolescents met virgins. I asked him why boys his age carried out suicide bombing attacks, and he said, "There are a lot of boys who were arrested. Seventy percent of them were convinced with lies. They give them a bag or a belt and explosives and twenty or thirty shekels [around seven dollars]. They tell them to take it someplace else. They just want to kill little kids, for example, at the Hawara roadblock at Nablus [where several suicide bombing attacks were carried out by adolescents]. I'm not in favor of that. A wanted man who is afraid something will happen to him sends a little kid. The Sharon Jail[1] is full of kids like that. I wasn't one of them. I was convinced and I asked to be sent, but they force the little kids to do it. There was one kid, fourteen, they arrested him at the Hawara roadblock. He didn't even know where he was going. Adults go of their own free will, but they force the little kids to do it. Their parents don't realize; they then see it on TV and go into shock. They take kids from weak families. Most of the kids in jail are from weak families. In school they talked to us about religion, about *shaheeds* and paradise. Little kids didn't learn about it, it's forbidden."[2]

Religious preachers do not brainwash small children lest they carry out suicide bombing attacks too early, which for them would be a "waste" of potential candidates. They prefer to postpone the process and indoctrinate older children, those who will cause more damage. They target adolescents who are looking for excitement and a way to prove their masculinity. "You feel more like a man, and you also do it to release tension," Fawaz said, and raised his eyebrows.

As for women in terrorism, Fawaz was of the same opinion as most of the others: "It is forbidden for girls to blow themselves up or take part in terrorist attacks. We are against that, because *banat* [girls] are unsuitable for it. Girls are forbidden in Islam. It is promiscuity—a girl isn't allowed to expose her body to anyone, and when she blows herself up it isn't exactly her body, it's little pieces of it, her whole body doesn't blow up. For us, in the Palestinian community, it is hard for a girl to be a suicide bomber because it isn't 100 percent certain that she will succeed in blowing herself up, and she might get caught. There is a problem with girls in jail. There is a problem because they killed a lot of people and because men prepared them and damaged the family honor. In a lot of cases there is a mess between the girl's parents and the men who recruited her. The parents are very angry with them . . ."

I asked him what he would do if his mother had asked him not to carry out a suicide bombing attack. He hesitated for a minute and said, "Maybe because of my mother I wouldn't do it, but first I belong to Allah and then to my mother. I do the right thing for Allah and then for my mother."

I went to visit Ayisha, Fawaz's sister, in the women's wing. Samira, the wing spokeswoman, sat down next to her and across from me. I knew who Ayisha was, but I had never spoken to her. She smiled in welcome, and from the other side of the table we were sitting at, she touched my hand. "You can speak to her freely," Samira told her in Arabic. "Can I really say everything I want to?" Ayisha asked, a look of surprise on her face, and was told she could. Ayisha was wearing a brown *jilbab* that completely enclosed her body, and a black *hijab*.

Ayisha smiled and giggled throughout the interview. She was relaxed and happy that a rare opportunity to express herself had been provided. There was something innocent about her, emotional and easy to manipulate. I was surprised because she was an adult woman with a certain amount of experience, not a child. I gave her regards from her brother and said I had come to talk to her to keep my promise to him.

Samira left the room every so often to tell the girls to stop making noise so that we could talk in peace. "I asked them to be quiet. You can't talk to the men." The prison staff visited the wing during our conversation to check complaints that the commissary had run out of certain items. "They're talking very loudly but I don't feel comfortable asking them to lower their voices," she said.

Ayisha was thirty, divorced, and the mother of a twelve-year-old daughter, by profession a hairdresser. She had already been in jail for four years and seven months, arriving just two months after Fawaz was arrested. She lived in Tulkarm and married a cousin at the age of seventeen, giving birth to a daughter the following year. She told me that they divorced when the baby was three months old. I asked why, and she said, "He went abroad, to Romania, and married a Romanian woman. I wanted a divorce, but he refused because he was my cousin. But in the end I did get a divorce, and I went to live with my mother and father. My daughter calls them mommy and daddy. I worked all the time, I learned to cut hair, and my husband didn't help with money or with bringing up the baby. At first he didn't see her at all, not until she was four, because he went to Romania. When he came back I didn't let him see her. I wanted to teach him a lesson because he left me and didn't ask about the child at all."

Ayisha broke out laughing, and other women came in and joined the conversation. There was a kind of "we're all sisters" laughter. She felt she had been treated unjustly but that she had fought back. I knew that similar stories could be found at any time, in any place. She kept laughing as she talked, enjoying the empathy of her fellow inmates, showing her white teeth and stroking the *hijab*, pushing a wayward curl back under the fabric. "And guess what happened," she continued. "He divorced the Romanian as well. She had two children by him here and returned to Romania. We live in the same building, and her children love me more than their own mother. And then he married again, and the third wife started raising the Romanian's children."

In the middle of her story Sabiha came into the room with her pink-clad baby, who didn't smile and seemed uninterested in his surroundings. Samira took him from her and put him straight into my arms. I knew him and his mother from previous visits but didn't recognize the baby for a moment. I bounced him on my knee. Other women came in, and we talked about children. The baby held my finger and looked at me for a long time. At first I thought he was a girl, but as the conversation developed I realized he was Bassam. I told them I hadn't been sure it was Bassam because of the pink clothing. They explained boys were often dressed in girls' clothing to ward off the evil eye. I remembered that when I saw him in the exercise yard for the first time he had been wearing a pink overall. Samira took him back and put him in his favorite spot, in front of the aquarium, and he watched the fish swim back and forth. He still tried to catch them through the glass, making the sounds all babies make when they are happy.

The atmosphere in the room was easy and made it possible to speak freely, and Ayisha continued her story: "At first my parents wouldn't accept a divorce, because my father is the oldest sibling and my husband was his brother's son, so they didn't agree to a divorce, only my older brother helped me." In Arab society cousins commonly marry, and every marital problem tears the family apart and creates conflicts within the extended family. Ayisha kept talking, voicing complaints about her husband and his lack of fidelity. Her husband divorced his Romanian wife and married again, and since in Islam the father's religion determines that of the children, they are Muslims, regardless of the mother's religion. The children grow up in Arab households and their mothers, who come from another culture, usually Western, are often forced to abandon their children because it is hard for them to adapt to the traditional Arab culture, which so blatantly oppresses women. They are faced with an impossible dilemma: to stay with their children and suffer a lifestyle that oppresses and humiliates them and that often includes physical violence, or to turn their backs on the past and abandon their children and return to their countries of origin. It is only the case for Muslim men and Western or non-Muslim women. On rare occasions, Muslim women marry Christians and Jews, and as soon as they leave the bosoms of their families they find their lives in danger, because Muslim women are forbidden to marry out of their faith.

Ayisha said that until sixteen she was a tomboy, and that she only became religious in jail. Prisoners often become religious. Sometimes a female Arab security prisoner arrives in jail wearing jeans and a T-shirt and within a short time has traded them for a *jilbab* and *hijab*, part of a desire to blend in with the other prisoners. Security prisoners feel the need to be part of a group, and wearing traditional clothing is one way of doing it. The change is important and obvious, and I often saw it with my own eyes, a kind of public statement that the woman was part of the group and accepted its rules.

I asked Ayisha how her family reacted to her volunteering to be a *shaheeda*. She said she had been recruited by a cousin because they were friends. Her brother Fawaz did it before he was fifteen, and now it was her turn, a kind of family behavior pattern. "My father yelled. He didn't understand how I could do it. Everyone thought I loved life, liked to go on trips, dress nicely, so they didn't believe I was going to do it. I wasn't thinking about anyone. I told my daughter not to cry if they arrested me. Now the hardest thing is that I miss my mother and daughter. When I think about them I am angry and I weep. When I first wanted to be a *shaheeda* I didn't think about them at all, but only about what I was going to do. I saw Wafa Idris [the first female suicide bomber] on TV. I only thought about one thing, about what the martyrs had done, and then I thought about carrying out an attack."

Like many other suicide bombers, Ayisha kept her family in the dark about her involvement in terrorism and what she planned to do. It is reasonable to assume that had her family found out, they would have stopped her. Ayisha described the robotic, obsessive thinking, the "worm" described by other would-be suicide bombers. They have obsessive thoughts that never leave them. All they can think about is blowing themselves up, like the worm, *duda* in Arabic, described by drug addicts inside their heads when they can think of nothing but their next fix. Their mental processes gave birth to a new expression in my mind, "*shahadamania*," the obsessive desire for *istishhad*, a mixture of euphoria, sexual appetite, and extreme hunger.

Ayisha continued: "When my brother Fawaz was arrested I was afraid something would happen to the family, but my motive was revenge. I was supposed to blow myself up in Netanya, to blow myself up and kill a lot of Jews. My brother knew a lot of Jews and had good relations with them at work. I used to get merchandise and makeup from Israelis." Did she feel anything for her potential Israeli victims? "I saw the blood of Palestinians and I didn't think about my mother or my family, so how could I think about Israelis I didn't know? My brother tried to blow himself up before me. It was hard for my parents and for everyone. They were in shock. They didn't know anything about it, only after I was arrested. You know, a girl is forbidden to go out when she wants to, but a boy can be away from home for hours at a time. The most important thing is for a girl to study. That way her parents may know where she is, but at least she is out of the house.

"Finances are not the reason people blow themselves up. Even people who had no money worries did it. It comes from religion and revenge. The *shaheeds* I know about are exceptional people who finished school and were well off. They did it because of our people's lives." Most prisoners I interviewed did not give a depressed financial situation as one of the reasons they decided to carry out terrorist attacks. The financial reasons were secondary and helped recruit them but were not decisive factors.

I asked Ayisha how she would feel if her brother had succeeded. She said, "I grew up with him, so obviously I would not be happy about it. He was young, and when I married I took him with me. I was like his mother." Even though she herself wanted to be a *shaheeda*, she didn't want her little-brother-almost-son to die. She wasn't the only one who was willing to blow herself up but who didn't want someone close to do the same thing. I asked her about what her brother had said, that a woman's body was exposed during an attack. She said, "After my body blows up, everyone sees it, but Allah hides it. There are religious girls who take public transportation to attacks and take off their kerchiefs." She was referring to women who wanted to look non-Arab for the success of the attack, since it would make it easier for them to enter crowded locations without calling attention to themselves. On the other hand, there is still a great deal of sensitivity, both within Arab society and among the women themselves, about the idea of exposing their bodies in public, even after an attack. Ayisha found a traditional religious solution to the problem: "Allah hides it," and no one sees anything.

I asked her about paradise and hell. She got excited and started waving her hands: "That was my goal, to succeed and go to paradise. I wouldn't have gone to hell. I think I will be more than the virgins in paradise, because they are human and humans make mistakes. In paradise I will be like a queen and sit in my kingdom and marry anyone I want to. I want someone who is handsome [giggling], and Allah will receive me. I hope I reach that degree. There are people who believe that not everyone who sacrifices himself goes to paradise but that there are different degrees. A man gets seventy-two virgins, but I don't want to talk about that. I want to carry out an attack and get revenge on the Jews and enter paradise." I asked again, "What about hell?" She said, "Fire, screams, thorns, no water, just very hot water. People stay in fire all the time. They die and come alive again and go into the fire and get their punishment. They have no choice. In paradise you rest. People in paradise don't even pray. The person who doesn't believe in Allah, an infidel, turns into sand, but that's better than to enter hell."

Hell was as real for her as paradise. She seemed terrified just by talking about it. When we finished discussing it, she smiled at Samira and said how much the girls liked her. "I am the jail's hairdresser," she said. I asked why they bothered with hairdos when their heads were covered by *hijabs*. Samira said, "The other girls in the cell see it." Ayisha told me that Islam forbids women to tweeze their eyebrows. I asked her whether she also took hair off the girls' legs. She could hardly stop laughing, and said, "Why not?" I smiled and said that women, in order to feel good, had to be pretty regardless of the situation. Samira had been listening with half an ear and said, "It's not about beauty. It's about cleanliness." We summed up by agreeing that she was the security prisoners' beautician.

NOTES

1. An Israeli jail.
2. That is, it is undesirable for small children to know about *shahada*.

7

❦

Special Bonuses for Each and Every *Shaheed*

Facing dozens of young Arab men and women, is it possible to identify potential suicide bombers? The Israeli security forces look for tell-tale signs. Riyad, the Shari'a lawyer and Muslim Israeli Arab mentioned previously, had additions for the Israeli security force profile, other signs that make it possible to identify a terrorist. "You can tell by certain physical signs. For example, he can be overly secular in his dress. The way he looks at you, his passion betrays him. It comes from inside, and it betrays him. He will wear a silver ring, because it is against Islam for a Muslim to wear a gold ring. The prophet Muhammad forbade it. Anyone who wears a gold ring will burn in hell, and even to camouflage yourself is forbidden. There are people who encourage the suicide bomber to camouflage himself by shaving his beard." Riyad told me that shaving reveals skin that was not exposed to the sun and is therefore white, and a fresh shave is another way of identifying a potential suicide bomber. A member of the Israeli security forces told me that sometimes the hair on the arms of suicide bombers is shaved and they are bathed. Sometimes they have prayer books in the right-hand pockets of their shirts and pray before the trip and when they enter the target site, and they also have a *siwak*, a special toothbrush similar to that used by the prophet Muhammad. They mumble prayers as they walk, a way of motivating themselves. They wear their watches on their right wrists, the preferred side. I was reminded of my father, who retained Iraqi customs even after he came to Israel and insisted that my little sister, who was left-handed, write with her right hand. He felt there was something wrong about writing with the left hand, despite the fact that forcing left-handed children to write with their right hands may impede their development.

Riyad noted that a terrorist could be identified "by his eyes. He isn't thinking about the present. There is excitement in his look, and a smile. It is a nasty smile which says that he who laughs last laughs best, that's he's going to get the best of you . . ."

There are other signs as well. Suicide bombing attacks were often carried out by terrorists with gel on their hair and shirts with things printed on them in Hebrew and English, which would make it easy for them to blend in with the Western crowd. There were those who wore nonseasonal clothing, like winter jackets in summer. Sometimes they used musk, a nonalcoholic perfume, as did the prophet Muhammad. They believe that after they blow themselves up their bodies will smell of it, and there are folktales to the effect that not only does the aroma of the perfume rise from their graves, but that their bodies do not rot. There are those who don't smoke before an attack or who want to meet Allah on an empty stomach. But there are no hard-and-fast rules. Hanadi Jaradat, who blew herself up in the Maxim restaurant in Haifa in 2003, ordered and ate a full meal just before she activated the detonator. However, the smile and automatic behavior are signs of alienation and dissociation, the desire to separate the body from the soul with smiles and mumbled prayers. The suicide bombers feel they are on their way to paradise, while the Jews and other infidels will go to hell.

Riyad wanted to talk about the Jewish people. He said, "In my opinion, no people have ever suffered from persecution like the Jews. The Jews want to lead good lives. They want to rest, and as a nation they can't do anything to hurt others. For that reason Barak was willing to give in to Arafat. If the Jews find an understanding with the Palestinian side and security for the Jewish people, they will give up half of Jerusalem and the territories, if there are guarantees for their security. Preparing Muslims for peace has to include understanding that the Jews are not a cancer, don't want war, are not invaders, but a people who were almost wiped out seventy years ago. They are no longer willing to have one more drop of Jewish blood shed. They already paid their dues, when their women and children were slaughtered. You have to bring Al-Jazeera TV to Yad Vashem."

I was surprised by his attitude about the Holocaust, especially in view of the increase in the number of Holocaust deniers in the Muslim world, foremost among them Iranian president Mahmoud Ahmadinejad. Various Islamic elements use anti-Semitic stereotypes, camouflaging them as "anti-Zionist": large-nosed, fang-toothed monsters. At trial, several terrorists have made remarks such as, "It's a pity Hitler didn't finish the job."

Riyad continued, "Israeli soldiers come with a lot of emotional baggage from home. They have no relatives because they were killed in the Holocaust. The Arab world has to understand the Holocaust. As part of a minority group, I owe it the Jewish people, because of racist dilemmas and my very deep feelings of empathy for the history of the Jewish people." He ended by saying, and it was obviously painful for him to say it, that "there is a dichotomy in Islam. On the one hand, it wants to kill people, on the other, to pity them. I disagree with things Muhammad said, but in the end, my father is named Muhammad and so is my son."

His speech seemed to have upset him. He said again that jihad was the personal duty of every Muslim and that whoever did not carry it out was a hypocrite or even a kind of infidel. "A woman who participates in jihad automatically receives mercy when she carries out a suicide bombing attack and is spared the agonies of the grave. The pain felt by a woman whose body is blown to shreds is like an insect bite. It doesn't hurt when you die like that." According to Islam, every true believer prays to the prophet Muhammad, through whom Allah forgives his sins. Only Muhammad can be a Muslim's advocate, but the *shaheeds* are automatically advocates, and those who sacrifice themselves for the sake of Allah go directly to the most exalted place in paradise and do not suffer in the grave, nor do the members of their family. Benefiting others is reserved for the prophets, the messengers, and the *shaheeds.*

Riyad asked, "How does a suicide bomber get on a bus in Tel Aviv, look a seventy-year-old woman in the eye and blow himself up? Because he is thinking about the special bonuses he will get. The first is described in a *hadith* [the oral tradition regarding the deeds of Muhammad]: As soon as the first drop of his blood is shed, he has atoned for all his sins. According to another hadith, the prophet was asked why the *shaheed* receives atonement, and the answer was because of the *fitna* [disorder, unrest] he feels at that moment. He receives atonement because of the agonies of his soul, because of the dilemmas and uncertainties which accompanied him, because he sees death before his eyes and still chooses to die, for the sake of Allah's desire and call for jihad against the infidels. How does a nineteen-year-old boy, whose friends don't have a care in the world and are only interested in chasing girls, how does he choose such a path? What does he think when he sits next to a pregnant woman on the bus or a woman old enough to be his grandmother? What goes through his head during the seconds before he blows himself up? He is thinking about what he will receive from Allah, what was promised by the prophet Muhammad, Allah's messenger.

"So when he is sitting across from the old Jewish woman on the bus, he is thinking about how he will be the advocate for seventy of his relatives, none of whom will go to hell, all of whom will go to paradise. That is a special privilege, because according to Islam a person is judged by his deeds. According to Islam, you pay the price for what you did, not for what your father, brother, or mother did. The *shaheed* has the unique right to save his relatives, to keep them from hell and make sure they enter paradise. So he weighs the two, his family on one side, his victims on the other. He prefers his family."

Riyad described the perquisites as though the *shaheed* had a shopping list. He related to the *shaheed*'s desire to get the bonuses that help the suicide bomber realize his goal. That prevents him from seeing his victims as people, and all he can think of is his objective. In criminological terms, *shaheeds* have an internal system of moral judgment that is situation dependent. They use neutralization and dissociation mechanisms to evade defining themselves as murderers. The only thing that can break the spell is the attack's immediate circumstances, for example, an external similarity between a victim and a relative. A would-be female suicide bomber told me she changed her mind because of a baby who resembled a nephew, causing her to see him as a human being.

In another instance, a dispatcher used promises of virgins in paradise to convince his younger brother to be a suicide bomber. In that case, the dispatcher tried to deflect claims made by Palestinians that dispatchers did not send their own relatives on attacks. The boy had his doubts and when detained said that he was sent to the commercial district in Haifa, where there were a lot of Arabs, and he did not want to harm them. He changed course and walked to a different area but decided not to blow himself up because he took pity on the women and children he saw, who reminded him of his mother and brothers. He eventually wound up in an abandoned building, where he took off the explosive belt and walked around aimlessly, arousing the suspicions of the police. His troubles ended when he was led to a place where he could put down the belt.

Dispatchers are not criminals and lead normative lives, but they dehumanize non-Muslims. Therefore, they can kill Jews or Christians without feeling they have committed murder and without being stigmatized as murderers by their environment. Only when something cracks the wall in their moral judgment, as has happened in certain cases,[1] is it possible to shake their determination to kill and look death in the eye, and even to smile, without seeing their victims as human beings.

Riyad continued his description of the bonuses received by the *shaheed*s. "The automatic mercy they receive does not include debts. An individual who wants to commit suicide has to know that if he owes money, Allah will not grant him mercy and that it is a crime between two people. If he does not pay off the debt and carries out a suicide bombing attack, Allah will not forgive him." Part of the psychological preparation dispatchers give suicide bombers is to pay their debts. The very act of paying the debt is preparation for the attack.

Riyad said, "The agonies of the grave are terrible, according to the Muslim tradition. The Prophet speaks of the 'embrace of the grave.' Coffins are not used in Islam, only a white shroud, like in Judaism. The dead person is placed in the grave, and people leave him. The grave hugs the dead man, presses on him until his ribs are interlocked. There is so much pressure on his chest the breastbone breaks, and then two angels come. Those are the strict rules of Islam. The angels say, 'Who are you? What is your name? What do you say about the man who was sent to you, the prophet Muhammad?' and the man has to answer. The average Muslim who wakes up every morning has to say the *shahada* [the creed: "There is no God but Allah and Muhammad is his prophet"]. The Islamic sages say it is worthwhile to repeat the prayer because like every other mortal you will eventually be in your grave, and when the angels hear the *shahada* they don't ask the questions. The angels are described as frightening creatures, angels of the grave, and that is the importance of the *siwak* [a toothbrush that looks like a small piece of wood, used by Muhammad], it encourages you to repeat the *shahada* [because it is part of the cleansing mechanism, it cleans the teeth and prevents bad smells]. When you are alive, you wake up in the morning and say the *shahada*, and when you are dead, it's like you're asleep. The angel removes the shroud and you say the *shahada*—it's like when you wake up from sleep. The angels hear you and don't ask the questions, so you avoid the interrogation and their deceit, and afterward the blows they deliver.

"*Shaheeds* don't go through all that. They blow up into little pieces and their souls go up to the sky. When a man carries out an attack he causes his own soul and those of others to fly straight up to paradise without the 'accounting in the grave.' Unlike every other mortal, Allah keeps the *shaheed*'s soul in the stomach of a green bird. The bird flies around paradise until Judgment Day. When Judgment Day comes and destroys the earth, the souls of the *shaheeds* return to earth, they join their bodies, and people are resurrected. What is special about the *shaheed* is that he did not experience the agonies of the grave. Everyone is afraid of that. Every Muslim child who reaches the age of five begins to hear about the tortures of the grave. It is part of the experience of every Muslim child. They told me about it and I was scared, too. Children grow up believing those ideas. They get inside them, into their brain stems."

Once a would-be female suicide bomber told me, "Seventy people from my family will enter paradise directly and will not suffer pain in their graves because I am a *shaheeda*."

Riyad tried to tell me what he meant by basic concepts inside the brain stem in an attempt to understand the secret, the *shaheed* who in point of fact acts for the good of his relatives and for his own sake. Is a suicide bomber motivated by altruism? There are emotional and impulsive aspects to their willingness to blow themselves up; however, it is an instrumental suicide, a way of getting concrete, material, tangible rewards in the next world.

Riyad said, "The *shaheed* knows that whoever does the deed is a benefactor for his parents and his people, but he is also doing himself a favor, because he is taking a shortcut and avoiding negative experiences. The *shaheed* suicide bomber knows he is freeing himself from experiences burned into his subconscious. His soul goes straight up. He is considered a *shaheed* and will go to paradise. He doesn't go to where Allah asks the questions other people are asked. The *shaheed* automatically receives mercy. From the instant the first drop of his blood touches the ground, it is written that he will enter paradise and not suffer the agonies of the grave as the dead do. On Judgment Day, when the sun comes close to the earth, and there is destruction and everything disintegrates, and the oceans catch fire, there are earthquakes and all the ecological things people talk about, that's Judgment Day. Allah gives the *shaheed* the cloak of faith. It's not a cloak of money or girls, but a kind of estimation. The *shaheed* will marry the virgins, the black-eyed girls, eternal virgins of divine beauty, not the kind of beauty we are familiar with in this world. It says in the Qur'an that 'No one touched them, neither man nor demon.' They are creations of Allah himself. He is the god of beauty, he can create such beautiful women. For the sake of the *shaheeds* Allah is noble, great. He is generous and does not stint on women for the *shaheeds*. He invests in creating such women and makes them unusually beautiful. Those women, as opposed to others, have never had and will never have a monthly period. In the descriptions of the prophet, their legs are so delicate you can see their bone marrow." I asked him how a *shaheed* could satisfy such special women. He said, "That is a question people asked the prophet: How can a man be enough of a man to satisfy seventy-two virgins? What will be the source of his sexual prowess? The prophet said it would come from Allah. This has to be understood within the context of Judgment Day, when people in paradise don't look the way they did on earth. They will be fifteen meters tall and according to the prophet will have thirty arms. All people, both men and women, have a different, very beautiful form in paradise."

I asked what happens to a *shaheed* after he blows himself up. The answer came immediately: "A black man from Shati [a Gaza Strip refugee camp] blows himself up in Tel Aviv and kills children and goes to paradise. There he receives mercy, bonuses, a beautiful new form fifteen meters tall, he gets a palace built especially for him by angels inside which seventy-two virgins are waiting, each one gets seventy-two virgins. When a woman with dark skin reaches paradise as a *shaheeda*, no one knows whether the color of her skin changes. It is reasonable to assume her skin turns white. Condoleezza Rice is known as the black spider, the black widow . . ."

Although there are many black Muslims, they are still discriminated against because of their skin color. The Muslims call their neighborhoods "the slaves' quarter." Sometimes "slave" is a racist epithet for a black man.

Regarding paradise, the terrorists did not seem to be describing something imaginary, but a kind of alternative reality, better than the life full of taboos, forbidden things, and shame (*a'ib*) that they live now. Riyad continued, "People care less about physical beauty, they are afraid of Judgment Day. They are willing to be monkeys, anything just not to go to hell. The men get women, and what do the women get? That question was raised only during the past decade or two. The Islamic sages claim that in the next world a woman can choose the man she wants to live with. Beyond that, Islam promises her nothing. The issue is embarrassing for the sages. A man can not only enjoy himself with seventy-two girls, there are also orgies with the women in paradise. As an incentive for women, promising ten men is not realistic, because women look for warmth from one man. It sounds bad even in secular terms: women don't exactly look for sex."

I am not entirely certain he was correct in his assessment of the needs of Muslim women. Women involved in terrorism whom I interviewed claimed that they would enjoy the delights of paradise, including "that thing"; most of them did not specifically refer to sex. One said, "There is no difference between what men and women get, it is almost the same thing. People say a man gets seventy-two virgins in paradise, and a woman definitely gets one, not seventy-two . . ."

Other women said that in paradise a woman can choose a mate, which she cannot do in this world, but only on condition that as a *shaheeda* she was not married. If she was married, she will meet her husband again in paradise, whether she wants to or not. If that is the case, she goes from bad to worse, because she will have to spend eternity with a man she doesn't love.

NOTE

1. A. Berko, Y. Wolf, and M. Addad, "The Moral Infrastructure of Chief Perpetrators of Suicidal Terrorism: An Analysis in Terms of Moral Judgment," *Israel Studies in Criminology* 9 (2005): 10–47.

8

Terrorist to Her Dispatcher: "Why Did You Betray Me? You Know I Love You"

Fadwa, a resident of Lod, sat on a wooden bench in a military court. On a separate bench behind her sat a male prisoner. She was about to be tried for her part in kidnapping an Israeli taxi driver. Male and female security prisoners never sit on the same bench. Even if they are being tried for the same crime, they sit separately. Only Fadwa's mother and sister were in court, waiting for the trial to begin. Although her feet were chained, she was wearing platform shoes, partially hidden by tight jeans. She had a green nylon windbreaker, and her curly hair was tied in a pony tail. She sat on the bench and stared vacantly at the wall. Her fingernails were long but unpolished. Occasionally she said something to her lawyer. The trial of the prisoner ahead of her finished, and he was led out of the courtroom.

Fadwa turned around, smiled, and began talking to her mother, who was sitting behind her with Fadwa's sister. The mother said angrily, "Just look at what you've done to us!" Fadwa broke out in tears and laced her fingers, laying her hands over her chest as if to say, "We have nothing more to talk about." She continued staring into space and then began crying again. Her lawyer tried talking to her, but she wasn't listening. She sank into herself, lacing and unlacing her fingers, staring at the wall, then at her hands, playing with her fingers to keep herself occupied.

Her lawyer, Rachel, was a well-known Jewish-Israeli lawyer who had represented many security prisoners. The trial had been held in Hebrew and simultaneously translated into Arabic. Fadwa was found guilty and her punishment would now be determined. However, she behaved as though the discussion were about someone else, sometimes abstracted, sometimes talking to members of her family sitting on the visitors' bench. When the court translator told her the prosecution was asking for a fifteen-year sentence, she jumped up as if bitten by a snake. "Me?"

she asked, pointing to herself. "Fifteen years?" She broke into tears and threw herself on the bench helplessly, her hands hanging down. Her mother also broke out crying, wailing, "She's my little girl. He took her, he exploited her. Muhammad knew she was in love with him."

Rachel was dismissive of the prosecution's demands: "They don't have a case." Rachel wore her black robe. Her hands were laden with heavy jewelry, and her hair was dyed. She occasionally made a comment to Fadwa in very basic, metallic-sounding Arabic, nothing designed to support her. She continued, saying, "None of the judges [there are three in Israeli courts] rejected that the accused was motivated only by something I cannot call romantic, but more the need to settle the matter of her marriage with the accused [Muhammad]. We know he dropped out of her life for two years and only reappeared on the day before the abduction, when he confused her and muddled her thinking with promises to take care of their engagement, which had been postponed for two years. In other words, he promised to restore her lost honor. That was no small thing for her—it was the center of her existence and made her blind to everything else. There is no evidence that the accused had any part in the abduction. The victim was never asked whether in his opinion she created illusions or tempted him into going away. . . . I appeal the conviction. She is being charged as though her presence contributed to the abduction, but when the entire story . . . is examined, it is in two parts: on the first day she expressed her surprise at the knife, and on the second day she came again and saw the crime, but all we have is that she appeared. . . . She was worried about the driver's safety. She told him the kidnapper would take care of him and also asked for a romantic trip to Jerusalem, and during it to show her the kidnapped Jew so she could see he was okay. 'Promise me nothing bad will happen to him,' she said to Muhammad. She also says she let the cab driver use his cell phone to call his family, and Muhammad was angry with her. She says he told her to take part in the abduction and that she refused and agreed only to a trip to Jerusalem. . . . She was only found because she called Yosef's [the kidnapped cab driver] wife, and she thought she was calling his mother. . . . She [Fadwa] was not in the army, she was not even in the pre-army program they have at school. She never went further than the fifth grade. Her father is Israeli by virtue of his father."

Rachel swept her robe back, turned to Fadwa, and said dismissively, "She is the fifth wheel, unimportant . . . hovering in the background." There was something arrogant and patronizing about the way she related to her client. Fadwa was asked whether she wanted to say something. She stood up, holding the rail in front of her. One of the judges said, "It is important for you to understand that this is your last chance to say something on your own behalf." Bending toward the judge, she leaned on the rail. She said, "First of all I want to say that what I did was not because I wanted to, I didn't want to do what I did and I'm sorry it ended like this. I didn't mean to be part of a kidnapping. I'm only sorry for one thing, that I went with Muhammad. That was all I meant to do, to go with him. I didn't have any other intention. I want to take matriculation exams and I want to go to university." Her statement sounded fairly ridiculous in view of the fact that she had only finished the fifth grade. Her saying that she only wanted to go with Muhammad reminded me of Fahima, the *shaheeda* in spite of herself, who said that all she wanted was to hang out with the guys, not to kill herself. Like Fadwa, Fahima only wanted to be around her boyfriend or with men in general, which is taboo in Arab society, and which involved both women in terrorism and led them into a situation from which there was no escape.

I looked around the courtroom and saw Fadwa's mother, who was obviously distraught. She was stout and wore traditional Arab dress, and she looked older than her years. She stood up and spoke emotionally: "I will tell you the truth. My daughter was young, she was only eighteen. When she met Muhammad from the territories for the first time, she was only ten, and he started wooing her when she was thirteen. Then he asked her brothers for her hand and they refused. Then they caught up with him and beat him to make him stop running after her, and after that a cousin from Jericho came, and he and Fadwa got engaged. She didn't see Muhammad for two years and he didn't have anything to do with any of my children. Then, when he heard she was getting engaged, he called and said, 'My parents agree, I want to marry you.' He came to pick her up in his car, and that was when it happened . . . Fadwa went with him and her little sister [her excuse to leave the house]. I will tell you the truth, because Fadwa loved Muhammad, but after her brothers were against it and rejected his marriage proposal, he wanted to get revenge on them through her. What we heard was that Muhammad kidnapped a Jew and told Fadwa, 'I'm going to get you involved in this, I'm going to destroy your life, and it's because you're getting engaged to your cousin.'" Fadwa's mother did not hide her disgust with Muhammad, calling him "the man who made fun of my daughter." As far as Fadwa was concerned, he wanted to get her into trouble. She told the judge, "All I want is for her to marry and have children." Even at a time like that, when her daughter was on trial and about to be given a long jail sentence, her only wish was for Fadwa to marry and fulfill her traditional Arab role as a woman.

I spoke to Fadwa before the trial. She was dressed sloppily in ordinary clothing, with no hint of religious inclinations. She smiled a great deal and did not seem aware of her situation, although, or perhaps because, at twenty she had already spent two years in jail. Her family was originally from the Gaza Strip but moved to Ramallah, under Palestinian Authority control, when she was ten. She did not mention that she currently was living in the mixed Jewish-Arab Israeli city of Lod. She slowly began to speak more freely, until it became hard to stop her to ask questions.

"I'm the third child in the family," she said. "I'm very attached to my family, to all of them, but especially to my father. But I don't tell anyone all my secrets.

We're six boys and four girls. My mother is forty-two and stays at home. My father is forty-five and sells clothes. I was happiest when my sister got married, even though I was in jail. The things that made me saddest were when I was arrested and also when my father divorced my mother when I was thirteen. All of us live with my mother. She never remarried. It's forbidden because she has children, so she can't marry again."

As often noted, when a man divorces his wife or dies, the children still belong to their father or his family. If their mother wants to continue raising them, she cannot develop a romantic relationship with another man and certainly cannot remarry. If she did, the children would automatically be taken from her and given over to their father or his family. The status of divorced women is particularly low in Arab society, and they are always under surveillance, considered problematic, and sometimes ostracized.

The story of Shafika is an example: her father was killed in a traffic accident in Jordan when she was a baby, and her mother brought her up until she was ten. After her mother remarried, she had to surrender Shafika to her late husband's family. Shafika often told me she felt she had been abandoned because "my mother preferred a stranger to me."

Before she was released from jail, Shafika told me of her fears: "I have no one outside . . . I am jealous of my mother's husband . . . May Allah take me! It is easier to talk to Allah than to people. Allah can understand me. I look up at the sky and say, 'Where are you? I want to talk to you!'" She hugged me, knowing we would never meet again, although she half-asked whether we could meet once she was "outside." She said, "I'm going back to Jordan . . . to live alone . . . to become the Shafika I was before jail. I miss being loved." I told her to take care of herself, and she said, "You, too, take care of yourself. Say hello to your daughters for me." We had spoken a great deal about my children during our meetings over the years, and I asked her whether I should say hello to my son as well. "Yes," she said, "to him, too," and smiled.

I hope life will treat you kind, and I hope
you have all you dreamed of ...& I wish you
Joy and happeness ,,, but above all this I
      wish you love ... & I will always love you ,,,

Shafika wrote me a good-bye note based on Dolly Parton's "I Will Always Love You."

Fadwa also grew up in a household without a dominant male figure. For women, the presence or absence of a father figure is crucial. Without a father figure they are considered defenseless, vulnerable to exploitation because in a patriarchal society such a family is perceived as weak.

Everything Fadwa remembered about her past life seemed tied up with her present situation. "My father remarried, but he has no children. He has good relations with us and he visits every week. We don't have anything to do with his new wife and we don't visit him in his new home. I don't know why my parents got divorced." Her parents' divorce was painful and influenced her life to a great extent. Her life had not been easy before then. They moved around and were insecure because her father collaborated with Israel. I asked her to tell me about her childhood and her dreams. She laughed and seemed happy to be talking about more pleasant things.

"I liked to play with a big teddy bear with my sisters. I want to marry and have two boys and two girls . . . I was engaged once, but he was also arrested. We were engaged until then. There were family troubles because we were together when we were arrested."

Her "fiancé," Muhammad, kidnapped an Israeli taxi driver. Until the abduction, Fadwa and he had not been in contact for several years. He refused to present her to his mother or get the engagement under way. In Arab society, that means receiving permission from the father of the prospective bride and a meeting between the two families to agree on the dowry paid to the bride's family, and both the permission and the meeting are necessary if the match is to be finalized. Fadwa loved Muhammad, and he knew it and exploited it to carry out the attack.

Fadwa continued: "My father was angry that I was seeing him. He said that I had shamed him because not only had I gone with a man but I was arrested with him as well . . . I was forbidden to leave the house alone so I took my sister. She was three years old and she came with me. I often take one of my sisters with me when I want to leave the house . . . I'm allowed out alone, but I'm not allowed to go far. I took my sister because Muhammad told me to go to Ramallah and said that we would be delayed there." I asked whether her parents were worried about them. "No," she said, "why would they be?"

Fadwa left early in the morning and came home in the evening to sleep. She went out again the next day, this time with a different sister, to meet Muhammad and to look for a place to hide the taxi driver when he was abducted. She said that when she came home that evening her mother yelled at her, but that was all. Her parents knew nothing of what had happened. "I hadn't sullied the family honor, but they were angry with me anyway."

She continued the story: "I didn't know what Muhammad wanted to do. He only told me after we left. I wasn't prepared to help him, but I went with him as though we were on an outing because I wanted to be with him, because I loved him. He told me to come, so I went. Now I know I shouldn't have gone when he told me what we were going to do, but we were already on our way . . ." It was obvious that she would have done whatever he told her to—the only thing that

mattered to her was to be with him. He invited her out, and on the way they kidnapped a taxi driver, but as far as she was concerned, the most important thing was
to be with him. I asked her what she especially liked about him, and she said, "I've
known him since I was twelve. He's from Ramallah, he's a friend of my brother's.
I used to look at him a lot and I loved him."

Fadwa dropped out of school in the fifth grade, after having been left back a
year. "I didn't like school because I was left back. I didn't like studying, and leaving school was ordinary for girls . . . Once I dropped out I stayed at home and
helped my mother." She could read and write, but not fluently or easily. She said
she could write letters, but didn't. Muhammad had graduated from high school
and exploited her innocence and ignorance to his own ends. "I don't know if he
exploited me," she said shamefacedly. "I miss him." She continued as though she
hadn't been in jail for two years because of the difficulties Muhammad got her
into.

She was not religious, she said, only her mother was. During the trial she
kept looking at her mother, who had covered her head with a kerchief but was
not wearing the kind of traditional dress that concealed her from head to foot.
Fadwa said she really missed her mother, whom she called her "best friend," even
though she didn't tell her all her secrets. She laughed, and told me she laughed all
the time. She only stopped during her trial, when she realized she was going to
jail for fifteen years.

The abduction carried out by Muhammad and Fadwa was a rare case in which the
IDF managed to rescue the Israeli victim unharmed from his Palestinian captors.
I wanted to interview him about the interaction between him and his abductors,
and between Fadwa and Muhammad. Yossi, the taxi driver, was only too happy
to talk to me. He was past middle age but still had a lot of energy, a small white
beard, and a good sense of humor. He spoke calmly and seemed to have worked
through the trauma of his abduction without the need for professional help. Married with children, he had been born in Iraq and fled to Israel with his family in
the 1950s. As a Jewish refugee he experienced the same problems of absorption
and assimilation all the immigrants did who came to the country after its founding, spending time in the transit camps, the temporary immigrant camps, and
even five years on a kibbutz, of which he had happy memories. Although he was
sixty-three, he was still in contact with some of the kibbutz members. He went on
to serve in the army, raise a family, and live the ordinary life of a taxi driver. He
still understood Arabic, his native language, but he was slowly forgetting it with
the passage of time. He spoke Hebrew with his abductors, noting that they spoke
the language very well, but he understood what they said to each other in Arabic,
a fact he kept to himself. He radiated calm and did not become upset, even when
talking about the abduction. His speech was reserved and careful throughout the
interview. I told him that not only had I met Fadwa in jail, but that I had been

present at her trial. I had been presented with the rare opportunity to hear both sides of the story and fill in some of the blanks, especially about the interaction between Yossi and his abductors, Fadwa and Muhammad. It all began, he said, on a summer's day in 2003:

"Two men and a woman and a little girl got into the taxi, Arabs. I didn't suspect anything because they looked like a family. They said they wanted to go to Jerusalem. We argued about the price and I told them straight off that I didn't go into Arab villages. Muhammad spoke to me in good Hebrew. The other man sat next to me, Muhammad was in back, and the little girl sat in the middle, between him and Fadwa. Before you get to Jerusalem there is a roadblock, and I asked them if they had ID cards. They said everything was ok. After the roadblock they asked me to turn off the road to the left near a village so they could relieve themselves and asked me to drive into an alley. I shifted into 'park' and waited for them to get out. That was when I felt a knife at my throat. It was Muhammad, and the one next to me had my hands bound in a second. I didn't shout, but I thought I could reach the panic button or my phone. They cut my safety belt, and then the little girl woke up. Everyone in the back seat got out of the car, and the two men pushed me between the front seats into the back. They didn't take me out of the car at all. They pushed me between the two front seats into the back. Then Muhammad sat in the driver's seat and the other man got in back and sat on me. I was on the floor of the car, and Muhammad started driving.

"The girl sat up front with the child. There was a lot of yelling. There was a ring in a box with some small change, and she took it and put it on her finger. [Israeli taxi drivers usually keep a box between the two front seats for things they find in case their rightful owners come to claim them.] They also took the money I had in my pocket. We kept going for a couple of minutes and then everyone got out of the car and we started walking. After fifteen, twenty minutes, we came to an Arab village whose houses were set far from each other. They freed my hands, but the other Arab, not Muhammad, put a knife to my ribs. It later turned out that he had a gun as well, but I didn't know about it at the time because I didn't see it. We kept walking until about 11 o'clock at night, and then we got into an Arab taxi, a van, larger than a regular car. I couldn't see the driver. Most of the time we walked in open country. Fadwa and the child walked a few steps behind, and the other man walked next to me with his knife in my ribs. Fadwa said she was tired and the child was crying, she was tired, too. Fadwa picked her up and carried her, and sometimes Muhammad carried her. The little girl didn't know what was happening, but Fadwa knew everything. She didn't hug Muhammad. They argued all the time, but I kept thinking about how I was going to get out of this.

"That night Muhammad sent Fadwa and the child to Lod, where she lived. The men were from someplace near Ramallah. We slept in a floor-tile factory that night, I guess it was also near Ramallah. I don't know exactly. The next morning Muhammad went to get a car. He was very tense and nervous. Someone came in a car and took us. She [Fadwa] came back on Saturday and was in the car at nine in the morning with a different little girl, one a little older."

It is hard to believe that Fadwa, who participated in the abduction, did not once dare defy convention and, even though she was in the midst of aiding and abetting a crime, still went to sleep at home so that no one would say anything about her conduct and her family would not suffer the shame and condemnation of having a daughter who stayed out all night. She returned the following morning with a different sister so that they would let her leave the house, but also to provide cover for the abductors, since a small child made them all look like relatives. On the day of the kidnapping, the little girl was moved the front seat to make it easier for them to pass through the roadblock and perhaps even to serve as a human shield.

Yossi continued: "From there we drove to one of the hills around the city and stayed there the whole day. We saw helicopters in the air. We were in a completely open area, and everything had been planned, where we were going, where we parked. We parked the car and started off on foot. The plan was to sleep in a greenhouse out in the open, but there were IDF patrols and roadblocks, so they changed the location. On Friday they brought fried chicken and cold drinks. They were very tense and aggressive all the time. They didn't hit me, but they threatened to kill me. Muhammad, especially, threatened me and said, 'Don't get any funny ideas, we'll kill you if anything happens. If something happens you'll die, you won't stay alive.' She [Fadwa] heard it all. On Saturday she stayed with us until 4:30 in the afternoon. Before she left she asked me if I wanted to call home, with the phone they took from me. We called my house. I told them the number and they dialed. There was almost no reception." After the call, Fadwa removed the battery so that the phone couldn't be located.

During the time he was with his captors, Yossi heard Fadwa and Muhammad arguing about romantic issues, and she didn't hide her jealousy. "For an entire afternoon they argued about his engagement to another girl. We were sitting under an enormous tree. I was on one side and they were on the other. They were sitting with the little girl, about two or three meters from me, not too close. Then they argued some more and asked me if I wanted to call home. I didn't have the time to say anything, just yell, 'Who is this?' and then Muhammad took the phone away from me. Letting me call home was apparently Fadwa's idea. She said, 'Don't worry, we won't do anything to you,' but he, Muhammad, threatened to kill me. She tried to calm him down and she tried to calm me down.

"When they talked about his fiancée the situation almost got out of hand. They screamed at each other, and she cried and cursed at him: 'Go to hell, what are you doing? How can you act like that?' Then she left with the little girl. I think they went by car, but she left. I didn't see her again. All the time she was walking away she was yelling at him about the other woman . . ."

Fadwa told me that she thought at the time that Muhammad was engaged to her, and that they only had to settle things with his mother, but it became apparent that he had fooled her, because he was already engaged to someone else. After throwing a fit of jealousy she left, everything openly said and done in front of the victim, although they didn't know he understood what they were saying.

Yossi continued: "At around noon Muhammad's friend went to buy food, pita bread and sour cream, and to see if there were any Israeli soldiers in the area. When he came back he said that there was a lot of army activity and that the soldiers were looking for them. I ate a little, but mostly I drank. Around five in the evening, after Fadwa left, we started walking again. We walked for a long time, and I felt like I was in basic training again. I couldn't even feel my legs anymore. At around 9:30, 10 o'clock at night, Muhammad let me call again. First he talked to my wife, and then he passed me the phone. He said, 'Take it, talk to her, your wife will recognize your voice.' I told her I was all right and then he took the phone back. He said to my wife, 'Don't worry, he's like a father to me, I won't touch him,' but at the same time he kept threatening to kill me. They asked me if I knew Arabic, and I said no. They didn't ask where I came from. They left all my documents and briefcase in the car and in my pockets. They just took the money."

I was surprised that Muhammad hadn't asked Yossi what his background was. Usually Palestinians ask Jews what their ethnic extraction is to show them they don't belong to "Palestine" but came to Israel from other countries. Some of those over sixty are Holocaust survivors, and some came to Israel as refugees from the Arab countries that expelled them after the founding of the State of Israel, as my parents were expelled from Iraq. However, the Jewish settlement in Israel is far older, and there are many families that have lived there for generations. Yossi told me the issue arose during his abduction as well: "Muhammad said terrible things about the Israeli government, about Ariel Sharon, about Israel, and said, 'You have no place here, what are you doing here? We will throw you all out!' After the phone call we kept walking and came to an inhabited area. They warned me not to make a sound. 'We won't kill you,' they said, 'but the locals will.' I was too tired to breathe. We came to a construction site. They were building something industrial. You could see concrete and smell it, too. I was outside for an hour and a half, and then they took me down to the basement. It was large and deep underground. It must have been meant as storage space. There was a small ventilation grille on the other side of a pit. They put down some boards and we went into the pit before it got light outside, and I was there until I was released. I couldn't fall asleep, and they spent the time talking quietly. On Sunday evening Muhammad went away and I was left alone with the other Arab until Monday evening. There was a third Arab who joined us, the building watchman. Everything had been planned. Even the factory gate had been left open so I could be brought in. We stayed in the same place until I was released, but late Monday night they took me out of the pit. They put down a ladder so I could climb up and use my mobile phone to call home. I talked to my wife for a minute, and then Muhammad took the battery out so I couldn't be located."

Yossi was lucky. He was rescued by IDF soldiers and went on with his life. Talking to him convinced me that Fadwa had been manipulated and exploited by Muhammad and that her motive for participating in the abduction had been romantic. She had no control over events, and she had even endangered her younger sisters. Attacks are often carried out by terrorists pretending to be an innocent family, using women and children as cover and passing freely through roadblocks. Using children is common, accepted practice among the terrorist organizations, even if it means endangering their lives, as was the case with Fadwa's sisters.

Gilad Shalit was kidnapped on June 25, 2006, from an army post near the southern Gaza Strip, and two of his comrades in arms were killed. The next day his captors demanded the release of all the male and female security prisoners under the age of eighteen. The day after that, a spokeswoman for the female prisoners was interviewed by Israeli TV, holding a baby, the son of one of them. The baby was supposed to make her look less threatening and to send the message that a mother's place was at home with her children and not in jail. Allowing her to be interviewed two days after the abduction was Israel's way of telling Hamas what the country was willing to pay for Shalit's release. As of this writing, Gilad Shalit has been held captive in the Gaza Strip and denied visits from the International Red Cross for almost five years. Hamas's demanding women and children was a way of making political capital and projecting the image of innocent, harmless women, some of whom were even mothers. The biological clocks of the women prisoners keep ticking, and they don't have time to wait for the customary Middle Eastern foot-dragging.

9

Clerics on Women in Terrorism:
"What Will She Get in Paradise,
a Couple of Virgins?"

Clerics, intellectuals, and other respected individuals in Palestinian society differ in their views regarding Muslim women who leave the private, family environment to enter the world of terrorism. There is no such dilemma regarding the participation of men in the "resistance" to Israel.

I discussed the issue with Riyad, who had a broad secular education as well as training in Muslim religious law. "In Arab society," he said, "people still respect and praise women who have taken part in terrorist attacks." However, it is impossible to ignore the many problems and embarrassing questions faced by Palestinians on such occasions. Riyad described it as follows: "On some of Al-Qaeda's websites people ask Khaled Mashaal [head of Hamas's political bureau] and Ismail Haniya [head of the Hamas administration] why they send mothers and women, why they sent an old woman [Najar, a sixty-eight-year-old grandmother, who blew herself up in November 2006]. They answer that as wanted men they consider themselves dead men walking, and that even if the Israeli security forces do not kill them, they are not immune." Studies of terrorist dispatchers have indicated an outlook of "each person has a role to play." "Dispatching a male or female terrorist depends on the proposed target site and the preparations made for the attack. There is no Islamic norm about sacrificing a woman for the sake of Allah."

Riyad told me about the moral commitment to jihad. Every Muslim is personally responsible when the *waqf*, the land comprising the Muslim endowment, is invaded. The responsibility of jihad is so important that a woman or child is allowed to leave the house without asking her father's permission. By contrast, a woman is forbidden to attend her father's funeral unless she receives permission from her husband. Many locations all over the world have been designated by

Muslims as part of the endowment and that they must be liberated by jihad. Spain (i.e., Andalusia), for example, which was under Muslim domination until 1492, is considered part of the *waqf.*

Riyad said, "Muslims are nurtured by the basic Islamic sources and influenced by people like Hassan al-Banna, Sayyid Qutb, and Abdallah Azzam, all of the Muslim Brotherhood. University students recruited for terrorist activities usually belong to groups [*usar*] in the *da'wah* [the Muslim social infrastructure, which deals, among other things, with propaganda]. If necessary, the cells can be armed and sent out on terrorist missions." Al-Qaeda, Hamas, and the Palestinian Islamic Jihad often use such cells. Abdallah Azzam, originally from a village near Jenin (a city in northern Samaria, controlled by the Palestinian Authority), provided Al-Qaeda with its name, which means "the foundation." He was killed in Pakistan in 1989 when his car blew up. Riyad admired him: "He was a walking nuclear bomb, and everything that happened in the world was his doing. He was the brilliant, creative mind behind the global jihad. He invented it. Al-Qaeda not only means 'foundation,' it is a fully formed concept. Azzam had a doctorate in Islamic law. Fourteen hundred years ago the prophet Muhammad began his mission and preached Islam, and he ran up against the same groups Muslims run up against today. There were Jews in Al-Madinah and infidels all around in Byzantium and Persia. Azzam said, 'Let's follow in the footsteps of Muhammad and do what he did, let's slaughter the Jews and Byzantines and Persians. Today's Byzantines are the Americans, and the Persians used to be the Soviet Union. Western Europe, the United States, and Israel, which represents both Western culture and the Jews, are considered by the Qur'an as Islam's worst enemies, because their stubbornness prevented them from accepting Islam.' One third of the Qur'an refers to the Jewish people. The verses in the Surah chapter called Al-Israa ('The Night Journey') outline all the terrorism in the world, including anti-American terrorism. One of the final goals, according to the Surah, is the destruction of the State of Israel. That is the terminology also used by Nasrallah, bin Laden, Ayman al-Zawahiri, the Muslim Brotherhood in Egypt, and others."

The position of the Muslim Brotherhood after the "Arab Spring" will solidify now that Mohamed Morsi has been elected president of Egypt.

Riyad mentioned the *shaheeds* who had attacked Israel, calling them marginal and dissociated from the hard core of Al-Qaeda, for whose members Hamas is not sufficiently radical. He said, "They are men who came upon terrorism by chance and not the hard core. We will eventually reach the men who are sophisticated, brilliant, whose interests motivate them to realize their aims. Thousands of them will realize the jihad."

After Israel disengaged from the Gaza Strip in 2005, its character changed, and it is now under the rule of Hamas, the Palestinian branch of the Egyptian Muslim Brotherhood. Weapons and global jihad terrorist operatives, including those with ties to Al-Qaeda, are brought into the Gaza Strip, into the "Islamic emirate" forming there. The situation was similar in Iraq, where *mujahedeen*, jihad fighters, from all over the world streamed in to fight the Americans and the new Iraqi regime. Immediately after IDF forces entered the Gaza Strip during Operation Cast Lead,[1] an operation prompted by Hamas's firing eight thousand rockets and mortars at Israeli civilians over a period of seven years, terrorist culture became firmly established in the Gaza Strip, aided by the massive amounts of weaponry sent from Syria and Iran and smuggled in through the tunnels under the Egypt–Gaza Strip border. Egypt is constructing a steel barrier above and below ground that will impede the flow of weapons into the Gaza Strip and sabotage the close physical ties between Hamas and the Muslim Brotherhood that threaten the Egyptian regime. Following the Egyptian revolution, the army's intervention in smuggling has weakened, and massive numbers of weapons now flow into the Gaza Strip and Sinai area. In August 2012 global jihad terrorists carried out a joint attack against Egypt and Israel. They killed sixteen Egyptian soldiers, commandeered their weapons and two APCs, which they used to break through the Israeli border, an attempt to carry out a mass-casualty attack. The Sinai Peninsula, although Egyptian, has become a largely unoccupied area, attractive to terrorists who are aided by local Bedouins. The attack on its soldiers during Ramadan shook Egypt to the core, to the point at which even its president, Mohammed Morsi, himself a member of the Muslim Brotherhood, realized that the danger was real and had to be fought against with determination.

Riyad said that in the Middle East, the Hanafi school of Islam, one of the four Sunni schools of Islam, named for Abu Hanifa and considered relatively moderate, is dominant, and the Palestinians belong to it because the Ottoman Empire adopted it when they ruled here. "Ibn Taymiyyah [who lived in the late thirteenth to early fourteenth century] said that if there was a battle between the armies of Islam and the infidels, and the infidels took the children of the Muslims and hid behind them as human shields, then it was not only permissible but also a duty to kill the Muslim children used as human shields to attack the infidels." In conflicts between factions, especially between Sunnis and Shi'ites in Iraq, beside the attacks on American, British, and other coalition soldiers, Iraqi civilians are often killed. Riyad's discomfort was obvious, and he said, "People claim that the jihadists misinterpret Islam, which is the religion of peace. . . . But the Qur'an is the source of hatred for the Jews. I have read the Qur'an many times and the exegeses as well, and the Jews are described as cursed and corrupt, as hard, stubborn enemies who will always persecute Islam and Muslims, as subversive—everything evil is attributed to the Jews." He felt the need to explain himself: "In a certain way, Islam is close to Judaism, in that both are monotheistic. They both have rules governing every facet of life, from the minute you get up in the morning until you go to sleep, and even how you sleep. In Christianity, if someone strikes you, you should turn the other cheek. Christianity is a religion which doesn't invade the bedroom. The Jew presents himself as belonging to the chosen people, and the problem is that Islam considers only itself and negates the others, the Jews, Christians, and atheists. The Qur'an makes it a religious duty to hate the Jews."

Abu Tawfiq was well educated, a graduate of Karachi University in electrical engineering, familiar with life in Israel but attached to the Palestinian Arab experience. He had visited many countries, and his worldview was unusual, simultaneously distanced and close up. He was sixty, took care of his appearance, and looked Western. He moved effortlessly between English, Hebrew, and Arabic.

I wanted his opinion on *istishhad* (martyrdom for the sake of Allah), especially among women, which is more prevalent among Shi'ites than Sunnis. Sunnis began implementing *istishhad* only during the past fifteen years. "Once," he said, "it would take six months to recruit a suicide bomber. Later it became just another way to kill, one that didn't have to be taught. Only brainwashing was necessary. It's easy. Today, you can just take anyone off the street and send him straight to a suicide bombing attack. It's a method of fighting. Instead of taking a machine gun, they strap on an explosive belt and blow themselves up. If politics enters Islam, Islam turns politics into ideology. They fool people to get outside support."

He continued: "Arabs are like other people; they have good qualities and bad qualities. A professor from Hebron University told me he had read the works of Ibn Battuta, a fourteenth-century Algerian traveler who visited most of the known world and prophesied what would happen." I told him Ibn Battuta was not a prophet, just an observer of men who described what he saw, and that people hadn't changed since then. "We live like Bedouin, and are blood-thirsty." The saying has often been repeated in reference to the fact that Islam does not renew itself,[2] and was said here unequivocally.

"I have a Jewish friend who told me that he saw a butcher in an Arab village slaughter a lamb, and that the butcher's children were standing around and watching the lamb's blood spurt. He said that if his own children saw something like that they would be frightened. I said, 'You're being stupid. The sight of blood is natural for us.' Islam is very primitive, and blood is something ordinary." Abu Tawfiq meant that Islam was based on an atavistic code that had essentially remained the same despite the way the world had changed, and that Islam had become habituated to violent external stimuli, which made Muslims ignore and even accept violence from a very young age. Another example is criticism of Iran over children attending public executions.[3]

He said, "Fear is deeply seated among Arabs. It is so deeply rooted that it cannot be excised. Despite the fact that Israel attacks buildings and people because the Palestinians fire Qassam rockets at Sderot, no one talks about being afraid." He was referring to Palestinians who lived in Beit Hanoun in the northern Gaza Strip, from where terrorists launch Qassam rockets at Sderot. Since then, longer-range Grad rockets have been launched that reach as far as Ashqelon, Ashdod, and Beersheba, the three largest cities south of Tel Aviv. The IDF's responses are painful, but the local residents either cannot or do not try to get the launchers out of their settlement and are in turn used by the terrorists as human shields.

"Politics ruins religion," he continued. "If you are a politician, you have to do what all the politicians do all over the world, you have to lie to people. Abu Ammar's [Yasser Arafat] view was, 'More blood, more publicity.' He was overjoyed when Palestinians were killed and used to say, 'Tell every woman to have ten children, one for her and nine to send to war.' He was ready and willing to sacrifice 90 percent of the people, and that was what he did. In my opinion, Islam has to be fought the way communism was fought: on every front and in every corner. Otherwise you will say, 'That is a good Muslim and that is a bad Muslim.' There are several verses in the Qur'an which say, 'Go out and kill!' If that is the kind of education people get for hundreds of years, it has to blow up in your face someplace or other.

"Even now there are people in Afghanistan who support the Taliban. How can that be explained? By brainwashing. I was in the region of Baluchistan [a district of Pakistan] in 1971 when they held elections. I had friends who belonged to the Socialist party, and they asked me to help them. Once someone from the party pointed at me and said, 'He is an Arab, close to the prophet Muhammad. If we hadn't chosen the right path, Abu Tawfiq would not support us.' People would kiss me and touch my arm to receive a blessing because I was an Arab, and Arabs were considered close to the prophet Muhammad and able to read the Qur'an in Arabic. So they like me there, and the Socialist candidate said I came because they were 'on the right path.'"

I suggested that perhaps they honored bin Laden because as an Arab, they considered him close to the prophet, and Abu Tawfiq agreed. He continued his discourse: "An Arab will go into a rose garden and step on the flowers, because the Arabs have not developed to the point where they are interested in flowers." He was outspoken and defiant, and clearly this was not the first time he was expressing his opinions. Several times during our conversation I wondered how he had avoided getting killed. I wanted to get back to the grandmother who had blown herself up in the Gaza Strip a few days previous. He said, "Fifty-seven years old [it was uncertain whether she was fifty-seven or sixty-eight]. A woman with a deviant personality. Maybe she did something wrong when she was thirty, and they came to her and said, 'You did so and so,' or, 'Let's talk about what you did,' or, 'Either you'll be slaughtered or you go and die as a *shaheeda*.' They do the same thing with children. If they catch a child talking to an Israeli from the security forces, they tell him, 'Hey, you! You work with the Israelis. If you don't kill an officer in the security forces or blow yourself up in a suicide bombing attack, we'll kill you.'" By "something wrong when she was thirty," Abu Tawfiq meant some sort of sexual transgression, or possibly that she was emotionally disturbed. Many of the people I interviewed spoke about the grandmother who blew herself up, finding it hard to understand or accept, and wondered where and when the wave of female suicide bombers would end.

He continued: "Maybe she was crazy [*majnuna*] in the past or deviant. She had forty children and grandchildren. She did it so people would say she sacrificed herself. She was fifty-seven years old. Maybe they found she was running a whore-house from her home, maybe she was crazy. Hers was not the action of a natural, normal mother. The girls who participate in terrorism are either not good girls or their father or brother was killed. So they tell one of them, 'Get revenge!' There is no other reason. Anyone who thinks differently or has a different idea in Arab society can't say anything. The only people who dare to speak have machine guns.

"They really believe in *Jana* [paradise]. They say to someone, 'Take three thousand dollars and carry out an attack. If you die you will go to paradise and if you live you will receive the money.' Otherwise, how can you explain that a woman sends her children to blow themselves up in suicide bombing attacks and then sings?"

I said, "I don't think she really sings. The people who force her to display joy don't let her mourn her children. The mother of a *shaheed* once told me that it's all for the cameras, and as soon as they stop photographing, the women scream and curse the people who sent their sons or daughters to blow themselves up."

He said, "A woman who acts that way, even in front of the cameras, is not normal. People think either that she received something or that she is afraid of something. Or that she will be punished, or that they will give her something. If she doesn't cooperate she will lose both her child and the monthly allowance they promised her, and that isn't normal. Whenever I hear that a child or a woman blew themselves up, I think it is something unusual, that they were exploited. You cannot find religious people behind this. None of the suicide bombers were imams in mosques or doctors of Shari'a. They are religious—they don't go and kill themselves. None of those who blew themselves up had a serious religious education. Those who blew themselves up were always exploited on some pretext or other. They exploit people with an Achilles' heel where pressure can be applied. *Shaheeds* are not washed, they aren't wrapped in shrouds, but they are buried in their clothes and go straight to paradise. Who would agree to have his mother go and blow herself up? A mother is something special. If they gave you millions of dollars and said, 'Send your mother to blow herself up,' who would agree to that? Even if my mother died I wouldn't let her coffin be blown up, and certainly not while she was alive. Everyone values the body of his mother, and no one would do anything like that, send his mother to blow herself up."

For Abu Tawfiq, sending a mother to blow herself up was going too far. On the other hand, he related to the *shaheeds* as victims of society. He did not have one word to say about the Israeli civilians who were the victims of suicide bombing terrorism.

Marwan, a Palestinian journalist, had a different perspective on the suicide-bombing grandmother: "She was one of the women sent to the mosque to hide wanted

Palestinians. They left the mosque [as a group], hid and protected the men with their bodies, and she was there and was angry about what people were doing. Her daughter said on television that after the incident she took everything personally. Two women were killed there. There was also the story of the Othmana family in Beit Hanoun who had ten of their members killed, a tragedy in which the IDF killed them by mistake in response to Qassam rockets fired at Sderot. The general atmosphere in the street, the pictures of body parts they showed on Al-Jazeera, everything had an influence. After that happened there was a woman on TV who said, 'Curses on your father, Mahmoud Abbas and Olmert.[4] Give me an explosive belt and I'll go blow myself up right now.' Maybe it was she. It was broadcast by [Israeli television's] channel 2. It was a classic case of someone exposed to incitement, and especially prone to revenge. On TV they showed the Qur'an she left open before she went to blow herself up." Marwan was deeply shaken by the story. People noted that although she killed herself, she barely managed to wound one Israeli soldier, so maybe suicide bombing wasn't a task for women. Many Palestinian men told me that about women in terrorism, especially women suicide bombers.

"What will she get in paradise, a couple of virgins?" Marwan asked with a laugh. "There is an Arab joke about that. As far as I'm concerned, this incident was an aberration, it crossed all the lines. You don't know anymore who will blow themselves up. It changed the profile of the suicide bomber. He could be a fourteen-year-old child or a fifty-eight-year-old woman. The AP said her real age was sixty-eight."

NOTES

1. December 27, 2008–January 18, 2009.

2. Irshad Manji, *The Trouble with Islam: A Muslim's Call for Reform in Her Faith* (Hebrew) (Or Yehuda: Kinneret Zmora-Bitan Dvir, 2005).

3. http://www.memri.org/report/en/0/0/0/0/0/0/6563.htm.

4. Chairman of the Palestinian Authority and at that time the prime minister of Israel, respectively.

10

⚜

Salima, Mother of Seven: "My Husband Only Thinks about Himself, I Don't Love Him"

One winter's day in 2006 when I went for interviews, there was a lot of noise coming from the Tanzim-Fatah wing, where the prisoners identified with the Palestinian Authority were held. They were sitting in a circle, trying to get a little sun and talking to one another. The office I usually received was locked, and I suddenly heard someone call "*Doctora* Anat!" from the kitchen. I turned and saw a woman in traditional Arab dress from head to foot leaning her elbows on a table covered with a colorful plastic tablecloth. She stood up, dragged over a chair, and invited me to sit with her. She was fiddling with a *masbaha*, worry beads, a chain of engraved wooden prayer beads. She showed it to me and explained how she used it to pray, praising Allah several times a day while holding it.

I smiled and told her that my grandfather also had a *masbaha* and that as I child I had watched him move the orange beads from side to side, as was the custom of the Jewish community in Iraq. She seemed confused and asked hesitantly, "Are you Jewish [*Yahudi*]?" I said I was but that there were Jews who fled Iraq and had come to Israel as refugees, and that my parents had been born there. She smiled and said, "I like Jews and Christians and all people. I don't have a problem with anyone."

She was a simple person. My feelings were important to her and she had not wanted her question to offend me. I was amazed she was surprised I was Jewish, because we had spoken in both Hebrew and Arabic. She offered me candy, and I took one and thanked her, sucking on it as we spoke. She was easy to speak to and responded without hesitation.

Salima was thirty-two, a large woman who looked older. She had seven children and had been in jail for three years, cut off from her children and family. She lived in a village near Nablus in Samaria, and her family had olive trees, cattle, and sheep.

She told me about herself: "I am a *fallaha*, a farm worker. I went to school for five years, but I know how to write. My mother was sick, so they took me out of school so I could take care of her—I was the youngest child in the family.

"I didn't think I would go to jail and that there would be trouble. If only we could have peace. Enough people have died, it's a shame. The most deaths occur in Palestine, Iraq, and Lebanon. People are killed in Iraq every day. I am most scared for the children. My oldest child is sixteen, and after him I have daughters aged between fifteen and four. I like the girls best, because I also got married very young. When I went to jail, my youngest daughter was one year old, and Houda [the wing spokeswoman] didn't allow me to bring her with me. So I haven't hugged her for three years, and she hasn't come to visit in two months. She didn't receive permission. My mother and father died a long time ago; I was only thirteen at the time. My mother died of diabetes, and my father died of leukemia when I was five. I got married when I was thirteen, and I had only been menstruating for one year. The *fallahin* marry their daughters off young. My older brother married me to a cousin. He was fifteen at the time. He married again in 2003 and did not divorce me, because we come from the same family. First he married a Christian woman from Ramallah and she went to France, so now he is married to a woman from Hebron."

Young marriage is acceptable, especially in the Arab villages, and polygamy is common. Women like Salima have short childhoods and then marry and start their own families. Salima was an orphan, and her older brother simply transferred responsibility from himself to his cousin. The fact that she was still a child didn't bother him.

Salima was full of grudges against her husband, especially since despite the fact that she was in jail, he still would not take responsibility and care for the children. His parents were also dead, so he sent five of the girls to a children's home in Jerusalem. "If I argue about anything with my husband when he comes to visit, it is that he doesn't bring the children with him." She made a gesture of turning a key over her lips, the Arab equivalent of the English "zip your lips," to describe the way she felt her husband was blackmailing her. She could not fight with him, fearing he would prevent her from seeing her children. She told me about other ways men pressured and controlled their wives, even though the women were in jail. She said she was tired of being in jail, worrying all the time about what was happening to her children. Most of the women prisoners said they were afraid their husbands would marry again and abandon them and the children. The men I interviewed in jail, on the other hand, were in most instances convinced that the situation at home was well taken care of and that their wives would come to visit them soon.

Salima's oldest daughter, who was fifteen, took care of the other children and filled the role of mother. The Palestinian prisoners' authority paid Salima 1,200 shekels (around $325) a month, which she had her lawyer remit to her daughter. She became very emotional when she spoke about the heavy burden on her daughter's shoulders. I could not quite understand how a working woman with seven children had found the time to get involved in a terrorist attack. Salima said, "They gave me a suitcase and told me to bring it someplace, and I didn't know what was inside. I don't make trouble, but when you know people who are problematic, the trouble comes by itself." Salima did not mention that in order to carry out her mission, which was smuggling weapons, she took her youngest daughter with her to make herself look innocent.

I asked her what her dreams were, and she said, "I will take the children far, far away to a new life. They will go to school and work and have nice homes, cars, and a lot of money. If it could only happen! Sometimes the neighbors make food for the children, but not every day. My daughter makes food and cleans the house, my brother visits them and talks to the little ones and tells them about me so that they don't forget me." Salima's dreams do not include her husband. She did not hide her anger with him: "Actually, I don't love my husband. I had a hard life with him. He only thinks about himself, not about me or the children, and I see he lives only his own life. I don't feel he is my husband, and I would divorce him if I didn't have children. The girls are growing up. I have to educate them and get them married. I won't get a divorce. If I do, they won't let me see the children, and I don't have parents to go to, so I stay married." The decision to stay married for the good of the children is more or less universal. The difference is that Salima was afraid that if she asked for a divorce, her children would be taken away from her and she would be forbidden to see them. In addition, once divorced there would be no place for her to go, because in Arab society a divorced woman returns to her father's house, but both of Salima's parents were dead. Often relations between Arab husband and wife are based on authority and fear; the woman has to be submissive and obedient, and many times she is the victim of continuing physical and emotional threats. Salima also felt that a divorce would make it harder for her daughters to marry and cause damage to their reputations.

A divorce stigmatizes the entire family. From a young age Palestinian women internalize their need to be submissive and accept humiliation quietly lest they be perceived as rebellious and disrespectful of their husbands. That is the behavior pattern dictated by society. One of the women prisoners told me that in her opinion the perfect husband was "muscular and strong . . . who would rule me and not be ruled by me," that is, a strong husband who would protect her from the outside world around whom family life would revolve. According to Islam, the husband divorces the wife, although in certain circumstances the woman can ask for a divorce, for example, if her husband is given a long prison sentence.

Toward the end of our conversation Salima waxed nostalgic: "We had chickpeas and *ful* [broad beans], and a good life. . . . We baked our bread on a *tabun* [a convex metal plate placed over a source of heat]. . . . Jail is no place for women. It's a shame. I like all people. I was sick, I had gallstones, and they took care of me in a hospital in Israel, and the women guards worried about me. I felt good about that and wanted to go back to jail from the hospital. Everyone lives and then they die. No one takes anything with him to the sand [i.e., the grave]." She smiled when I nodded in agreement and offered to make me coffee.

I left the kitchen and was on my way to the exercise yard when Nawal called me from the other side of the fence. She was young, slim, and pretty, but she had no teeth. I sat on one of the plastic chairs in the yard, and one of the women brought coffee and a table from the kitchen to put it on. Jemilla, about whom I have written in an earlier chapter, came over, more prisoners joined the group, and we began to talk. While Nawal was talking to one of the others I asked Jemilla why Nawal had no teeth. She said that Nawal had a gum infection that made her teeth fall out but that Houda had prevented her from going to a periodontist, and only now was she receiving treatment.

It occurred to me that had Nawal not been in jail, she probably would not have received such expensive dental care, entirely paid for by the Israeli prison system, that is, the Israeli taxpayer. Nawal came closer, clasped the fence with her thin fingers, and told me how much she liked and admired Jemilla. I complimented Jemilla on her jeans, which were decorated with studs, and asked her whether she had sewn them on herself. "No," she said, "I bought them like this." She jumped up and said, "Wait a second," and went back to her cell. Out of the corner of my eye I could see the women in the cell pass her something through the opening in the door. She came back holding a white woolen teddy bear with button eyes and a red satin heart. "It's very pretty," I said, "did you make it?" "No," she said proudly, "the girls made it for me."

We kept talking and then, in the middle of our conversation, she jumped up again, saying "Can you wait for me again?" and before I could answer, she was gone. I watched her go from one cell to another, collecting various items. She came back and placed them carefully on the table. They were pictures in improvised frames made of cardboard pasted together and decorated with small sequins, made by the women. There was Arabic writing on the cardboard. We looked at the pictures together, most of them of sweet-looking small children, the brothers and sisters of the prisoners, most of whom were unmarried. Jemilla explained that relatives brought the materials for the frames when they came to visit. Jemilla read aloud what was written on the frames: "You are in my heart," "I miss you," "When you are in my heart it is hard to forget you," and the names of the children. On the pictures themselves were red hearts. The security prisoners had arts and crafts groups and invested a lot of effort in them. They were pleased with my admiration, and I couldn't help thinking that ten-year-old Israeli girls produced the same sort of thing in summer camp.

All of a sudden, Jemilla asked me whether I ever went to the hairdresser. "No," I told her with a smile, "I just leave it in a braid." "Don't you ever feel like changing it?" she wanted to know. "I keep changing my hair style." The close relationship we had developed over time gave her the confidence to say something she had wanted to for a long time: "I want to ask you a personal question, is that okay?" I told her she could ask whatever she liked. They wanted to know how old I was. The women whispered to one another, and I was sure my age was an issue that had figured in many of their conversations. "I'm forty-seven," I said. "No!" she said. "I wouldn't have thought more than thirty-five!" Music to my ears!

I wished them "*Eid saeed*" (happy holiday) for Eid al-Adha, the Feast of Sacrifice, a Muslim holiday that celebrates Abraham's sacrifice of a ram instead of his son Ishmael. From there I went to the wing where the Hamas and Palestinian Islamic Jihad security prisoners were held. Samira, the wing spokeswoman, was standing with her back to me and talking to another prisoner. I waited until she had finished and then called her name. I told her I hadn't come to talk, only to wish them a happy holiday. She kissed me on both cheeks and I felt the folds of her *hijab* brush my face as she thanked me.

11

≈≈◉≈≈

Nawal, Palestinian Knife Wielder: "Jail in Israel Is Better Than Hell at Home"

Several months after our first meeting, Nawal, the prisoner with no teeth, asked to speak to me again. She had previously been in the Fatah wing but had transferred to the one for Hamas and the Palestinian Islamic Jihad prisoners after the women had quarreled among themselves and opposing camps had been created in each wing. During our first meeting she had tried to hide her empty mouth. But now she sat across from me and smiled, exhibiting a perfect set of false teeth, courtesy of the Israeli prison system. I complimented her, and she said she was under the care of the prison dentist, and was obviously grateful. Since our first meeting she had managed to be released from jail, only to return after she tried to stab an IDF soldier at a roadblock.

She was wearing a black V-necked shirt and slacks, and her black hair was loose around her shoulders. She was twenty-three years old and had two sisters and three brothers; their father was dead. We talked about her life. "I am alone and I don't have a cell mate. The girls don't want me, not those from the Palestinian Authority, not those from Hamas." She had gone from one wing to another, still trying to find her place. Her Hebrew, learned in jail, was good, although sometimes she resorted to Arabic. "I left jail and then I came back. There are problems with my being at home. My mother doesn't want me, and curses at me all the time, and hits me with a pot. Jail in Israel is better than the hell at home." She picked up her shirt and showed me her stomach, which was covered with bruises. As she spoke, she became increasingly emotional.

"My brother is twenty-five; he rapes me and doesn't want me to tell anyone. I'm twenty-three. My father died four years ago. I told my mother and uncle about my brother, and my uncle hit me and said my brother hadn't raped me. My brother said he hadn't done anything. I asked them to take me to a doctor. I went

113

to the Palestinian police and a policeman said, 'I can help you, but your brother is a friend of mine.' He wanted to have sex with me, and he said, 'Your brother won't know anything.' And I said, 'If you, the police, say that, what should I say to all the women outside?' I didn't know where to go.

"The Jews put me in jail. I was alone for two years, and no one said anything bad to me. But we are Arabs, we are of the same blood. Why do the Jews take better care of me than us? The Jews help me solve problems; they don't do it for money or to get something." Nawal said that the Israeli judge was afraid to release her from jail lest her family harm her. She said that when she went to the Palestinian police and asked to be sent to a hostel in Jerusalem, they told her, "The hostel is not for Arabs."

In September 2009, twenty-one female security prisoners were released in return for a sign of life from abducted Israeli soldier Gilad Shalit. During the German-mediated negotiations for their release, those who wished to stay in jail were not forced to leave. In light of Nawal's history, it is not hard to understand why a significant number preferred an Israeli jail to their own homes.

Nawal continued: "My brother who is twenty saw everything [i.e., the rape] and told my uncle that I was telling the truth, and my older brother hit him so hard he couldn't stand up for two hours. I told him I was going away and I went. They got into the car and looked for me, and I went to the police, and after that I went to the IDF roadblock. I had two knives. A soldier saw one of the knives and asked me what I wanted. I said, 'I don't want anything, I want to go to jail.' He asked me if I had trouble at home.

"My father was forty when he died of high blood pressure. My brother wanted to rape me for a long time but my father beat him and threw him out of the house and set up a girls' bedroom near his own. He protected us from our brothers." Nawal told me that one night she felt someone taking her bra off. As she spoke, she pushed her shirt aside and showed me her bra. "I was asleep. I took a sleeping pill, and my father pretended to be asleep, and then he discovered my brother going upstairs to the girls' room. After that he threw him out of the house and didn't let him come back for three months. In the end he let him return and told him that after nine o'clock at night he was forbidden to watch television in the girls' room and that when we were alone in the house he wasn't allowed in." She was proud of the way her father protected especially her. "He held the whole house in one hand and me in the other." As far as her father was concerned, she believed she was more important than the rest of the family put together.

"There are a lot of women prisoners who were raped. Safia came back here because her family wanted her to die, and her boyfriend made fun of her and raped her. Their families say they should die and then they can show everyone that she was murdered to save the family honor. I would rather be in jail. They help me here, and I like the guard named Mira." While we were talking, the head guard of the wing came in holding a fan. "You see," said Nawal, "he is like a father to me, bringing a fan."

Our conversation was apparently both physically and emotionally draining for Nawal. All her reactions were emotional and accompanied by gesticulations. I suggested we stop and continue in a few days.

The next time we met, Nawal was brought out of solitary to talk to me. She was wearing a sleeveless white top with a very low neckline and tight pants. She was happy to see me and continued the story of her family drama, which had led her, in the end, to jail. "My brother [the one who raped her] had friends who were thieves. They used to look at me. I'm not a man, I couldn't say anything to them about looking at me [a man would have told them looking at her was not respectful behavior]. My uncle beat my brother with an electric cord after my father died." She pointed at the cord on the fan in her cell.

"When my brother was sixteen he was beaten by the whole family. My father didn't say anything because it was his own older brothers who were hitting him. My uncles spoke to me nicely while my father was still alive, but after he died they stopped. When my father went to the hospital, the doctors said to my mother, 'Your husband doesn't feel well. Bring the children to see their father.' One of my uncles hit me because I went to the hospital alone to see my father. He cursed at me and yelled when I asked to see my father. He came to our house and said, 'He's my brother and I don't want any of you children to visit him!' and he said to me, 'You did this to him!'"

Nawal's uncle had a lot of influence over the children of his sick brother, sometimes more than the brother himself. As Jemilla told me and as I knew from my own family, the father's side is closer and has a lot of influence on the children, regardless of who their father is. Terrorist operatives often told me that their parents and uncles were more important to them than their children. In Nawal's case, the uncle decided who would and would not see the dying father and did not even let his children say good-bye. Nawal refused to accept that and sneaked in the back door of the hospital to see her father. The uncle beat her and her brother and did not allow them to visit again.

"After that I didn't believe they were telling me the truth about my father, so I called my uncle, and he said, 'Your father is dead and I hope you die too.' I rushed to the hospital and went in for a couple of minutes. My father's temperature was 104. The doctor didn't know I was his daughter. He had a heart murmur and he couldn't see anything. The doctor told me to pray, maybe Allah would help him.

"He died the next morning. My mother came home from the hospital in my uncle's car and said, 'Nawal, your father, who always loved you and gave you what you wanted, is gone.' My father's mother said that my mother went with men, and that was a problem for us. My uncles didn't help us, and when I left the house there was a mess. I had a boyfriend who wanted to marry me but my father said I was too young. In the end my uncle married me off to a boy who was no good and didn't work. He is in jail in the Palestinian Authority. I was only married for fifteen days and then I saw boys and girls together and my husband in a room with another woman, all of them naked. I said I was sorry they had "work to do" and left. I was screaming and crying and very upset. I called my uncle and told him, and he told me my husband was a good-looking man and I was forbidden to talk like that. My uncle also visits prostitutes, so he doesn't believe anything women tell him."

Her uncle took her home by force. It turned out that in addition to the house of prostitution her husband had opened, he took drugs and gave her Ecstasy: "I took them because he exchanged them for my blood pressure pills . . ."

Nawal fought her family and appealed to the religious court for a divorce. Eventually she was granted a divorce and returned to her mother's house. She was a divorcée and not a virgin, and considered damaged goods by one and all. From that time on she was the victim of severe mental and sexual abuse. She prostrated herself on her father's grave and wept. She said, "My uncles' children and my brother told me I wasn't a virgin and wanted to rape me. I kept going to my father's grave, and I even slept there. They came to the house when my mother went to work and I was alone. They didn't let me go to work. My cousin raped me, and then my brother. I spilled boiling water on my cousin and he told people it was an accident at work, but I said I had done it.

"My mother said my cousin wouldn't enter the house anymore, but no one asked my mother. They only asked my uncle. My mother said I couldn't be at home without a man [meaning the brother who had raped her had to stay at home with her, because he was the man of the house after the father died], but he didn't understand anything, and she [even] gave him money for cigarettes. That was why I went to jail, why I went to the roadblock and said to the policeman, 'I have a knife, I want to stab an Israeli soldier,' and I was sentenced to two years and they let me go, but I came back because of my brother."

Nawal's case is not exceptional, especially regarding Palestinian women who go to roadblocks and wave their knives in the air without trying to hurt a soldier. They want to go to jail to solve personal or family problems. Reading court records reveals that many of the girls in jail were trying to escape from forced marriages or were accused of improper behavior or beaten at home. They tried to stab soldiers or waved knives in the air or threw acid in the general direction of an Israeli soldier at a roadblock and were sent to jail in Israel, which for them was a safe haven.

12

❧

Women under Interrogation

To get as comprehensive a picture as possible, I spoke to Israeli security service personnel in charge of interrogating terrorists. Interrogating a woman is different from interrogating a man, as Yosef and Shlomo, both senior personnel, told me. I have held many conversations with them in the past six years.

Yosef discussed various issues regarding women in terrorism. He said, "Until the middle of the 1990s only a tiny percentage of those interrogated were women. We tried not to interrogate them, only in cases where they clearly had exact information and someone was a 'messenger.' There were periods when women served as couriers from the headquarters in Jordan and Syria. Elements within Fatah also knew that the Israelis didn't rush to interrogate women. At the end of the 1990s and during the *intifada* women began participating in suicide bombing attacks and aiding and abetting. In recent years we have seen a change in behavior patterns."

At the end of the 1990s women interrogators were brought in to respond to the number of women becoming involved in terrorist attacks. The interrogators are careful not to offend or insult the woman during questioning. According to Yosef, "The criteria for questioning and female interrogations are decidedly different. For the same sort of information, a man will be detained but not a woman. When a woman is interrogated, she will be treated with kid gloves. We try not to offend her status as a woman, to treat her kindly, you know, 'the enlightened occupation . . .' It is always harder to interrogate a woman than a man."

Questioners differentiate between village women older than forty, who usually serve as couriers, and urban and student women. Today the female terrorists are younger. In the past, almost all the women involved in terrorism belonged to the Popular Front for the Liberation of Palestine or the Democratic Front for the Liberation of Palestine. Today there is a significant increase in the number of women in Fatah. In addition, their organizational affiliation is not as clear as it was in the past.

Yosef seemed to indicate that less effort was invested in interrogating a woman: "The interrogations of women are much shorter because the interrogators give up quickly. 'What can she tell me?' they ask themselves. There is contempt for the place of women in the terrorist organizations, and a female terrorist is perceived as not being able to give much intelligence information, and even if she can, it won't be worth much. Women are no less dangerous than men, but after they have been in jail the chances that they will return to 'active duty' are far smaller than for men."

When terrorists are asked during interrogation whether they aren't ashamed of sending women to do a man's job, most of them say that there are many advantages to sending women; they are not examined as carefully at the roadblocks and do not arouse suspicion. Yosef added that "women are used less frequently when it is a question of Arabs attacking Arabs, because it is a matter of honor." (That has changed, for example, in Iraq, where there has been a significant increase in the number of women involved in terrorism.) When he spoke of "honor," I thought of the suicide bombing attack at the Maxim restaurant in the northern Israeli city of Haifa in 2003, carried out by Hanadi Jaradat, a lawyer from Jenin. Yosef interrogated her handler and had the following to say: "Jaradat was an anomaly in Palestinian society. She was very well educated and very attractive. She had to support her father, who had cancer, and her sisters. Her fiancé, Muhammad Jaradat, and her brother were killed by the IDF. Muhammad Jaradat was handsome and considered a hero, a fighter, a knight in shining armor, and from the same extended family. There was no way she would find anyone like him in the Palestinian elite, young and from a good family. She was in love with him and he died in her arms, and with him died her dreams. Everyone knew they were having an affair and were planning to marry."

Female terrorists are perceived as easy to infiltrate through the roadblocks, but operationally speaking, they are generally unsuccessful. The case of Hanadi Jaradat was different. The suicide bombing attack in the Maxim restaurant was one of the worst in Israel's history. Whenever female suicide bombers are discussed, hers is always the first name mentioned. First she ate lunch at the restaurant, watching the Israeli families as they ate, and then she stood up, walked to the middle of the restaurant, and blew herself up, wiping out entire families, in one case six members spanning three generations. I spoke to a woman who was there, who is crippled; she lost almost her whole family. She clearly remembers the split second before the explosion: Jaradat leaned over the woman's father as though she wanted to ask him something. Then she detonated the explosive device.

Shlomo, the former head Israel Security Agency interrogator, had a different style. He injected humor into the conversation, and I sensed that many people gave up their information without quite realizing what they were saying.

Shlomo said that in the past, nationalist Muslims disliked the idea of using women. They were included in leftist political activities but not in terrorism. The change came during the first *intifada* (1987–1993), when schoolgirls and female university students went out into the streets with the men. One girl was killed during a riot. We spoke about Dalal Mugrabi, who actively participated in the massacre on Israel's Coastal Road in 1978, which resulted in the deaths of thirty-five Israelis and the wounding of seventy-one, and for whom a square was named in a town near Ramallah in March 2010 and a street in Nablus in November of the same year. We also spoke about Wafa Idris, the first female suicide bomber. Mugrabi and Idris were turned into role models by the Palestinian Authority.

Shlomo said: "They exploited the women for terrorist activities instead of realizing that they had a relative advantage when it came to smuggling messages in and out of prison in intimate places, moving wanted terrorists, sending messages abroad, using mothers. . . . They thought, and they were right, that we had limits when it came to interrogating them, kept them in separate cells, had female soldiers in the room with them during interrogation. The police and we are afraid of what will be said if we interrogate a female terrorist. They thought we would forgive a woman, and they were right—interrogating a woman is a logistical difficulty for us. . . . As terrorism stopped being small, compartmentalized cells and became more popular, there began to be cadres of women, and the same happened with the media: Internet, television . . . the struggle is photographed and broadcast."

Shlomo flushed angrily. "The worst thing," he said, "was that Israel stupidly brought the guerrilla party from Tunis [He meant Arafat, who was expelled from Lebanon and relocated in Tunis until 1993.]. For all those years we separated the terrorists from their headquarters and made sure there were no communications between them. And then, in complete stupidity, in the Oslo Accords Israelis linked up the Palestinians' popular struggle to their headquarters and armed their divisions. And at the street level everyone participates, even women. Their trademark is the word 'popular.' That seems to be what motivates them. When we didn't talk to the Palestinians there was only terrorism, and when we started talking to them they used terrorism to achieve things. . . . I interrogated a lot of female terrorists, and not one of them used nationalist slogans. They all talked about being forced to marry men they didn't want, about troubles at home, husbands who beat them, being thought of as *sharmoutas*, whores."

Shlomo talked about the marginal position of women in terrorism and in Arab society in general: "Have you ever seen a woman fire a gun?" It was his opinion that Palestinian women first got involved in politics and then used the political platform to get involved in terrorism. He told me about a female terrorist who rode in a car during a drive-by shooting. She was not active in the attack and did not fire a gun herself, and was only there because the terrorists used her foreign passport to rent the car.

By the end of 2010 more than fifty women had blown themselves up in Iraq. It is important to study the behavior patterns of female terrorists. The distinctions, as described by Yosef, are made between village and urban women, educated or uneducated, married or single—and if married, first wife or not—liberated or rumored to be liberated.

Women from villages are far less sophisticated and more passive, and accept and carry out orders. Their roles have been relatively simple, usually along the lines of acting as couriers. They often are told to take their children with them to reduce suspicion. Village women are usually poorer and regard terrorist activities as a way of improving their economic conditions; sometimes they are threatened and forced to comply. Generally speaking, they come from weak families and lack either parents or a protective male figure.

Shlomo said that suicide bombers chose terrorism primarily for social reasons and that the financial motive was secondary. They are, he said, looking for a way to stand out, to make people notice them, and instead of being considered criminals and then forgotten, after they die a "mourning tent" is set up at their family's home. Often terrorists were car thieves and small-time criminals who underwent "vocational retraining." As opposed to common crime, terrorist activity "for the sake of liberating Palestine" brings honor and prestige to the terrorist and his family.

According to Shlomo, "A man who fails as a suicide bomber whimpers and weeps during interrogation. I say, 'A minute ago you wanted to blow yourself up, and now you're crying?'" He told me that there were discrepancies between the video clips the suicide bombers make before the attack explaining their motivation and the real reasons, which are revealed during interrogation. As for women, he said that "anyone who is considered wanton or has a personal problem is known to four or five people, but put an explosive belt on them and the whole world knows." Women react differently from men and see causing pain to other people in a different way. Many women got cold feet or hesitated or failed on their way to a showcase attack, and technical difficulties kept them from causing many casualties. Jaradat did so much damage because she was intelligent. That wasn't the only reason she was exceptional. She was about to get married, and Israel killed her fiancé and shattered her dream. She was planning to carry out the attack somewhere else. It was only a matter of chance that she blew herself up in the restaurant.

The Israel Security Agency, just like terrorist operatives and Palestinian Arab society, does not hold the abilities of the women involved in terrorism in high regard. The Israeli security forces are aware of the terrorist organizations' readiness to use women for suicide bombing attacks, but they are still considered marginal. The Palestinian organizations do not use them for "masculine military activities" because they are "limited," "incapable."

Shlomo recalled another case: "There was a *sharmouta* from Jenin who was married, but she was the lover of a wanted terrorist from there. Her husband kept quiet because he collaborated with Israel. She and her husband moved to Ramallah, and one day she met her lover in the street and he took her along on an attack. She only did it because they were lovers. Her motives were romantic, not nationalistic." His story reminded me of Fadwa, who helped abduct the Israeli taxi driver because she was in love with the terrorist who abducted him. Often women find themselves involved in attacks as an excuse to be near the objects of their affection.

I asked Shlomo to describe the behavior of a woman suspected of terrorism during an interrogation. He said, "The stress and emotional pressure often bring on their monthly periods, it doesn't matter what time of the month it is. An interrogator wants to have some kind of connection with the person being questioned. Women sometimes fall in love with their interrogator. He isn't just an enemy, he is Israeli, Jewish, belongs to the Shin Bet, and they flirt anyway. It's a kind of puppy love. 'Stay, don't go away . . .' They will ask a certain interrogator when he is coming back, leave him little notes, drawings, it's like they have to find something, anything in a hostile environment, a connection to something, intimacy. Being interrogated is like being in solitary confinement. There is no one else there, no witnesses, just she and the interrogator, although there is a policewoman present at all times as well. If she says anything in jail, the other prisoners will get after her, because it was done publicly. Being imprisoned, as opposed to being interrogated, is a group situation, and the prisoner undergoes a process of socialization. There are many stations on the way to jail: there is the police 'filter,' the courtroom, the media, processes which influence her. . . . On the other hand, during interrogation it is hot or cold, good or bad. During interrogation the terrorist is alone with himself or herself and there is no one from a support group to protect him. There was one case in which a female Palestinian killed a child and only agreed to confess after a cosmetician gave her a facial."

Who would have thought that Houda, who tempted an adolescent boy though an Internet chat and then murdered him, would only admit her guilt after a facial in a hotel, and after her Shabak interrogators had papered the walls and floor of her cell with pictures of the victim? Interrogators have to be creative, and sometimes the little things that no one would attach importance to can change everything and make women give the interrogators information that in many instances helps prevent the next attack. In this case, despite Houda's difficult personality—she was assertive, educated, and sophisticated—what made her talk was something utterly feminine. What the interrogator did was create a temporary, alternative, pleasant situation, a cosmetic interlude, and then return her to her cell, from which the face of her victim looked at her wherever she turned. The change of venue shattered her resistance, and she agreed to talk.

Shlomo said that many of the people involved in terrorism suffered from various disabilities. For example, Abdul Rahman, the sheikh involved in the first attack on the World Trade Center in 1993, was blind; Sheikh Ahmed Yassin, Hamas's ideologue and founder, was confined to a wheelchair. "The worse the hand they get dealt by Allah," he said, "the more they want to screw the Jews. They find some kind of confirmation in their religion and use it to vent their hatred. The commander of the 'Night of the Pitchforks' [when Israeli-Arab terrorists infiltrated an army camp near a kibbutz in the north and killed Israeli soldiers, February 14, 1992] was sterile. He tried to poison his second wife because she said she would tell everyone he was sterile, and she had to be hospitalized. His first wife died. She had no children, and it was never proved that he killed her.

"What happens with women is interesting. Is there some physical cause of self-destruction? Ugliness, scars, a limp, infertility, some defect? There are a large number of recidivist men, but for women it is usually just one incident: did she do it or didn't she, with the exception of political activity or work in women's organizations. I never saw a brigade of women fighters in Hezbollah, despite the fact that their marches are full of veiled women. The religious Muslims have a problem with women mingling with men: in the camps the fighters train together. And when it comes to suicide bombers, one brother will strap an explosive belt onto another, but no brother will strap one onto his sister. I have never heard of a female suicide bomber who was a relative of a high-ranking member of a terrorist organization. Within a family, when a dispatcher sends one of his female relatives to blow herself up, it is an admission that she is a *sharmouta*. For men it is an act of honor, but for women it is an act of catharsis. How many women orchestrated terrorist attacks or sent other women to carry them out? They aren't part of the system."

Shlomo said that a person being interrogated frequently behaves like a child, and that among women there are a lot of emotional reactions: weeping and hysterics, stress-induced menstruation, worry about physical appearance. Women from conservative rural environments where women do not smoke usually do not ask for cigarettes during interrogation. Urban women, however, and women with criminal backgrounds do. He continued, saying, "I don't know of any women who shut up during interrogation. For women, talking is a way of releasing tension. Sometimes they curse, but they don't use the same four-letter language men do. It is hard for women to function in the dark, and if they are isolated they want to go back to the interrogation room. Women are not used to being alone, so solitary confinement is hard for them. The men are more resistant. They are more independent and can be alone for longer periods of time." As noted, a woman is not left alone during interrogation; there is always another woman present, usually a policewoman. She supports the woman being interrogated but does not take an active part in the process.

"There is a difference between the interrogation of a woman who has been accused of something and one who only helped. Even the way men and women sit is different. Men usually sit with their legs spread, while the way women sit depends on whether or not they are religious and how they perceive themselves. If the woman knows she is pretty and attractive, she will push her breasts out, smile, bend over, some of the women, at least. If she comes from one of the villages or is religious, she will be dressed and act modestly. The urban ones are usually younger and almost flirt. If a Palestinian man is known to be sexually active it increases his macho status, but a woman is afraid of being thought of as loose."

In one episode of an anti-Semitic Turkish television series, one of many episodes demonizing the IDF, soldiers were shown raping female security prisoners. The security prisoners in Israeli jails became angry and asked the prison administration to contact the media and tell them that no IDF soldier had ever offended their honor.[1]

The underlying disdain in Shlomo's voice was apparent when he said, "An interrogation is a conversation controlled by an investigator. In the final analysis, people are people, and if you know which buttons to press, in the end they all talk."

NOTE

1. Dina Aboul Hosn, "Controversial Turkish TV Series to Air Tomorrow," *Gulfnews*, March 19, 2010, http://gulfnews.com/news/region/palestinian-territories/controversial-turkish-tv-series-to-air-tomorrow-1.600013.

13

❦

How to Talk to Terrorists

People have often asked me why terrorists are willing to talk to me. I tell them that if you know how to create the right atmosphere, you can't get them to stop talking. If the first contact is positive, subsequent ones are regarded, by both male and female security prisoners, as visits, not interviews, and visits are very precious to them. The security prisoners waited to speak to me the same way as they waited for visits from friends and family. I became part of the jail scenery, and they felt they received something from our conversations because they were for research purposes and not interrogations.

In an article Dr. Post and I published,[1] the fruit of our individual experience of direct meetings with terrorists, we discussed several aspects important in communicating with them. The discussion here will center primarily on the methods I used to build relationships with terrorists sentenced to many consecutive terms.[2] The most important elements were universal humanity and finding a common ground. That enabled me to reach an emotional level where the person I was interviewing did not regard me as an enemy, but simply as a person, a woman, a mother, a friend, an intelligent woman who was pleasant to talk to. In that way authentic communication was possible and the insights I gained were genuine. At the beginning of every interview I said something about myself and about my parents, who were born in Baghdad and fled as refugees to Israel as soon as the country was founded. I said that I had grown up with Middle Eastern culture, speaking the ancient Jewish Arabic of Iraqi Jews. Sheikh Abu Tir, deputy head of the de facto Hamas administration, immediately seized on the fact that my parents were from Iraq, saying that the Iraqi home was Arab and believed in values and principles, and was very strong and conservative. I agreed and said that my late father only needed to look at my siblings and me and we did whatever he wanted, and that we respected him but feared him as well. He never let us curse because it was shameful (*a'ib*).

Saying the word "shameful" was like using a secret password. Abu Tir grinned and said, "I like, really like your Iraqi father. . . . Iraqis know how to educate their children properly." Once we had established a common ground, the atmosphere was relaxed and we could talk, and I asked him about the integration of women in terrorism. He said, "I would never agree to let girls go to jail. It's hard for them and for their families and for us. According to Arab ideology, those two things don't go together. You know that because you grew up with those values." It was easier for him to relate to me as a woman who had grown up with Arab values than as a Jew and an Israeli, and I was no longer an enemy but one of the tribe (*hamoula*) and could now understand what he had to say. For creating closeness and openness, it was important to have a basic understanding of Arab culture, the way it communicated, its greetings and compliments. He said that he was certain I came from a good home and that he thought it was a good thing that we were afraid when our father looked at us. He wanted to know whether my mother was still alive, and if she was, "Tell her Abu Tir says hello." Before we parted he invited me to come visit him at his home with my children, saying that there wouldn't be any "problems." I looked him straight in the eye and said, "I know there won't be any problems. Why should there be a problem?"

It is important not to broadcast fear, and the researcher has to treat the person being interviewed with respect, while being professional and assertive. There are prisoners who are dominant and very manipulative, and they cannot be allowed to direct the conversation into channels that do not contribute to the research.

Whenever I went to visit jails I always wore modest clothing, nothing tight, nothing colorful, usually just black. How I dressed was very important because I knew that the first thing a traditional Arab man would do would be to judge my attire, so I made certain to wear clothing compatible with the Arab women's conservative dress code.

One of the most dangerous dispatchers, a man sentenced to eleven consecutive life terms, told me that he had worked in a restaurant in Tel Aviv and found it hard to look at "female flesh" all day long, meaning Israeli women in bathing suits. He smiled as he sipped his coffee and said, "Sitting and talking to a decently dressed woman like you is really pleasant." Sometimes the prisoners I spoke to began by asking me whether I had read a certain book, and one said immediately, "I don't want to talk about my childhood, it weakens me," and we talked about other things that were relevant to my research, but beyond as well. The fact that other prisoners could see we had a good relationship was also important, because in addition to the easy feeling the prisoner had, it made it possible for other prisoners to participate without feeling that they were doing something wrong by talking to me.

The approach I usually use is one of "I know why you are in jail, I read the indictment, and I don't want to talk about what you did. All I want to know about is you, your life, your family, mother, father, sisters and brothers, your childhood, what you like, whom you love. Everything is fair game, and you can talk about anything." The secret was not to let them focus on religion or politics or what they thought about the Palestinian-Israeli conflict but to make them feel that I was really interested in them as people.

In certain instances I had to deal with sophisticated terrorists who tried to manipulate me by showing they were superior or to frighten me so that they could take over the discussion. For example, I spoke to a would-be Hamas suicide bomber who pushed the button on his explosive belt but failed to detonate it. In the beginning he stared at me with hatred, and I felt that he was thinking evil thoughts. I looked right back at him and moved a cup of tea toward him and said, "Why? Did I do something bad to you? I only came to hear about your life," and in an instant he deflated. I made him feel like a thug who was menacing me, while all I had done was ask to speak to him, without handcuffs, even though he was serving several consecutive life sentences and he had nothing to lose by killing another Jewish woman. It was out of the question for me to project fear or lack of control, and from that moment on the conversation moved ahead freely.

I also interviewed a suicide bomber dispatcher who was a heavy smoker, and after a few hours he asked if he could light a cigarette. I suggested we postpone the rest of our discussion, but he decided he would rather postpone the cigarette and continue sitting there, pouring his heart out. When we finished talking he asked when I would return, and when I eventually did see him again he said that he had waited impatiently to continue our talk.

That kind of relationship leads to openness and the desire of the person being interviewed to make himself heard, and also to have the catharsis of having expressed his—or her—emotions and revealed intimate details about himself.

A different kind of communication was created with another suicide bomber dispatcher. After we had spoken for many hours, we began talking about more personal things, like children and even the Middle Eastern foods we had both grown up on. All of a sudden he said, "You are Jewish from an Iraqi home, a Sephardic home. Israel has never had a Sephardic prime minister. Sephardic Jews are discriminated against, just the way the Arabs are."[3] He was trying to use the relationship between us to undermine my status as interviewer and to alienate me from my society in order to make me identify with him. I had to answer him, and I said that as far as I was concerned it made no difference, as long as the country was run properly. My husband's family, I told him, is Ashkenazi, his family was destroyed during the Holocaust, my family were refugees from Iraq, and my children don't ask themselves whether they are Sephardic or Ashkenazi. The dispatcher was surprised by my answer, and said that he had thought about it a lot and asked himself how immigrants from such different cultures had managed to create something shared in the State of Israel.

When the situation was right, I allowed them to be chivalrous. I let them help me open bottles of mineral water, carry my bag, or bring chairs when we moved from one office to another, because even though I was on the other side, I was still "only a woman" as far as they were concerned, and they were stronger, and even in jail they maintained their relative advantage. There are various other examples, like the cooking lesson I received from the sheikh's wife in Umm el-Fahm. It is important to be creative and bond with the person interviewed, often through things close to his heart or significant to him in some way.

When interviewing prisoners, the focal points of power have to be identified. I visited the prisoners often, so it was important to make them feel I was part of the scenery and that every visit wasn't something unusual. Most important are the wing spokespersons; they are the moving force, and a personal link has to be created with them. Every visit I paid to a women's jail began with the spokeswoman, and even if she was in solitary confinement, I made sure to talk to her through the door. No security prisoner, male or female, will talk to anyone unless the spokespersons have authorized it, so a great deal of attention must be paid to them. Talking to someone without that authorization, even to a prisoner's lawyer, is considered collaboration with the "Israeli-Jewish-Zionist" enemy. Only prisoners who are respected and charismatic, who were responsible for many mass-murder terrorist attacks, have a certain amount of freedom of action and will never be suspected of collaboration. One particularly important prisoner was Hamas founder and leader Sheikh Ahmed Yassin (who died in a targeted killing in 2004), who was viewed by Israel the way the United States viewed Osama bin Laden. I met Yassin in jail in December 1996 and interviewed him for five hours. His only condition for speaking to me was that I cover my hair. We only stopped talking because I didn't want to make him miss lunch. Toward the end of our conversation he said he would be willing to meet me anywhere, including the Gaza Strip and including the moon. Often when prisoners were hesitant to talk to me, I would tell them that even Sheikh Yassin had spoken to me.

I had to locate the powerful, important prisoners and use the utmost patience while talking to them. The leaders in jail have to be respected, since it can be assumed that in the future some of them will be part of a legitimate Palestinian government. What is meant by patience is, for instance, to arrive without a strict timetable, to conduct what will be considered everyday conversations, not to fidget, and to accept the Middle Eastern pace, without the Western approach of "time is money" and that everything has to be done now.

Years of interviewing terrorists in jail taught me that the interviewer has to be empathetic and aware of nuances, to understand the other person by absorbing his or her feelings, thoughts, motives, intentions, and objectives. Sometimes it is very difficult just to listen. There were times when would-be female suicide bombers wrote me letters, drew pictures, and threw themselves, sobbing, into my arms. One of them wept on my shoulder and said, "All I want is my mother!" I hugged her and comforted her as I did the others, knowing that only yesterday any one of them was capable of blowing herself up anywhere and killing my children. However, I disregarded my emotions and did not let such thoughts make me physically or mentally push any one of them away.

Even a dispatcher who felt the desire to express himself received pencil and paper and could draw or write while we were talking, because the better the people being interviewed felt, and the easier the situation and interaction were, the more productive the conversations were. The prisoners felt they were important, that they received priority and the space to express themselves freely without being judged, even if they said things I didn't find particularly pleasant. They felt I understood but did not necessarily accept what they said. The key was respect: to listen quietly and politely, and to show that I was listening, to nod, look them in the eye, smile, and touch the hands of the women.

Even an aside to a female terrorist, such as "Stop biting your nails," was received as an indication that I cared and an expression of maternal warmth. As far as female security prisoners were concerned, as soon as their initial suspicions and hostility were dispelled, we spoke about love, our mothers-in-law, the children, the family, our hopes and fears. They asked ordinary questions and wanted to know how old I was, how many children I had, whether or not I believed in paradise, and I always answered them. Sometimes they wanted to know about Israeli society and women's place in it. Once they felt our conversations were sincere and genuine, they slowly shed their defenses and began expressing themselves. I often found myself sitting in a prison yard holding a prisoner's baby or sitting at an arts and crafts table while a prisoner proudly displayed her creations.

Some of them tried at first to make the point that we were on opposite sides: I was Jewish, they were Muslims, Arabs, I was the "occupier," they were "occupied," we, the Israelis, had things, they had nothing, I was free, they were in jail. The challenge was to neutralize their feelings and to conduct an authentic conversation without condescending to them, and to neutralize my own feelings as an Israeli woman and mother, a potential victim of their terrorism.

From the outset I tried to get them away from stereotypes and into discussions about universal themes, and to use empathy to help us see each other as two people without relating to what they had done or tried to do. I would give my daughter, who was then an instructor in the army, as an example. Once she was on her way to her base with her rifle and two large bags. It was a long ride, and she found herself on a bus sitting next to a traditionally dressed Arab woman. She could tell how the woman felt about IDF soldiers by the way she looked at her. She said it was hard to find a place for the rifle that wouldn't annoy her neighbor, who kept shifting uncomfortably in her seat. My daughter took a pack of gum out of a pocket, smiled at the woman and offered it to her. The woman relaxed in her seat and a few minutes later offered my daughter *baklava*, a kind of Middle Eastern pastry, and the rest of the trip passed without tension or hostility.

I began creating bonds the first time I walked into the women's wing and picked up the baby crawling on the floor. He was the son of one of the prisoners, but he was being watched by Samira, the wing spokeswoman. He was the first link between us as women and made later communication easier. When I visited after one of the Jewish holidays, they asked the standard Israeli questions: where were you and how was it?

Many prisoners asked to speak to me, and not always those whom I needed for research purposes, but I was always willing to meet with them, regardless. Sometimes what they said led my research into new channels and strengthened the trust and bonds between the prisoners and myself.

Body language was also important in creating an empathetic, supportive atmosphere. They had to be listened to attentively and responded to, and I had to nod, look at them, and express genuine interest. What both sides had in common also had to be emphasized. Drinking coffee or tea or even water together helped create an open, natural atmosphere and alleviated apprehension on both sides. It was also important to dispel hostility, distrust, and pressure by making it clear that I was doing research and not conducting an interrogation. I made sure that whenever I spoke to prisoners they were not handcuffed, even though the staff often told me that for someone who had killed so many Jews, killing one more Jewish woman wouldn't make a difference.

I had to make it clear at the outset that I was not part of the system and that I needed authorization from the staff for everything. Sometimes we had to end a conversation in the middle because it was time for a headcount or a meal, and I always said, "Rules are rules, and that's the jail timetable. I also have to abide by it—we'll continue later." It was also important to let the staff know that I appreciated them and their help, and that I did not mean to disrupt their daily work, which was hard enough without my interference.

To succeed I needed an understanding of the background, language and culture, and especially the manners of the prisoners. They knew I had a basic knowledge of Arabic and felt it was easier for me to understand their way of thinking. Drinking coffee from the same cup with a would-be suicide bomber was considered breaking bread together and a sign of closeness and cooperation and also a way to test me. Even drinking water together was important: the dispatcher Nabil said, "If I heard that something bad happened to you I would be shocked, because we drank water together." I always came prepared with mineral water, which I shared with the prisoners I interviewed, and when they offered to prepare coffee, I was always happy to accept. They treated me like a guest, whose status is high in traditional Arab culture. The day Gilad Shalit was abducted I was invited to the cell of some women security prisoners. We sat on their beds, drinking grapefruit juice and eating wafers. The following year, one of them reminded me about the day, which they all remembered very well. Every time I came they made sure to update me about their fellow inmates, especially those whose small children were with them in jail. More than once a prisoner would hug me and tell me she "loved" me. Obviously, she didn't mean love, and that was never my objective, but something in our relationship helped foster openness between us and even helped them view the Israeli enemy in a different light. If I am an enemy, then maybe the enemy is not really so terrible. Such positive feelings led to an atmosphere that made it easier for me to do my work.

To conduct research, the process of turning free people into prisoners has to be taken into consideration. Some of the prisoners I spoke to had been in jail for only a few weeks, had not yet been accepted into the prisoner subculture, and were frightened. They had not internalized the mind-set of security prisoners or been indoctrinated into the jail lifestyle. During that time they were much more vulnerable and defenseless, and it was easier to reach them. When prisoners had spent a long time in jail and felt more confident in their surroundings, I had to invest greater effort to remove the defense mechanisms they built up. For the recidivists, jail is less threatening. They are familiar with the environment and feel comfortable as opposed to the anxiety and uncertainty felt by first-time prisoners.

Concepts of time are different in jail. The hours pass more slowly. It is pointless to hurry; the prisoners aren't going anywhere. In addition, the Middle Eastern concept of time is different from what Westerners are used to. Anyone who conducts research in a jail cannot show impatience or do things quickly. It is important to give every person interviewed the feeling he is supremely important, to make him feel that his life is interesting and that all the necessary time will be invested in him.

Men and women conduct themselves differently in jail. Even the way they sit is different: the men sat across the table from me, while the women sat at a ninety-degree angle. The women sometimes hugged me and cried, while the men tried to keep a stiff upper lip. But men too became emotional at times, especially when talking about their families, particularly their mothers. Hardened prisoners serving life sentences cried when we talked about their mothers, and the tears were accompanied by emotional outbursts.

As a woman conducting research in a jail, I had a distinct advantage. I was perceived as less threatening and reminded the prisoners of a wife, a mother, or a sister. It created a situation of delicacy between the terrorist and me, and the men's macho coarseness gradually faded. Sometimes all it took was asking a male prisoner to help open a bottle of mineral water: they were happy to do so and felt their masculinity was reinforced by helping the "doctor." She, like other women, needed their help because she did not have their physical strength.

I always made sure to be aware of what was going on around me during an interview. Often the person being interviewed would not tell me if he was uncomfortable lest he insult me, especially after we had established a bond and he felt some kind of commitment. On one occasion there was a radio program featuring prisoners' families, and the woman I was speaking to wanted to listen to it because her mother was supposed to participate. She didn't say anything but I felt something was bothering her. Only after I asked her what the matter was did she tell me that she wanted to listen to the program with her friends. I told her there was no problem and to come back when it was over.

Avoiding political and religious arguments was very important, despite the fact that in the outside world things happened that both the prisoners and I were exposed to via the media. Some of the prisoners with whom I spoke will someday enter or return to positions of power in the Palestinian Authority, and the time they serve in jail is a kind of training for and legitimization of those positions.

Many of the people I interviewed considered my visits as social, an important privilege. They often asked me why I hadn't come for a long time, or asked me to come more often, or said they would draw a picture or do needlework for my next visit.

NOTES

1. J. Post and A. Berko, "Talking with Terrorists," *Democracy and Security* 5(2): 145–48.

2. A. Berko, *The Path to Paradise: The Inner World of Suicide Bombers and Their Dispatchers*, trans. Elizabeth Yuval (Westport, CT: Praeger, 2007).

3. Berko, *The Path to Paradise*.

14

⚜

Arab Lawyer: "Every Woman Involved in Terrorism Is a Romantic"

I paid several visits to a military court where security detainees were tried. I watched trials and spoke to Arab-Israeli defense and military lawyers. One of the Israeli military lawyers was a Druze named Akram. He told me that "every woman involved in terrorism is a romantic. Once there was a woman whose entire family were terrorists, and so was she. She was married but she let men into the house, which is not acceptable behavior in Arab society. There was another woman once, and they said she was meeting with Rayid Karmi [a terrorist assassinated by the IDF] even though she was married. Foreign sources even said Karmi was killed on his way to visit her."[1]

Akram gave me several other examples, saying, "Even Hanadi Jaradat [who blew herself up in the Maxim restaurant in Haifa in 2003] had a love interest. Okay, it was never proved it was anything that would damage the family's honor, but she was romantically involved with a terrorist operative named Muhammad Jaradat. He was her fiancé and boyfriend, and she carried out the attack because he was killed. Akhlas as well, the one who escorted the suicide bomber to the Sbarro restaurant, now she has found religion, but she was in love with Ahmed, one of the operatives, and that was how she became involved. She was unmarried, and in 2001 all Hamas members were very religious Muslims and they didn't accept everyone into their ranks, and she was secular. Nevertheless, because of her love affair with Ahmed she took part in an attack. Since then Hamas has changed, and they accept anyone who is willing to attack Israel, even those who are not religious."

Akhlas was a university graduate who was sentenced to fifteen consecutive life terms. She was the first woman to join the Izz al-Din al-Qassam Brigades, Hamas's military-terrorist wing, and accompanied the suicide bomber to the attack at the Sbarro restaurant in Jerusalem on August 9, 2001. Fifteen Israeli civilians died in the attack, many of them children, and 122 were wounded. Akhlas is known for her eternal smile, and she even smiles when she calls the women in jail to prayers. In court she faced the families of her victims and the judges and said defiantly, "I do not ask forgiveness from the Jewish family here, because many of us also lost those who were dear to us. With the help of Allah I will be lucky, if not here on earth then in paradise, when I see you and him [pointing to the judge] in hell. And if my smile gets on your nerves, I will smile it forever because I won. Even though we are not allowed alcohol, I will drink a toast, because I conquered you."

Akram continued, "There was one woman whose husband was in jail, and all the operatives in jail had erotic phone conversations with her. Her husband found out about it because he got an enormous phone bill. There was a woman from Jenin who agreed to transport a bomb and it was another love affair, this time with an operative from Hebron, and even the famous security prisoner who is the spokeswoman [Houda], before she tempted the boy in the chat room and lured him to his death, had a sexual relationship with a boy from Jerusalem and met him twice in his apartment. They hugged and kissed and touched each other. She had a boyfriend named Salah who goaded her into killing that Jewish boy, and he found out she had met the boy in Jerusalem. If her motivation really was ideological, why didn't she kill the boy in Jerusalem when she was making out with him? Obviously, he was too embarrassed to testify at her trial because he had gotten married in the meantime, and she was famous and he didn't want people to say he had any contact with her."

Not even Akram had anything good to say about Houda, nor did other lawyers who represented Palestinians accused of terrorist activity. He said, "Houda, for example, even though they call her a little whore who wanted to sleep with the boy who was killed, today they consider her the leader of the female security prisoners. When she was fifteen she turned herself in to IDF soldiers and said she wanted to confess to belonging to the Fatah youth movement and to throwing stones. They asked her why, and she said a girl who wore jeans didn't exactly follow Arab tradition. For that reason she fought with her father and wanted to rebel.

"There was one prisoner who had slept with her entire neighborhood and even had an affair with a policeman. She wanted to stab someone to clear her record. There were also cases of terrorist operatives who exploited Israeli-Arab women. For example, Samira [the spokeswoman for the prisoners affiliated with Hamas], who didn't have a lot of luck with Arabs in Israel, tried her luck with Arabs in the territories. She brought them mobile phones, and her phone bill was tens of thousands of shekels a month, and she was afraid her parents would find out about her relations with them and her debts. The wanted men told her they would send her the money if she came to work with them. There was another girl who was recently detained on suspicion of attempting to abduct an Israeli civilian. She came from a poor family in Nablus and worked as a cleaning woman at Hamat Gader [a spa with hot springs to the east of the Sea of Galilee, close to the borders of Jordan and Syria] and got to know a lot of people. Terrorist operatives gave her a sleeping pill to give to an Israeli man she knew. She dressed like any other girl, jeans, a shirt, her head mostly uncovered, just a scarf. During interrogation she broke down, cried, and said she was sorry and asked what her punishment would be.

"There is even a man named Nabil who was romantically involved with several women who are in jail today. There were two, Layla and Abir, who were rivals for his attention. Layla is married to all of Jenin. She comes from a broken family and grew up in an orphanage in Azaria [East Jerusalem neighborhood], even though she was originally from Jenin. She married someone *dardali* [weak, insignificant] and hung out a lot with wanted men. Her husband wasn't much of a man. They have four children. Even during her trial she flirted with the judge and the police. She is careful about her appearance, and she came very nicely dressed and with makeup every time she came to court. Once during an interrogation she said to me, 'Give me half an hour with Nabil and I'll be willing to confess . . .'

"Layla and Houda quarreled in jail, and you know how women quarrel. Houda used to tell her she was a whore and slept with everyone. So Layla ran to lodge a complaint against Houda, saying *she* was the whore, that she wore shorts and a sleeveless shirt, didn't fast on Ramadan, flirted with the guards, and even asked for the Playboy Channel in her cell. There was also talk of lesbianism, and they didn't want to put underage girls in with the older ones. There was a complaint that the younger girls were being corrupted by the divorced women. When the women fight, their language is right out of the gutter. Even the notes they write to each other use the same language.

"Abir was also in love with Nabil, and he exploited both of them to infiltrate a suicide bomber. Nabil, on the other hand, was in love with his wife's sister and fooled around with her, and his wife's family found out about it. So his wife's younger sister strapped an explosive belt onto Darin, the suicide bomber who carried out the attack at the Maccabim roadblock."

Nabil tried to convince Manal, his wife's sister, to carry out a suicide bombing attack. For him it was the solution to the family trouble he was entangled in. However, she told her family. She said that Nabil suggested she join them and help them carry out a suicide bombing attack. He proposed that she commit suicide, but she refused. She said, "I met Darin again, and Nabil said that she meant to carry out a suicide bombing attack and the explosive belt had to be strapped on. He asked for my help because I was a woman, and I helped put it on her, and I remember that her shoulder strap was loose so I held it in place with a safety pin. After the belt was strapped on, Nabil took her, I don't know where, and came back about half an hour afterward. Later I heard she blew herself up at a roadblock."

The passive way Darin stood there while Manal strapped the explosive belt in place reflects the traditional role of women in Arab society. Manal's story is another example of a suicide bombing attack in which another woman was involved, in this case as a support figure.

Rania, who was pregnant, recruited her cousin Suad. According to Suad's indictment, "Rania was a jihadist activist who headed the wing called Women's Action. The accused knew that Rania was the contact for women who wanted to carry out suicide bombing attacks. She told Rania she was willing to carry out an attack inside Israel to kill Israelis because they were Israelis. Rania told the accused to talk to a jihadist operative named Abu Amjad. One week later Rania told the accused that Abu Amjad agreed to allow her to participate in a suicide bombing attack."

Akram continued: "It wasn't over. Abir had trouble before. Her brother carried out an attack in the Central Bus Station in Tel Aviv. She became intimate with Nabil during their detention and entered into a *jawaz muta'a* [a "pleasure marriage," a short-term marriage acceptable in Arab countries; for example, businessmen marry young girls for a few days in return for money and then divorce them]. They asked to have conjugal privileges in jail. Before that, they were found making love near Nablus." From his and other stories, Nabil was apparently an attractive man, and he exploited the attraction for terrorist purposes. Akram said that in many instances, such as the suicide bombing attacks in 2002 carried out by women in Mahane Yehuda, a market, and Kiryat Yovel, a neighborhood in Jerusalem, one terrorist network was responsible for dispatching the women, and they were sexually exploited before the attacks. He said it was accepted practice in the Fatah networks to which Layla, Abir, and Nabil belonged. It was, he said, less acceptable in Hamas and the Palestinian Islamic Jihad, both of which made sure to find women to strap the explosive belts in place.

"Sometimes they want to force a girl to marry someone against her will, and then she is willing to participate in an attack. I have been dealing with this since before the *intifada*, and I never met a single woman who was motivated by ideology. The men, yes, but not the women."

Samir and Fuad are both Arab-Israeli lawyers who represent terrorists. I asked them how Palestinian society regarded women who got involved in terrorism. Samir said, "If the woman goes around with men, is not well educated, and her family has a low socioeconomic status, people will talk about her. But if she is educated and participates in a military action, even a suicide bombing attack, and she has a good family supporting her, even if she gets sent to jail, when she comes out she will be stronger." As an example he gave Houda, who came from a strong family, but because she sexually tempted a Jewish youth, people now relate to her as though she is cheap and wanton. Thus the division can be ambiguous.

Fuad was more emotional. "It is true that in Arab society the family is a closed unit, but since 1967 the security situation in the territories has changed the notion of family a little. There was a time when Arabs in the territories got married, the man established a family, he stayed at home for three or four months and then went to Kuwait to work and came back six years later. There he would find a six-year-old child who was seeing his father for the first time. At that time, families earned their living in the Arab countries, not in Israel. That's what it was like until the 1970s." Because of Arafat's support for Saddam Hussein, Palestinians from the territories were expelled from many countries in the Persian Gulf, especially Kuwait (which was invaded by Iraq in 1990).

As an aside, Samir said, "It was the one they call 'the house slave' [Condoleezza Rice]. The slave sits in the shade and does what the master tells him but doesn't accept the conditions [set down by the master]." We were holding the conversation in July 2006, during the second Lebanon war, when Rice, who was then the secretary of state, was brokering a cease-fire between Israel and Hezbollah.

I asked him whether he didn't think he was being racist. There are, I told him, many black Muslims, and the Arabs call them "the race of slaves." Was it hard for him to accept Rice because she was well educated and impressive and he wasn't used to assertive women, finding it easier to marginalize her and her efforts to bring democracy to the Muslim world? He said, "It is impossible to ignore the fact that Condoleezza Rice is a woman, and it would be a lie to say that it didn't affect the way people look at her. But the important point is that the blacks and Arabs feel like underdogs and basically have to stick together . . . Like the Arabs and Sephardic Jews in Israel. Sephardic Jews treat the Arabs worse than the Ashkenazi Jews because they are mistreated and they need someone to mistreat even worse in return. Even Colin Powell was referred to as a slave, but they say it about Rice a little louder."

Once I interviewed the mother of a *shaheed*, and when I was introduced to her I was told she came from the "slave neighborhood" of Jerusalem. I asked what that was and was told that there was a neighborhood with a high percentage of black Muslims from Nigeria who came to Jerusalem in the nineteenth century. In 2002,[2] Dr. Muhammad Bassam Yusuf, a Syrian writer living in exile and the mouthpiece of the Syrian opposition, attacked Rice on the Akhbar al-Sharq website, saying, "Perhaps the black Condoleezza Rice, the American security advisor, has forgotten her African origins and why she was in America and not in Africa, her original homeland. She has to be reminded that she is a descendant of African slaves and that the Americans enslaved millions of them and led them to America in chains from their homeland in Africa.[3] The Americans killed millions of them as they killed millions of Indians, the true owners of the American land."

Neither Fuad nor Samir could accept that a black woman could tell them what to do. It was peculiar to hear such sentiments from well-educated men, Arab citizens of the State of Israel with respectable professional and personal status. Their opinions were conditioned by their upbringing and the traditional Islamic mentality of their environment. They rejected the idea of a woman in a key position who could influence world events and who was sure of herself. It is difficult for an Arab man to cope with such a woman, the antithesis of what he is used to, that is, that women are inferior and their roles begin and end with raising children and taking care of the house. Arab lawyers spoke about Barack Obama with hope because his father was a Muslim, but also thought that a black president would be a puppet in the hands of whites.

Nabil, the suicide bomber dispatcher, had a different opinion of Rice. "*Sauda tuchkum ala'alam*? A black woman running the world? She makes the Arab world furious. We have never seen a woman in such an important position. There has never been a Jordanian or Egyptian woman president. What is the difference between Rania [the queen of Jordan, a woman of Palestinian extraction] and [King] Abdallah? They're the same. Even she can run the country better than he can." I wondered whether Nabil was being so disparaging of the Jordanian king because his wife had a Palestinian background. About 60 percent of Jordanians, about five million people, are of Palestinian extraction, so was he hinting at future events? He continued his diatribe against Rice: "That black woman does something bad to Arab sensibilities. Both black and a woman and running the world? That is unacceptable to Arabs. She accepts it. She did more than Bush to bridge the gap between the two sides."

A source in the Israeli judicial system, who preferred to remain anonymous, said of women in terrorism, "The classic crime is stabbing soldiers. Every time a woman has a problem, she solves it by wanting to die or going to jail in Israel, so she stabs a Jewish soldier. You can never know what is going on at home, and she claims she's fed up with her life and would rather be in an Israeli jail than at home. To get there she takes out a knife, and some of them don't even know what to do with it. Most of them don't actually reach the stage of stabbing anyway and are accused of attempted stabbing. What I don't understand is that if they want to die, there are a lot of ways to do it—why stab an Israeli soldier? I don't remember a lot of women who carried out suicide bombing attacks. Some of them are very successful and blow themselves up, so we don't get to see them in court. . . . They use their wives or their mothers to pass through the roadblocks or to take things from one place to another. They also open bank accounts in their wives' names as a cover. Women are also the link between their husbands and the outside world. They withdraw and transfer funds and information between prisoners still in jail to those outside, and in general."

Another lawyer involved in trying terrorists told me about a woman and child involved in a terrorist attack in Rishon Letzion, a city in the central part of the country. She was nineteen, and he was sixteen. He blew himself up, but she changed her mind. Their escorts were a young couple who took their little daughter with them. The wife was a Russian named Silvia, a Christian who had converted to Islam. He said that "at the trial Silvia looked like the picture of piety in traditional Arab dress, but before that she had been a prostitute in a massage parlor. Her husband was one of her clients, and he rescued her from a life of prostitution. They went abroad and got married there. After that they went to live near his family in an Arab village and started a family. He apparently loved her but had no respect for her. The prosecutor asked him if he had told his wife everything, trying to understand if she was an accomplice or not, and he said, 'You know how it is with women—they have one quarter of the brains of a man . . . but you know, they see a woman, they let her pass through the roadblock.' When the woman who had changed her mind went back to the car, Silvia told her in broken English, 'When you got out of the car I felt sorry for you, you were going to die, and now I think you are a coward. Look at how many people worked hard on the attack and you didn't do it.'"

I met Silvia in jail, her pale eyes prominent, framed by her black *hijab*. There was something obsessive about the way she clutched a copy of the Qur'an and prayed. As a convert from Christianity, she had to prove to all the prisoners that she was no less a genuine Muslim than they.

To complete the story of the suicide bombing attack in Rishon Letzion, I met with Shafiqa, the nineteen-year-old would-be suicide bomber who changed her mind. Hers was a classic story of the suicide bomber who recognized at the last minute that her potential victims were human beings and decided not to kill them.[4] She was a very intelligent woman and told me her story with tears in her eyes and hugged me. She had a strong desire to live but had internalized the oppression inflicted on women in Arab society, even though she was attending university. She described herself in the following terms: "I see myself as a white rose, even if I am black [the accepted ideal is a woman with fair skin]. . . . A woman has the right to work for herself and succeed in Palestinian society, but I'm not in favor of her being a director of a company or president. Our religion tells us it isn't good for a woman to be a leader because she does what her heart tells her, not her head. Muhammad, our prophet, said that a woman is not like a man. According to our religion, a man is more than a woman because we have monthly periods, and when we do, we don't pray. That makes us less than men. We have less in our heads because we think and decide with our hearts because we are more sensitive than men. . . . A woman in our society is not respected, and that goes for me as well . . . Men should respect me . . . They should respect what I did." As for the man of her dreams, she said, "I want a strong man who will control me," similar to what another terrorist told me: "I want a man stronger than I who has control, who can control me. I don't want to be the strong one while he is weak. That's the most important thing. There are a lot of men like that."

According to her indictment, "The accused claimed she had a connection with a man named Fadlallah who was a Tanzim operative. He was killed by the IDF and the accused wanted to avenge his death by carrying out a suicide bombing attack. She stated that when she arrived in Rishon Letzion she walked around with the explosive device on her back. She saw people on the street and some of them were very young children, and she decided she did not have the right to take away their lives, that she had to think in a more humane way. She changed her mind about the attack. When she saw Sawid [the boy who went with her to carry out the attack, and who in the end did blow himself up] she told him she had changed her mind and was going back. He also said he did not want to blow himself up. The accused said she used her mobile phone to call her escorts and that they tried to convince her to go back and carry out the attack, reminding her about Fadlallah and paradise, but she still refused. In the end they gave in and came to pick her up. The driver, Silvia's husband, wanted to give her five hundred shekels so that she could get to Bethlehem by herself but in the end he took her in his car, along with his wife and little daughter. She asked him about Sawid and he lied and said that he had given him two hundred shekels so that he could get back to the Palestinian Authority by himself. In reality he had not picked him up and the boy had nowhere to go, and feeling boxed in, all he could do was blow himself up. Silvia and her husband bluntly told her that she had been singled out and the Tanzim would kill her, because she was egotistical and had not killed Jews as she had been supposed to. The accused added that as far as she knew at that point Sawid did not intend to go through with the attack and that she was only told later that he actually had."

NOTES

1. Amos Harel and Avi Issacharoff, *The Seventh War* (Hebrew) (Tel Aviv: Yedioth Aharonoth Publishing, 2004).

2. "Arab Press Reacts to National Security Advisor Condoleezza Rice's Statements on Democracy and Freedom," Middle East Media Research Institute Special Dispatch no. 427 (October 11, 2002), http://www.memri.org/report/en/0/0/0/0/0/0/742.htm.

3. In point of fact, the slave traders were Arabs.

4. A. Berko, *The Moral Infrastructure of Chief Perpetrators of Suicidal Terrorism: Cognitive and Functionalist Perspectives*, unpublished dissertation (in Hebrew), Bar Ilan University, 2002.

15

⁂

Nabil, Dispatcher of Terrorists: "A Pity I Sent Her to Blow Herself Up, She Could Have Given Birth to Three Men Like Me"

Nabil's name often came up in conversations with would-be female suicide bombers and Arab-Israeli lawyers. He was a very important figure in Palestinian women's terrorism. I spoke many times with suicide bomber dispatchers who were serving consecutive life sentences, and I wanted to interview him in particular to understand whether they made a distinction between male and female suicide bombers, and if so, what it was.

Nabil, who had been sentenced to four consecutive life terms, sent Darin Abu Ayisha to blow herself up at an IDF roadblock in 2002. I met him in a little cell reserved for meetings between prisoners and lawyers. The walls were white and unadorned, and the only furniture was a Formica-topped table and two chairs. When he came in, I stood up and extended my hand. He was of medium height, brown-eyed, and had not recently shaved. His hair was rather long and uncombed. He wore a brown jacket and the brown prison uniform of Israeli jails. He was relaxed during our conversation, sometimes sitting with his arms folded across his chest and sometimes resting his elbows on the table. He had a great need to talk, and our meeting gave him the chance:

"I am thirty-two years old, live in Nablus. I have been married for eight years. My wife teaches school. I have a daughter six years old and a son who is four and a half. My mother is fifty-five and stays at home. My father is sixty. There is no work in the territories and the situation is as bad as it can be. I grew up in the Al-Farah refugee camp. Both my father and mother are from Haifa. There are six of us, three boys and three girls, and I was born third. When I was little, I had good grades and I didn't have any problem with school. I never finished. I dropped out when I was fourteen. I know how to read and write, and I'm studying political science at the Open University [while serving time in an

Israeli jail], using the time well. The Palestinian Authority pays for it. When I was at school I was detained once for six months for disturbing the peace during the first *intifada*. I threw stones. When I was released, I dropped out of school and went to work in one of the markets in Haifa. I worked there for almost three years. I had trouble with Hebrew, but eventually I got along. I slept at my boss's house. His name was Yossi. He liked me, and once he even visited us in the refugee camp. Every two or three weeks he used to take me home. He was a good person. I opposed the Israeli occupation and the humiliation it brought us. I don't see Jews and Arabs the same way. I'm against Zionism. I belong to Fatah. I miss my children. I've been in jail for four and a half years. My son was one month old when I was arrested. They don't let my family into Israel to visit me. My wife has only come to visit me three times." I nodded and said, "It must be very hard for you." "It is," he answered.

"I study, I kill time before it can kill me. We live in jail with the same hopes we had outside, to live, that there will be peace, to live in our own country. To establish our own institutions like other people." Nabil said that his brother had been killed in 1992, while he himself was in an Israeli jail. His brother's death made him change his outlook and escalate his struggle against Israel. "After the *intifada* there were the Oslo Accords, and then there were ten quiet years, maybe only a couple of attacks. Hamas and those of us from Fatah would stop the attacks, but the IDF shot at the jail we [Fatah] put them [the terrorists] in."

I said, "How can you say it was quiet after the Oslo Accords? There were a great many terrorist attacks inside Israeli territory during those years, including suicide bombing attacks." He wanted to say something but hesitated. Then, out of the blue, he said, "I sent a woman to blow herself up at the Modiin roadblock, Darin Abu Ayisha. She was twenty-two. I don't want to talk about it. I find it very painful. I was against sending women on attacks. Now I'm in jail, and I'm still against it. I was in a situation where I felt it had to be done. She was studying at the university in Nablus, and she told me how she felt and why she thought about killing herself. The *intifada* had a great deal of influence, people getting killed and seeing it on television. The media have a lot of influence on people on both sides. Each side enlists the media for its own approach. Darin saw women and children being killed on television by IDF rockets and wanted to do something. She appealed to me a number of times because I sent her cousin on a suicide bombing attack, and she escorted him to the site, and that's how she met me. I didn't feel that the parents of the suicide bomber I dispatched were angry with me. I went to visit them. They gave me *baklava* and we had a party."

Nabil didn't waste time and exploited every opportunity to meet women and recruit suicide bombers. In that way he met Abir, the sister of a suicide bomber he dispatched, and they began a romantic relationship. His name was mentioned in romantic contexts by many female security prisoners I spoke to. The unpleasant circumstances didn't prevent him from romantic overtures, even as he paid condolence calls to the homes of parents whose sons he had sent to their deaths. In his head, he was already working on the next attack.

He was quick to justify himself: "The attack was in Tel Aviv in 2001. One blew himself up, and one was caught at the central bus station. At that time the entire Palestinian nation demanded attacks. I brought the video of the bomber to his parents' home and played it so they could see it . . ."

Most parents do not want to lose their children to suicide bombing attacks. In addition, after an attack, the IDF sometimes destroys their house, leaving them homeless until they are given alternative housing by whichever terrorist organization dispatched the bomber, which usually happens fairly rapidly. They have to present a happy face because their children are *shaheeds*, knowing that the only thing left for them is respect from Palestinian society and financial rewards from the terrorist organization that dispatched their child to his death, including pensions and new houses.

I asked Nabil how he felt when he went to the home of a *shaheed*, whether the parents treated him as though he had murdered their son. He said, "The parents weren't happy, not at all, because it was their child. But they were proud that their son was a fighter. He was twenty, worked in Nablus installing windows. It was the same story as Darin. The media reported that three days previously, four people were killed in an apartment, and he saw what the bodies looked like. He asked one of the people who knew me well to introduce us. I told him to wait, but he called me every day and asked when I would be ready to send him on a suicide bombing attack, so I sent him . . ." Nabil referred to the suicide bomber as "him" and never once mentioned his name. As far as Nabil was concerned, he only acceded to the boy's request, and he was far removed from his death and not responsible for it at all.

Nabil did become emotional when he spoke about Darin. "It's different to send a girl. If I could turn the clock back, I wouldn't send a girl. It's very different and very painful. After all, she's a girl, even if she was a pest. She called me every hour. I was exiled to Ramallah in coordination with the Americans when Arafat was in the *Muqata'a* [his headquarters], and she came to Ramallah."

I said that maybe she was simply in love with him. The expression on his face said that it wasn't the first time someone had said that. He smiled slyly and said, "If she was in love with me, she wouldn't have left me. People tell all kinds of stories like that. The Tanzim influenced people, and the situation in Palestinian society was difficult, but there is no truth to the stories that she loved me. When a girl is in love with someone, does she leave him and blow herself up? That doesn't happen."

Later, during his trial, he said that he dispatched a girl on a suicide bombing attack because "it was easier," and he wanted to prove that despite the fact that there were roadblocks and the IDF was operating in Ramallah, it was still possible to carry out a suicide bombing attack. He said that after Wafa Idris died.[1]

"Darin's story is different because there was pressure from the people in the cell that was working to organize an attack. I sat with my friends, and Darin was with us, and we decided to send a girl, because the week before there was a woman who gave birth at a roadblock where there were IDF soldiers, and she died but the baby lived. The media gave it a lot of coverage and it had a lot of influence on all of us, not just Darin. A girl is a message—if a girl can give birth at a roadblock, a girl can also blow herself up at a roadblock."

I asked him how a Muslim Arab girl could sit in a coffeehouse with three strange men in broad daylight. The question made him uncomfortable, and it was hard for him to explain. In the end he said, "Darin's parents were in Nablus, they didn't know she was with us or that she was going to do such a thing. Two days before the attack she ran away from home. She was with me in Ramallah in a friend's house. She stayed with the friend's wife. Whenever a woman carries out an attack, there is another woman present. There is a woman who was sentenced to eight years. She is my wife's sister, and they said she was the one who strapped the explosive belt on Darin. It is out of the question for a man to do that because the woman has to take off all her clothing."

When women are involved in terrorist attacks, there is always another woman in the background. She helps recruit the would-be suicide bombers and escorts them to the site of the attack or stays with them to encourage them and keep them from changing their minds. Sometimes she is a mother figure and puts the explosive belt on the terrorist's body, as was the case with Darin.

He continued, "After I dispatched Darin, all the organizations were angry with me. It was strange, you know, to send a woman. It was something strange for the Palestinians during the *intifada*. It wasn't that Darin had to blow herself up, it was that you, the Israelis who push everyone into violence, for you it was a message.[2] Darin's story was a very big deal. She took a knife and called me every day and said she was watching television and saw Palestinians who had been killed, and that she wanted to feel she was doing something. I told her she didn't have to die, she shouldn't commit suicide, and she said, 'Prove that you can do something if you don't want me to kill myself.' I was in Ramallah and she was in Nablus with her cell phone, and I said, 'There is a gun. Bring it to Ramallah—you can help by bringing a weapon. If you are alive you can help every day. If you kill yourself you won't be able to do anything.' She brought the gun, and I said, 'Do you want to do something else?' I gave her an explosive belt that had been disassembled and told her to put it on so that she would feel she was doing something. I swear on my daughter's life, it was so that she wouldn't think about committing suicide."

He seemed to be reliving the trauma: "I also met her at the university when I was there visiting friends. There is a restaurant across from the university. When I spoke to her I changed my mind. I felt sorry for her. She was studying at the university, she was very pretty, she had good grades, and all the students, her girlfriends, everyone liked her. She told me about the woman at the roadblock who according to rumor had given birth and died, and I changed my mind, and I promised I would avenge the woman, but Darin started being a pest. She took a knife, and she wanted to attack settlers, so I took her back from Ramallah, and she said, 'If you don't let me do something, I'll do it by myself.' The owner of a knife store knows me. He saw her and knew I knew her, and he called and told me she bought a big knife. He said there was something funny about her, something wrong, and that she was very emotional. After he called, I told her that a police-woman had seen her, and I packed her into my car, and I saw the knife and she said, 'I told you that if you didn't let me do something I would do it myself,' and I said, 'Okay, you're going to die.'"

On the one hand, he packed her into the car like a piece of furniture, with no regard for what she was thinking or her operative capabilities, but on the other, the way she challenged him, manipulating him by telling him, "Prove you are a man!" goaded him into action. He related to her, a potential *shaheeda*, as an annoying child for whom something had to be found to keep her occupied and make her feel she had achieved something. He therefore gave her little missions to carry out, smuggling weapons, wearing a disassembled explosive belt. He claimed he did so to make her forget about committing suicide, but I could see that he enjoyed toy-ing with her and feeling his power over her, and there was nothing more powerful than sending her to her death.

Again and again he called her a pest, emotional, and he kept saying that his only crime was to give in when she pressured him and dispatch her on a suicide bombing attack. I asked whether people had talked about them, he, a married man, in the company of an attractive, single young girl, something that is unac-ceptable in Arab society. "People knew I had dispatched her cousin and that I had connections with the family, and that it was preferable to send a girl on an attack because she could pass through the roadblocks. It would be easier than sending a man. She wasn't angry with me for dispatching her cousin. She was twenty-two years old, not a grandmother, and she didn't have children. As far as the prisoners are concerned, and the organization as well, the only thing I'm sorry about is that I dispatched Darin Abu Ayisha. If I am released, I will continue doing the same thing. I'm sorry I sent a girl because I shouldn't have done that. A girl has to be at home, go to school, be a PhD, an engineer, in the kitchen, at home, bring up the children. She could have gotten married and have three children like me and help the Palestinian people do more than what I did."

I said that since women bear children, maybe it wasn't worth it to send them to blow themselves up. Nabil said emotionally, "A terrorist attack isn't a woman's job. It is forbidden for a woman to touch weapons and commit suicide. War is not a job for women. There are people who don't know all the circumstances and what exactly happened. They think it is a boy-girl thing because she was with me. I'm against it. It is the occupation that pushes us into it." I asked what he meant, because there had been no so-called occupation in the Gaza Strip since the disengagement and the IDF's withdrawal in 2005. He said, relating to the pre-2005 era, "The Gaza Strip is a jail larger than this one. Every city in the territories is almost a jail. There is no work, nothing to eat, people live in the streets. The situation was better at the time I was arrested, but today there is no work, there is a roadblock every ten yards; you wait three, four hours at the roadblock, get out of the car, and then you wait some more. Go to Jenin, Ramallah, what kind of life do they have there? It's crappy, it's not a normal life. I'm certain it will be different for Israelis and Palestinians as well. People don't have patience for all this killing. It's unbearable. Both sides are getting slaughtered."

He went back to talking about Darin. "When it comes to Darin, I am very angry with myself, because she was just a girl. A journalist asked me in front of a camera about Darin and myself, and I told the camera what happened. He also asked Jaradat [who dispatched Hanadi Jaradat to blow up the Maxim restaurant in Haifa] how he felt when he heard she had blown herself up, and he said he felt nothing. I was shocked—how could he not feel anything? That isn't true, he was wrong. I also dispatched a suicide bomber." He surprised me by saying, "You're Jewish. If I heard that something bad happened to you, I would be shocked, because we drank water together. Even though you're Jewish, I wouldn't want anything to happen to you. So if something happens to a girl I know from my village, of course I'm shocked.

"To this day, every night I look at a picture of Darin and cry. I have her picture in an album, and I think about her day and night. When I prepared the attack and a car came and took her, I wanted to bring her back. I called the driver and told him to come back, and she said she would blow up the car if it brought her back." The assumption that female suicide bombers bear a moral stain was made for Nabil because of Darin. Palestinian society often suspects that the dispatcher had a romantic or sexual relationship with a female suicide bomber and found an elegant way of getting rid of her to lay suspicions to rest. Nabil repeatedly claimed that only Darin herself could be blamed for the attack, and that all he had done was accede to her demands because he had no choice.

I said, "You sent a woman, Darin, to blow herself up, yet you claim that the pain you feel is greater than her parents'. You're a father. Do you think that someone can feel a greater pain than parents whose children have been harmed or who have lost a child?"

He answered, "My son is five years old, and in five more years I am willing to have him put on a belt and be dispatched, but I could never send my daughter to blow herself up. Never! Palestinians asked me if I would have dispatched Darin had she been my sister. The answer is no. It was a message sent to the soldiers at the roadblocks, that they could turn all the Palestinians into Darins. I don't think they got the message, because the occupation continues.

"I put her in a house and dispatched her. When I heard she had done it, it hurt me so much, and I cried so much I almost went crazy! Most suicide bomber dispatchers don't have the courage to tell the truth. I am against terrorist attacks, especially those carried out by women, but I have to do it. The Israelis killed my brother, and he was only twenty-two. My other brother was hit by thirteen bullets—he's a cripple. He was in the *Muqata'a* with Yasser Arafat. I went through a terrible period. I saw a family get killed in Ramallah. The IDF wanted to kill the family, so they fired a rocket at their car and killed the wife and children. The father wasn't even there; he had gone to the supermarket."

In some unfortunate instances Palestinian civilians are harmed because the terrorists find shelter among them and use them as human shields. Throughout most of the world an effort is made to keep civilians away from conflict areas, but the Palestinian terrorist organizations use civilians as human shields and their homes as places to hide weapons and fire rockets, assuming, correctly, that Israel will not attack civilian targets. That leads to a situation of moral asymmetry and a double standard: the terrorist organizations deliberately target Israeli civilians, and Israel's law and morality do not permit it to respond because the attacking terrorists have mingled with the civilian population.

I asked Nabil why he dispatched suicide bombers and hadn't carried out a suicide bombing attack himself. "I couldn't sit still for a minute. I would take my weapon [the suicide bomber] every day, my friends and I would, every day. It was enough that I came with the weapon [escorted the suicide bomber] to the central bus station in Tel Aviv, and I'm a wanted man, and I got home again. That was enough. All my friends couldn't believe it—how did I get there and back? What I do earns me more respect in the eyes of the Palestinian people. I am willing to dispatch my son and my brother. I suggested dispatching my brother when he was younger. I asked him to be a *shaheed*. It was the first time I asked one of my brothers to do that. That's my answer to all the people who ask me why I didn't dispatch my brother. In Palestinian society people always say, let's see if he's willing to dispatch his brother or his son. That's a question that gets asked all the time. I know other men who have dispatched their brothers." Suffice it to say that the adrenaline rush of living on the edge aside, he never actually dispatched one of his brothers.

I asked whether he thought he was more of a man than other men. He smiled. "The Palestinian people respect us, and that gives us courage. My wife is against it because she almost never sees me. In the beginning my parents were against it, but when they saw I had made my decision they let it alone. I want us to have our own country alongside Israel. Can anyone destroy Israel? No one can."

I said that Hamas did not recognize the State of Israel, and he said, "For the media, Hamas says what Khaled Mashaal [head of the Hamas political bureau, located at that time in Damascus] says. But listen to what the man in the street says. Everyone says we can't destroy the Israelis and they can't destroy us. My dream is to be with my children and wife at home. My wife's parents help her. She has been living with them since I went to jail. They help her with the children. She is a teacher and goes to school every day." What did he think, I wanted to know, about polygamy? He said, "The economic situation is so hard, how can someone marry three or four women, what, just to get married?" (Arab men have to pay the bride's dowry to her father, and a wedding entails considerable expense.)

I asked Nabil whether it was hard for him to find suicide bombers for attacks. "I never looked for them, they all came looking for me. The problem was to pick just one out of the crowd. Not everyone who wants to be a suicide bomber finds someone who will be his dispatcher. If you and I go to Nablus now and walk around, thirty, forty potential suicide bombers will approach me. To choose one, I would talk to them and say, 'If you need money, or money for a wedding, we will arrange it. If there is a problem in the family, I don't want you to blow yourself up because of it.' He has to believe that Palestinian people are being killed day and night, that he is a soldier who puts on an explosive belt to defend the Palestinian people, Jerusalem, the women who wait at the roadblocks and give birth to their babies there."

It was easy to understand what kind of people approached him. He decided who would live and who would die, with victims on both sides. Like many of the others I spoke to, Nabil never expressed sorrow or regret for his victims. Another dispatcher told me that he asked people to seek "sad young men" for suicide bombing attacks. The dispatchers are fully aware who the likely candidates are for committing murder and suicide, and potential terrorists know where to turn for help in carrying out an attack.

I asked him what he thought about using children to carry out suicide bombing attacks. "It's not true. I am positive that the Shin Bet coordinates it because there are people from the media at the roadblocks. I dealt with things like that and I know that it isn't easy to dispatch children." I said I meant how he felt about the moral aspect, but he answered only that using them prevented the roadblocks from being removed. As far as he was concerned, using children harmed the Palestinian media struggle. He said, "Not all the young people in jail were potential suicide bombers, maybe there are five or six, and they were all caught. Everyone was also against the suicide bombing attack carried out by a child in the Carmel Market [in Tel Aviv, 2004], not just his parents, the whole village."

I wanted to know whether the *shaheeds* really believed in paradise. He said there were those who told him they wanted to go to paradise, and those who also wanted to defend the Palestinian people. "I believe in paradise as described in the Qur'an and I honor it. There are virgins and all the other things. We believe it because it is our religion, according to the Qur'an. The main problem is the humiliation caused by the occupation. Before the *intifada* the situation was better, but why should I work for the Jews, until when? And why can't we have our own country? Why should an Israeli soldier be able to examine me in my own village? Would you accept it if someone asked you for your authorization to be in Tel Aviv? It's unacceptable. A Palestinian policeman should do it, we should have a country. We are the last people in the world still living under an occupation." He was wrong about Tel Aviv. Israelis are examined in every city in the country, day and night, every time they go into a shopping mall, a movie house, a restaurant, a supermarket, a hospital, a bank, or any public building.

I asked him what he thought about dispatching women to carry out suicide bombing attacks. In any case, it was a pressing issue as far as he was concerned, and gave him no peace because of Darin Abu Ayisha. He took a deep breath and began. "There is no *fatwa* against women blowing themselves up. There is no *fatwa* from al-Azhar or Tantawi or Qardawi [sheikhs who issued famous *fatwas*] against suicide bombing attacks, and not from those who belong to a political religion like the Muslim Brotherhood. If there were such a *fatwa*, girls would not come to us asking to commit suicide, Darin wouldn't have, either . . .

"I prepared seven girls who blew themselves up in this *intifada*. The media have the greatest influence on recruiting suicide bombers. One told me that he waited at a roadblock for six hours and they made him take his pants off, and he swore he would take revenge. There are also suicide bombers whose social and economic situations are good; they even have nice cars. But most of them are in the middle of a difficult period or something, they were humiliated at the roadblocks or influenced by the media, a child was killed, their father or mother. My parents told me not to dispatch attacks because my brothers were hurt, but if the suffering hadn't reached my own house I wouldn't have taken part in it."

Nabil was confused over the issue of *fatwas*. On November 11, 2006, on the eve of the Muslim holy month of Ramadan, Sheikh Yussuf Qardawi issued a *fatwa* regarding the use of women in terrorist attacks. Abu Hilal of the Palestinian Islamic Jihad, a graduate of Al-Azhar University in Egypt, explained: "People say that Sheikh Qardawi is the secret head of the global Muslim Brotherhood. His *fatwa* says that there is nothing wrong with a woman taking her veil off before an attack. A short time before the attack, just at the last minute, so that the enemy won't notice her. What is in and of itself forbidden is permissible when the need arises.

"Sheikh Qardawi did not say a woman should take her clothing off. He was speaking in general. She is allowed to do things to confuse the enemy, like taking off her veil and exposing some of her body. What difference does it make what happens after she dies? In writing the *fatwa* the sheikh could not go into every single rule. He says a woman may remove her *hijab* and even a lot more than that. He hinted, he did not say a woman should take off her dress and underpants. Anyone who reads the *fatwa* will understand that a woman can take off everything.

"The sheikh supports and allows *amaliyyat istishhadia* [suicide bombing attacks]. He issued a *fatwa* specifically for Hanadi Jaradat which says she blew herself up to take revenge. He also talks about Rim Riyashi [who carried out a suicide bombing at the Erez crossing in the northern Gaza Strip] and explains that it was defensive jihad, and he also mentions Wafa Idris. Bin Laden said women were forbidden to carry out suicide bombing attacks as long as there were men to do it, and Qardawi says the opposite, that there are women fighters in the army of Islam and there is no problem with that, they can take their clothes off and do a lot of things that Islam usually forbids."

"So," I said, "the *fatwas* enable the dispatchers and other terrorist operatives to exploit women sexually before an attack?" He answered, "There was a girl from Ramallah who was sexually abused by someone from Fatah, so he sent her to commit suicide. She had serious emotional problems. They did a lot of things to her and dispatched her. The Islamic organizations don't do that, but it is well known that men from Fatah do. How do their men put explosive belts on the bodies of women? By telling them, 'Take your clothes off . . .'"

There is a lot of confusion about the limitations and religious laws regarding the inclusion of women in terrorist attacks, especially about the disagreement over exposing her body, before and after the attack. For that reason, Nabil thought there was no *fatwa* regarding the issue.

Toward the end of our conversation, he told me he liked to draw. I gave him a piece of paper from the pad I used for taking notes and handed him a pen. He quickly and skillfully drew two hands shaking one another and two doves, one holding the Israeli flag and the other the Palestinian flag.

I was genuinely impressed. I told him how well he could draw and how talented he was, and he was delighted with the compliment. I promised I would visit him again. He said he would make me more drawings. We shook hands on it and continued talking until a guard came to take him back to his cell. We shook hands again, and he walked out the door.

Our next meeting was like a reunion of two old friends. He was happy to see me and began speaking immediately. "Jail is one of the reasons I am against involving women in attacks. In Palestinian society it is hard to accept a woman's being in jail. Sometimes, when a girl blows herself up, not all of her body is destroyed, parts of it remain, and it is very hard for her [that people see them]. I don't know what Islam says about that, but I think it is forbidden. We talk about it here with each other. There is no *fatwa* that says it is permitted or forbidden. I don't know how Islam regards it. While it is true that I sometimes pray, I don't know the ideology of Islam."

Nabil was no different from many others who opposed dispatching women on suicide bombing attacks because it seemed to them that they were "taking their clothes off in public," and they worried that people would see their bodies, or rather, what was left of them after the explosion, lest their private parts be exposed. I said it was known that the terrorist organizations kept a head count that told them whether the attack had been "successful" or not. Maybe women weren't as successful as men because they didn't kill enough Israelis.

"No, it's because her body is exposed, it's not because fewer Israelis are killed. The success of an attack is not determined by the number of people killed. It's not as embarrassing to see a man's body ripped to shreds as it is a woman's. A woman

"Two Bleeding Peoples. Let Them Live in Peace. To Dr. Anat from Nabil. 21.12.06."

should be at home and not off someplace acting like a man. She should bring up the children, raise fighters, oppose the occupation. She should be a teacher, not a *shaheeda*. I'm willing to be a suicide bomber because that's my role. To prepare and dispatch a suicide bomber is not easy, so the organization guarded me more than I guarded myself."

The lives of dispatchers are far more important to the terrorist organizations than those of the suicide bombers, who are disposable. The role of the suicide bomber ends when he blows himself up, but the dispatcher will continue to orchestrate attacks, and there will always be another potential *shaheed* waiting to step up and take his place in line.

Nabil tried to draw a parallel between the Israeli victims and the suicide bombers by saying that not only were Palestinian bodies exposed, so were those of the victims. It is true that after an explosion the workers from ZAKA, Israel's volunteer Disaster Victim Identification organization, often find it hard to distinguish between the bodies of the victims and that of the suicide bomber.

He did not praise Darin after her death lest people say he sent a woman to carry out an attack, that he used her, that they suspected he was involved with her sexually. The fact that he dispatched a woman to an attack did not raise his status, either with his organization or with the Palestinian public in general. Quite the opposite: his masculine image was damaged, and he did everything he could to hide it. He didn't have her picture on his dresser, although he did have pictures of the men he had dispatched, and was not proud at all of his act, afraid he would be perceived as a pimp.

I told him about a meeting I had with the mother of a *shaheed*. She deeply mourned her son's death. He showed no empathy, simply saying, "It was her son, but we have to fight against the occupation. Why should my son live a life of humiliation under the occupation? Maybe it would be better for him to die as a *shaheed*. Half of the Palestinian population is already in jail. We want our own country with the 1967 borders.[3] If we are there and you are here, there won't be any more *shaheeds*. If we had helicopters and tanks, we wouldn't use suicide bombers, but we don't have them, and the Israelis go into every city and village from the air and on land. The children are scared day and night, so why shouldn't the children in Tel Aviv be afraid? They have to feel it, and then the Israelis will leave and stop attacking us.

"The children can't go to school—going from one village to another takes more than five hours instead of five minutes. Four, five women gave birth at the roadblocks. That's no way to live. It's a life of humiliation, of nothing. There is no work, no one works, no one does anything. Most of the Palestinian Authority are thieves. They stole the money that belongs to the Palestinian people. Who brought the thieves from Tunis? The person who knows what we feel is Marwan Barghouti [Tanzim leader], and he is with us in jail. Yesterday he was with us when we went for medical treatment. He is a prisoner in handcuffs. When he was in Ramallah he was with us in the street, and we found him here in jail, and he feels us. Mahmoud Abbas is all show and hot air. If there were no *intifada* against Israel, there would be one against the Palestinian Authority."

I asked Nabil why his name was often mentioned in connection with women involved in terrorist attacks. He seemed embarrassed but nevertheless pulled himself together and said, "In 2003 an Israeli journalist wrote that the girls were exploited. I knew lots of girls before the *intifada*. I had a great life. I have a lot of friends, male and female. In the villages it's unacceptable for a man to be friends with girls. In the big cities, Ramallah and Nablus, it also isn't accepted a lot, but people don't look as closely as they do in the villages and refugee camps."

At his trial, Nabil requested permission to speak, waving an article he cut out of the newspaper. He said that the article claimed he had sexually harassed and raped women while involving them in terrorist attacks, and he vigorously denied it. I felt he was now trying to deny romantic links with Darin. On the one hand, as a man, he felt complimented by the way women responded to him, Darin especially, but on the other, he knew that as a Palestinian man it could mean trouble, and therefore he denied the newspaper item. Not only that, he personally wrote to the military judges to protest.

I asked him whether it were possible that the women he had dispatched were in love with him, and I could tell he liked the question. He hesitated and said, "What women? The ones in the indictments? Not love, we were just friends. The Shabak said, 'She did it because she was in love with Nabil.' So if she's in love with me, why go off and commit suicide?"

Women often choose to carry out attacks out of love. Such a woman will carry out a suicide bombing attack to please the man she loves if she cannot have him. The women in Nabil's life apparently knew that he would never take them as his second or third wife, so as far as they were concerned there may have been something romantic in their willingness to die for him.

Nabil continued, saying, "There are more than one hundred twenty female security prisoners in jail, and I know more than seventy of them. At home, everyone I met on the street knew me and had heard about me. So if some woman wants to find me, it isn't hard if she wants to do something."

"Okay," I said, "but why did so many women who wanted to participate in attacks go looking for you? Were you more active, more macho? What made women want to reach you?"

He couldn't hide his smile. He even didn't try not to answer. "They all know that I am married and that I have a son. [He also had a daughter, which he did not mention when he answered the question.] So it's not a question of love. If it were, would a woman be willing to place a bomb for me or take a suitcase or an M-16? . . . Maybe she would, but to commit suicide? Never. Unbelievable. We talk about politics, never about love. My wife's sister is in jail for strapping the explosive belt on Darin, and my wife is angry with both of us. My wife didn't want to lose me because we have children. But in the end she was convinced that I chose this path because I believed in it, that there is a sacred goal I share with all my comrades, a sacred goal that must be achieved, even if I'm in jail. If I am unsuccessful today, my son will realize the goal. My daughter is seven. I tell her I want her to be a lawyer so she can defend the Palestinian people, defend her father's goal."

Nabil's wife was offended by his romantic associations with women, and for a while, until she calmed down, didn't send him letters. He convinced her that his popularity among women came from "relationships at work," nothing more.

I asked him to draw a picture of Darin for me. He said he couldn't remember what she looked like. Nabil, who was so enthusiastic every time he got the chance to prove his artistic talents, was not eager to draw Darin. "I don't like to draw her. It is painful. I don't want to remember her anymore. I try to forget her but I can't. It's not the same as for a *shaheed*. I talk about Muhammad all the time, about how brave he was, how he used to talk and laugh and eat, but I don't tell my comrades anything about Darin. I don't think it a great honor to dispatch a woman to kill herself. I am uncomfortable with it inside. It's a strange thing, a girl who goes and blows herself up. During the time of the Prophet, thousands of years ago [*sic*], women weren't used in war . . . I don't feel right, putting a belt on a woman's body and sending her to kill herself. She was the second *shaheeda*."

I asked whether he had seen her wearing the explosive belt and he said yes, he had. I asked him to draw her with the belt, and he said, "No, it's out of the question, to draw I have to be sitting in a coffeehouse with a cigarette . . ." but nevertheless he took a sheet of paper and began drawing. As he did, he told me that he had already tried to draw her in 2004, but without success. Over the drawing, he wrote, "If only you could come back to life." He drew Darin without an explosive belt, but the drawing was faint and hesitant, her image abstract and nonconceptual. I complimented him on the drawing and said that instead of holding weapons and fighting, he should draw. He said he was unlucky, but that with Allah's help his luck would change.

We kept talking. I asked him to tell me about Darin just before the attack. "Darin wore a white blouse, and the belt was strapped on top of it. There were wires hanging from it so I took them and led them through the button hole in the sleeve of her jacket. The belt weighed 12 kilos [26.4 pounds]. She looked like she was pregnant." As he spoke, he mimed pulling the detonator wires through the sleeve. It was frightening to watch him. It made me think of the pregnant Palestinian women who had trouble receiving authorization to pass through the roadblocks because of the female terrorists who had disguised themselves as pregnant.

After a short pause, he said, "Wafa Idris, I know her story. She was supposed to place a bomb, not kill herself. She blew up by mistake. The device was attached to her telephone, and using it was supposed to detonate it. The phone wasn't supposed to ring, so actually the first *shaheeda* was really Darin, and I told her about it. I told her when I was preparing her. She was ready and checked everything, and I told her at the last minute that she would be the first *shaheeda* because of what the real story about Wafa was." He made Darin feel special, the same feeling other female would-be suicide bombers told me about when I spoke to them. They said they were special, different from other Palestinian women. The way Nabil talked about Darin, it was as though he were telling her she was really the first woman in his life, first in the sense of virginity, which is so important in Arab society.

I told Nabil that in Israel, people said Wafa was barren and her husband divorced her, and that was why she carried out the attack. He had already heard something like that. He said, "The Israeli side tells the story the way it sees it, and we tell it the way we see it. Are you convinced that a woman without children would kill herself?"

I asked him how Darin reacted when he said she would be the first female suicide bomber. He said, "She was happy to be the first. I don't want this in the media, don't want to harm respect for Wafa, but I wanted Darin to feel she was the first. Doctora Anat, for us, the *shaheed* who goes to commit suicide and blow himself up, you know how that is received in the village or city where his family lives. The family is respected and people treat them differently from other families. Every day people ask them how they are, all the organizations, not only the organization which sent him on the attack. If the house is razed, they build him a new one and point to it and say, there, his son is a *shaheed*, he blew himself up. That gives them respect, you know that. I wanted Darin to feel she was the first. Not just for her to feel that way, because she really was. This is the Arab world, not America or Europe. Things don't develop here, there is no progress. *Khalas* [enough], we were born Muslims with the sword [*saif*] of the prophet Muhammad, and there is no progress. We look at a woman and say she should be in the kitchen. If she leaves the kitchen, it's only to do something bad."

It was ironic to hear Nabil, who sent women to their deaths and to carry out terrorist attacks, saying that a woman's place is in the kitchen. Did he think the women he was personally responsible for getting out of the kitchen had done something bad?

He said sadly, "The whole world is moving forward, and we in the Arab world are stuck in place. The occupations and dividing the Arab world in the Second World War didn't let us progress. The British Mandate and the French in Lebanon and Syria had a lot of influence.

"Before she left," he said, "we had dinner together. Then I left and got everything ready for the attack, and I checked the route. I called the comrades and told them to get the car ready. I wasn't in the same house Darin was. I tried to make her angry, so I called her and said, 'I have postponed the whole thing, it can't be done.' She started crying and said, 'I lost my chance, what lousy luck, you should have let me go with the knife!' She cried over the phone, and I wanted to be sure she was convinced she wanted to go through with it. She was with the wife of a friend of mine. They were making food." The friend's wife also had an important role in the attack. It was her job to encourage Darin and keep her from losing interest in *istishhad* (self-sacrifice).

"My friend's wife made dinner and *halawat* [cookies distributed on festive occasions]. It was seven in the evening. Darin said she would make me something to eat. So we ate, and she blew herself up at nine." There did not seem to be any anger between them, even though he said he wanted to make her angry. And until the last minute, the *shaheeda* still had not left the kitchen. She behaved like the perfectly trained woman, whose function was to serve the man and keep him happy. Nabil remembered the last meal very well. Usually, a man who is about to become a *shaheed* is invited to a meal and also receives money and does not prepare food for his dispatcher.

Nabil continued, saying, "I took the car and drove to a lone roadblock, one in Jerusalem. I said to her, 'This is our message, that a woman can blow herself up at a roadblock.' She got out of my car and into another one. I gave her a pen and said, 'Write whatever you like.' She wrote to her family, to her brothers and to her sister, who was studying at the university, and asked her to continue her studies. Her father was ill and she was worried about him."

The illness of Darin's father makes her story similar to those of other women who chose terrorism in the absence of a father figure or the presence of a weak father who could not protect his daughter. Darin's patriarchal family seemed weak and vulnerable, making it possible to exploit one of the daughters without risking a blood feud.

Nabil lowered his eyes, perhaps remembering things he would rather forget. "My friend's wife hugged her and then Darin said to her, 'I'm going and I won't be back.' Both of them were crying. I smoke all night long and write poetry. I have a book coming out in Ramallah."

"Come on, write something for me," I said, and he jumped at the chance. He had a need to express himself, write poetry and letters, draw. As he was writing, he told me that when he was little he liked to write and draw. Then he very politely asked whether it would bother me if he smoked. The female security prisoners simply took out cigarettes and lit them. None of them had ever troubled to ask whether it bothered me. I told him that since there were no windows, if he wanted to, we could stop where we were and continue some other time. He said it was okay, he would smoke later.

I asked him what he would write to Darin and gave him a sheet of paper and a pen. He began writing without hesitation. Suddenly, he couldn't continue.

"To the girl who left and took my soul with her, and made me cry day and night because she was gone. The heroine who proved to the occupation that their attempts to humiliate our women at the roadblocks, the occupation which will of necessity make every Palestinian woman and every Palestinian man living in this land turn into a bomb.

"My dear Darin,

"I am writing this to you and my pen is witness to the fact that I am writing all the sad and painful feelings in my heart because you are bleeding and not here. If I had any power over fate, or if I could turn back the wheel of history, then I would not agree to your dying as a *shaheeda*. That is because you went while others trade in your blood and the blood of heroes like you, they corrupted your blood and heroism in the streets of Gaza."

I asked him what the difference was between dispatching men and dispatching women to blow themselves up. He thought for a minute and said, "When I

.الى التي رحلت وأفضت معنا مهجة القلب . وجعلتني أبكي فراقها
ليل نهار . البطلة التي أثبتت لهذا الاحتلال . بأن محاولاتك ،ذلال
لسانا ونا بلا هؤلاء الاحتلال سيؤدب حتماً ،الى أن يجمع كل
.امرأة فلسطينيه أو كل فلسطيني لا هذه الأرض ،الى عيون غارقه

عزيزتي دارين .

أكتب اليك بهذا القلم شاهد أنني أكتب ما في قلبي لا مشاعر حزينه
وهي بقاء غيابك الدامي .ولو أن القدر ( ) كان يمدي أو
أن عجلة التاريخ هي الان بيدي .اعادتها للوراء . لا كنت قد
. وأفتدك با ثمارة الاستشهاد . لزلك رحلت وهؤلاء
الذين يهاجرون مع دعائك ،نزلك رحلت وهؤلاء
وبطولاتك هناك لا شوارع غزة منطلع شوهو دمائك

28 . 12 . 06

The letter to Darin.

dispatched Sawid, we embraced, man to man. I kissed him, and he kissed me. It was sad, but not like it was with Darin. When I let her out of my car, we turned off our mobile phones because of the tracking devices of the helicopters, I took her to the other car, and she went for about two hundred meters in it. If she were in my car, I could have turned her back, but I couldn't call—our phones were off." Apparently his unease with the situation caused him to contradict himself and indulge in wishful thinking.

"I regretted sending a girl. I never should have done it. She was a girl.

"We parted crying. I didn't hug her, but I kissed her on the forehead. She gave me her mobile phone and documents so I could give them to her family, and she wrote me a note: 'If you get to paradise I will thank Allah that we meet there and end this suffering.' She said, 'I see you are a person who cares about his people, who does everything for the Palestinian people.' I have the note at home. I couldn't sleep at night. No one did what I did. I couldn't look at my children."

Darin's incomprehensible surrender is still a mystery. Her image on paper was faint. All that was left was a theory of Darin as a passive provider of services who tried to satisfy and please her dispatcher, and Nabil as pulling the strings. She hoped to meet him in paradise. When they parted, she expressed her real feeling for him and the hope that they would meet in a world after death where their relationship would not be forbidden.

He continued, his voice quavering. "Darin Abu Ayisha was such a beautiful girl, everyone would want to marry her. She was pretty, well brought up, and she just died, just like that, by pressing a button. That was it, she pressed a button and there was no more Darin." He apparently felt that if he couldn't have her, no one could, and he distanced himself from her death.

I asked him what he thought women received in paradise, and the question seemed to embarrass him. It is described as full of alcohol and sex, an environment definitely not suitable for Muslim women. He said, "I don't know. I think they will be virgins. The women will wait for the *shaheeds* to arrive, that's according to our religion. The Qur'an says what there is in paradise, and I believe it because it is written there. If Allah wants me to be a *shaheed*, then maybe we'll meet, but it's not something you can know. Telling Darin's story makes me want a cigarette, ten packs of cigarettes.

"I dream about my children on the beach. Watching children on television running and playing on the sand makes me cry. Before the *intifada* Palestinians and Israelis had an employee-employer relationship. We didn't feel we were respected, and nevertheless I don't legitimize sending suicide bombers," he said, again distancing himself from what he did. "If we had our own country everything would be different. It would be one soldier against another, and we would either continue living the way we do now, in a garbage dump, or we would use all the legitimate and illegitimate means. Today I can't take my children to the beach, to a restaurant . . ."

While he missed his children, as far as he was concerned, suicide bombing attacks were a legitimate weapon even if they did not end the conflict with Israel and even if a Palestinian state were established. Once it might have been a moral dilemma, but he seemed to have come to terms with it. On the one hand, he wanted a normal life, while on the other he delegitimized Israel and justified the use of terrorism and violence against it.

"What about the Israeli soldier who pressed a button and killed fifteen innocent people because of Salah Shahade [a terrorist who died in a targeted Israeli Air Force killing, during which fifteen civilians were also killed]?" I said, "Then why use civilians as human shields? Is that a terrorist strategy, to hide behind civilians?"

Nabil complained that pregnant women were detained at roadblocks. I was put in mind of the woman who miraculously was not killed in the terrorist attack at the Maxim restaurant in Haifa, who told me that the suicide bomber was disguised as a pregnant woman. I said, "You yourself sent Darin disguised as a pregnant woman to blow herself up at a roadblock, so what do you expect, that pregnant women won't be examined?" It took him a couple of seconds to find an answer: "I understand what you are saying, so what do you think we should do? Just throw stones at tanks? Everyone claims ownership of the land. How can Israel be a country without borders? The Zionists regard all the Arab countries as though they should be the borders of Israel." That was the propaganda Nabil had been nurtured on and what he believed. He said he had read books in Hebrew by David Ben-Gurion to understand "what my neighbors think about me."

Nabil returned to his personal history. He leaned toward me as if he wanted to tell me a secret. "My wife was jealous of the other women and we almost got divorced. But then I convinced her that we just had a working relationship, and that it had nothing to do with love. She cried. She has faith in me, but every day people tell her I am with this or that woman, and she gets angry again. I convinced her it wasn't a question of a wedding or love, and in the end she believed me. If she didn't we wouldn't still be married."

I laughed and said it was up to him, that in his culture the man divorced the woman. All he has to say is, "You are divorced" three times and the marriage is dissolved. He laughed aloud and said, "How can I live with a woman who doesn't like being my wife? A woman can stand anything except having another woman around her husband. She can't stand that. Our religion permits us to have more than one wife, but I don't believe in marrying four women. I love my wife and I married for love. I did everything to marry her, I respect her and she respects me. We have two children. But since I have been in jail we haven't been able to be free.

"During my trial there was a girl named Abir who testified. She said things to the judge, and she didn't know my wife was in the courtroom. She made it sound like I was her boyfriend and that we spent nights in a hotel, that we went to restaurants together, and my wife was sitting there and listening to it all. The girl tried to prove to the judge that there was no military connection between us, that we had a romantic relationship, because she wanted to protect herself. She was in love with me and wanted me to marry her. My wife heard all that, and it complicated things for me with her. Before that, she used to send me letters to jail, and after that she didn't send me a single letter for three months. She was very angry. We had phone conversations on a phone smuggled into jail."

To extract himself from the romantic entanglement, Nabil told his wife that he had asked Abir to say what she did so that her punishment would be reduced. He also sent a letter to Abir rebuking her for having exposed their relationship. After that he didn't write to Abir for four years, although she continued sending him love letters.

I expressed surprise, and he said, "Yes, she loves me. She wants to marry me but I certainly don't want to. Everyone knows I love my wife. I don't want to marry another woman, even though in the beginning I felt guilty because now Abir is in jail. I was thinking about marrying her because she asked me to. I thought about it for a couple of months. We used to send each other love letters. She was sentenced to five years, and in another two or three months she'll get out, so I told her we would get married because she was in jail.

"When I was in Nablus she was captured with me because she brought food and cigarettes and coffee to where I was hiding. They told me, 'Give yourself up!' [Nabil brought his fist up to his mouth as if he were using a megaphone.] She was with me a minute before that with the coffee and cigarettes, and when the IDF broke in she was captured, too. She didn't have an ID card, and I said, 'Tell them you're my wife,' so they would let her go, but they didn't believe her and they took her too, they detained her." He shifted uneasily on his chair.

Nabil was faced with a real dilemma. He was married, and Abir was the sister of a suicide bomber he had dispatched to blow himself up. He met her when he paid the family a condolence call. He recruited Darin Abu Ayisha in much the same manner. "Shaheedism" has become a family trait among the Palestinians, the same way everyone in other families is a doctor or a lawyer.

Nabil exploited the aura of "attractive wanted man" to form so-called professional relationships with various women. Moreover, romantic liaisons are formed between male and female security prisoners, and time spent in jail takes on a new and exciting dimension when romantic messages are exchanged and prisoners dream of being a couple in the future. Exchanging letters turns the time in jail into something different, and a romance can be conducted without parental supervision or pressure.

Nabil seemed slightly embarrassed over the affair with Abir. "She said she wanted to commit suicide. She came to me a couple of times after Darin. She's one of Darin's relatives. I refused, because to this day I regret having dispatched Darin, I regretted it from the minute Darin got out of my car. Send another girl? Abir loved me, and I felt guilty. I sent her a letter [when they were both in jail] telling her that everything would be okay, that I was seriously thinking about marrying her. My wife knew there was something going on between Abir and me, and she said, 'If you marry someone else, I want a divorce.' According to our religion, if the husband is in jail for two years, the wife can ask for a divorce. I thought about it for a couple of months and then I changed my mind, and I told Abir that I didn't want to marry her." His wife threatened him with divorce, unusual behavior for an Arab woman. She was raising his children, and he did not want to make her angry, especially since he had been sentenced to a long prison term and needed her emotional support.

I asked him whether male and female security prisoners routinely sent each other love letters. He said, "We write to the female prisoners. Houda was a friend of mine on the outside. I know her, she will be a leader [when she gets out]. People admire her in spite of the story about the sixteen-year-old boy. What she wrote on the Internet was not respectable, but the goal was [to kill the boy]. While she was on the outside no one had ever heard of her. There are girls who were released from jail and got married and had homes and children, and there are men who don't want to marry women who were in jail. In the 1980s the family of a girl who was in jail would kill her on the spot—it was unacceptable in Palestinian society. Today female prisoners are an accepted thing. They are not respected the way men are, because it is not a woman's role to fight. People look at them differently. In the end, the whole world is convinced that we did what we had to."

Nabil had a problem with admiring what Houda did because of the way she did it, that is, using the Internet to seduce a young boy. Even hiding behind political ideology won't do her any good, and she will be stigmatized forever. Palestinian society does not like such a woman; she is perceived as frivolous, problematic, and practically a whore.

I asked him what he thought about Najar, the sixty-eight-year-old grandmother who blew herself up. He raised his eyebrows and said, "A grandmother in Gaza, that's strange. I think that starting tomorrow every day a grandmother will blow herself up. If I were desperate I would dispatch my grandmother, but not my mother. There is no hope of work, a life, school, no hope of getting married. The principle is hope. You have to have hope, and for the past four years the Palestinians have had no hope anything can happen. Today they fire Qassam rockets, and we know they don't do anything, it's just fireworks. The Israeli media have been recruited for Israel's interests. They never show the missiles the Israelis fire from helicopters and tanks. In Gaza they fire Qassams. Tomorrow they'll do it from the West Bank. If the wanted men in the West Bank become desperate, they'll use them.

"In jail, most of the time we talk politics. We have been following the news for years and say what we think should have been done. We will leave jail as political commentators. We talk about our children, but not about our wives. Who can I talk to about my wife? Telling a girl about my wife is not like telling another man.

She's my wife. You don't talk about your wife. That's what makes people go crazy. I'll talk about how much I miss her. I look at the pictures of my son and daughter. They're next to my bed."

What about his wife? I wanted to know. Did he have a picture of her as well? "No," he said, "I don't want other people to see her picture. It's not allowed for people to see her. Until a girl is fifteen or twelve [he meant as long as a girl is young], you can show her picture, but when she looks like a woman, no. Girls are hidden out of love, that's the difference between boys and girls. According to our religion, a woman can participate in jihad. I know the brothers of Hanadi Jaradat [who blew herself up in the Maxim restaurant in Haifa in 2003]. They're criminals in Jenin, thugs."

I said that her father had cancer. "Yes," said Nabil, "he was sick, weak, but her older brother was almost like a father to her. He gave out *baklava* when she blew herself up, shed a few tears, and that was it. He hung up a picture of her. She was engaged, that's like being married. The agreement had been signed in front of the sheikh until her father could decide the date for the wedding. She was considered a widow because her fiancé died."

Nabil was angry with the Israeli media. He claimed that it presented the women who carried out attacks as problematic, especially as having romantic problems. He said, "If an Israeli woman gets a divorce and leaves her boyfriend, does she kill herself? Why would she kill herself? Why do they say that a Palestinian woman who gets divorced kills herself in a suicide bombing attack?"

Conversations with Nabil revealed a sophisticated, ambivalent personality, a serial killer by proxy with no sympathy for his victims. He even justified the killing but was greatly frustrated because he did not receive the recognition he felt was due him because he had dispatched women to their deaths. In the eyes of traditional Arab society, anyone who uses a woman for his own needs is considered inferior, almost a pimp. The man is ashamed of what he has done, usually denies it, and looks for a way to conceal it. In such circumstances, a terrorist like Nabil finds himself hiding things and lying, and when his misdeeds are revealed, he tries to find excuses and justify himself. A dispatcher of women does not have the same sensation of achievement and success as when he sends a man to carry out an attack. Moreover, he tries to make it seem as though he was forced into recruiting women, whose role in life is not to "deal with military work." Even Nabil, who was a serial dispatcher of women, did not express admiration or recognition for what they had done. What, he claimed, could they change anyway in the never-ending struggle between Palestinians and Israelis? Nabil was stigmatized by the society he lived in as a man who "played around with women," and he tried to remove the stigma in every way possible. Using women to carry out terrorist attacks led people to wonder about the kind of relationship he had with them. Something in his Arab-Muslim masculinity, honor, and morality was damaged. A *shaheeda* is a second-class *shaheed*, and who knows what went on between them, why she had to become a *shaheeda*, why he dispatched her if he was trying to purify himself, and whether she had to purify herself for her family.

NOTES

1. The first female suicide bomber, who blew herself up in Jerusalem in 2002.

2. The message has not been received. In Israel all suicide bombers, male and female, are regarded with disgust, loathing, horror, and wonder at their stupidity.

3. Technically speaking, there is no such thing as "the 1967 borders" as applied to the Palestinians. The West Bank belonged to Jordan, and the Gaza Strip to Egypt, and people referred to Israelis and Arabs, not Israelis and "Palestinians," that is, two separate geographical entities with no territorial connection and with two different types of people. So what Nabil means is the creation of a new entity. Israel is in favor of two states for two peoples, with changes in the 1967 borders.

Afterword: Disrobe for a Terrorist Attack—Is the *Shaheeda* a Heroine?

The *shaheeds* feel themselves to be omnipotent, like a deity, like Allah. They decide when they will die and, moreover, when others will die. They make the decision who will live and who will die. While it is true that they are not responsible for the entire production, they play the part of the protagonist, the main character on the stage. Without them, the show cannot go on. Their stars shine for a brief moment and then fade and die. There is always someone behind the scenes, a director and producer who reap the fruits of their bloody acts.

The act of suicide-murder gives the terrorists, both male and female, if not the power to control life, then the power to control death, and not only their own, but that of others, the victims of suicide bombing attacks. That sensation of power and control gives the terrorists a sense of capability and self-worth while scorning the "hedonist others" of this world who "love the good life."

Suicide bombers do not have suicidal tendencies. Their entire society has openly avowed suicidal tendencies, verbally expressing their willingness to kill themselves if it means killing the hated enemy. For female suicide bombers, the desire is more practical and expressive. It releases them from their inhibitions and allows them to express their anger at their double oppression: political oppression entangled with their struggle against the State of Israel, and gender oppression, which is deeply entrenched in Palestinian Arab Islamic society. Those motives lead to a situation in which the use of women is more than operative-instrumental. The women become particularly lethal, both because of their need to prove they are able to act and sometimes out of the sensation that there is no way out of the situation they find themselves in. Once they have started out along the path to terrorism, there is no turning back.

Salem, a Palestinian intellectual, had the following opinion: "I don't understand how the *shaheeds* do it to themselves. It's something I can't understand, how someone can reach a stage where he gets it into his head to kill himself like that, knowing that he will be blown to shreds, and he does it anyway. It's something I can't comprehend. We, as Arabs, that we have someone who is willing to do that, it isn't human at all. It's not the way to change things. It won't change anything. The family comes first, my daughter and I, before everything!" That was strange to hear because he had nothing to say about the importance of the victims. He made no mention of his wife, just his only daughter. "I cannot imagine myself," he said, "going to die and leaving my daughter without someone to worry about her. It makes me shiver." Putting himself in the shoes of the *shaheed* and using a tone of voice that seemed to indicate a degree of identification with the role, he said, "I know the Israelis destroy the family's house, and the father's and the brother's. How can he allow himself to do it? Not only do I [i.e., the *shaheed*] die, but I cause suffering for those who are still living. Those who do it believe it is the only good way. There is no other explanation. It's as though he promises paradise to himself and those around him, and that satisfies him." Salem was nervous and upset as he spoke, and without a doubt he was angry at the suicide bombers for not having any consideration for their families. He went on to speak about the place of the mother: "The mother is the personality, something good in the house, the heart that waits for everyone. That's the mother. My mother influences me emotionally. My father influences me mentally, but emotionally, it's my mother." Thus the central emotional place of the mother in the life of an adolescent can be used to influence and prevent both sons and daughters from participating in terrorist attacks.

The suicide of a *shaheed* can be seen as a kind of anomie,[1] a condition arising from the disintegration of normative arrangement accepted by a society, blaming the other (in this case, the Israeli) for what happens to him and for what leads to the deterioration of his condition, which stems from normative expressive disintegration of the society. In such a situation the individual in society finds his self-expression in "murder and suicide," which have become the norm. The suicide bomber decides to destroy the "club" that perhaps did not accept him. Durkheim[2] says that anomie can be linked to altruism. One crisis may destroy a person's life, disturb the balance between him and his environment, and at the same time bring his altruistic tendency to the point where it will push him to commit suicide. That would seem to be the situation of the female suicide bomber, willing to both kill herself and take off her clothing at the same time and thus break through the bonds of oppression she bears both inside and outside the house. It is a way for her to express her rage and hatred for Jews and the West and to shatter, once and for all, the chains of oppression and humiliation binding women in Muslim society. The intimate parts of her body are exposed for everyone to see and mingle with the body parts of her victims, male and female, a horrendous circumstance for physical contact, bodies with bodies. It is a monstrous situation and completely forbidden by Muslim religious law. In interviews, clerics called it *a'wra*, "lewd." Moreover, the terrorists themselves, male and female, consider using women in terrorism as violating a taboo. For Islam, as was reflected by remarks made by men and women with whom I spoke, by carrying out the act of blowing herself up, the woman is performing an act of undress. It is an affront to her intimate honor and by extension to the honor of her family and relatives, who tried, throughout her life, "to preserve her modesty."

For the religious ideologues and the dispatchers (and it is often difficult to distinguish between the two), using women in terrorism in general and suicide bombing terrorism in particular is predatory. The objective is to achieve political, ideological, religious, or other goals. The joint objective provides the female suicide bomber with a solution for her personal and family problems. Society completely rules the woman in Palestinian Islamic society and forces her to make the "right decision"—to commit suicide or to carry out a suicide bombing attack as a way out of the dead-end dilemma she finds herself in. It is a meeting of needs and a bargain with the devil: the dispatchers send a human bomb to her death in a way that "honors" her and that for her is a solution to her problem. The dispatcher is relieved of an unfortunate physical entity covered in shame, using her suicide and broken body, exposed to all, while he chalks up points in the race to a future paradise. "The woman knows she has to die, and in the case of a killing in accordance with the tribal cultural code, it is always better to be a *shaheeda* than a *sharmouta* [whore]," said an Arab journalist who accompanied me to some meetings. "Women make news, and those who dispatch them know it."

In fact, the world media do focus on stories about the women, giving the Palestinians coverage and making the world aware of their cause. However, it undermines the established social order in Arab-Muslim society. As female suicide bombing develops, it challenges the patriarchal family structure. When a woman is involved in terrorism, she marginalizes her father, and she is crushed by the anvil of terrorism. His personality and place in the family are neutralized and not taken into consideration by the recruiters and dispatchers who detour around the disgraced father, damage his status within the family and society, and take his daughter from him. Both society and the family sense that something terrible has been done to the daughter and the family beyond the terrorist act. In the final analysis, the daughter had to come into contact with men to carry out her mission, so that in addition to testing an area in which she had no place, her involvement in terrorism and moving about outside the home to meet with the "guys" might have meant suspicious meetings and sexual exploitation, beyond the use made of her for the attack itself. The loss of a parent at an early age—especially the paterfamilias— also increases the chances of suicide in general and jihadist suicide in particular. In the case of suicide bombing terrorism, a great deal has been said about the connection between the lack of the father, the patriarch who supports the family and guards its gates and moral norms, and the social, economic, and image deterioration of the family. The Arab family is completely dependent on the father, who is its social and economic force, and is perceived as shielding it from evil.

Relations toward the father in the Palestinian family are ambivalent, also a factor of the relations between mother and father. The mother is regarded as a victim over whom the father has complete authority. The polygamist Palestinian father, despite the fact that he is the breadwinner and dictates the family's norms, is often penniless. His status is undermined by the political and economic situation, and he becomes helpless, accused of failure and weakness, and is not a role model for his sons, but in fact is quite the opposite. A great deal of anger is generated toward the father, which, because of normative reasons of religious and cultural tradition and of physical fear, is not aimed directly at him but rather seeks other channels. For the women involved in terrorism, the situation is far more difficult. At first they feel empowered by their activities, especially by the feedback from the men around them, but later they do not seem to be as strong. The expectations and disappointments of exposing themselves to those orchestrating the terrorism and the influence of the reactions of their environment to them create an emotional polarity between the feelings of empowerment and pride in their contribution on the one hand, and the disappointment and weakness, or the sensation that they are going in one direction, to a dead end, on the other. Only in jail do they receive social support from one another, but they are weakened by the increasing awareness that they are not accepted "outside" or by the daily quarrels among the inmates. Those quarrels lead them to question the whole dramatic process they have undergone, and sometimes lead to a sense of having missed out on something, as well as the deprivations of imprisonment, or even of apology for the lives they have chosen.

That was evident in the remarks made by a nineteen-year-old terrorist, a student who helped wanted men. "I helped several wanted men. I have girlfriends at the university, but I don't speak to the male students. There is no reason for me to talk to them." On the other hand, she felt herself special and powerful: "What I did is considered something masculine. There are almost no other girls who did what I did, because it is usually something men do . . . Maybe the wanted men sent someone to blow herself up or help wanted men, or to transport weapons or to conduct surveillance."

After saying that, she felt the need to justify her actions and preserve her good reputation: "I did what I did, but another girl was with me. I didn't sleep away from home." Saying that reflected the insecurity felt by a girl who had stepped outside the very clear, firm boundaries set for women by society. (It was especially important for her to preserve the image of a protected girl who did not, even if it looks wrong to you, have dealings with men or sleep away from home, the kind of girl who did not spend time alone or talk with men but who was always accompanied by another girl.) At a time when it is well known that her reservations were impossible circumstances for a female terrorist, her aiding terrorism or a terrorist attack clearly violated most of her social taboos and norms, and she sometimes went too far on the assumption that, in any case, she would never return home.

The burden of tradition, the suspicion, isolation, and the separation of the sexes in Palestinian society lead to women's sometimes being recruited via the Internet because it is the only way they can break out of the "quarantine" and have contact with men. A nineteen-year-old female terrorist told me that in her lifetime, she "would not benefit anyone, so better to become a *shaheeda*. It is easier to chat over the Internet about what is in your heart. Sometimes you know the person you chat with, and sometimes you don't, but maybe he can help you in some way?"

Not only women are exposed to the influence of the Internet. The so-called Facebook revolution, which began in Tunisia and led to the revolution that deposed Hosni Mubarak in Egypt, spread like wildfire to Yemen, Libya, Bahrain, Algeria, and Syria, and there is unrest in other countries such as Jordan. Al-Jazeera TV has encouraged the demonstrators and played a significant role with the coverage of the events, i.e., the slaughter of the citizens in Syria by the Assad regime.

Demonstrators in Iran were also encouraged by the Egyptian revolution and are again trying to liberate themselves from the regime. Every demonstrator with a mobile phone with a camera and Internet connection has sent pictures of the events to the world.

I interviewed Benjamin Netanyahu, currently Israel's prime minister, who at the time was without a formal government position. He predicted an information revolution in the Arab world, but without knowing where it would lead. He said that things were changing and that the Arabs were emerging from the restrictions of the culture and religion, saying the effect would snowball. He was half right, since the revolution has led to the radicalization of the terrorist organizations, who exploit modern communications capabilities. On the other hand, there is a trend that may be positive for the oppressed masses in the Arab countries, that of allowing the "West" to enter every home with a television set and computer, and people know what they can attain and what they are fighting for.

In terrorism as well, most of the women have no ideological background or affiliation and randomly join terrorist organizations shortly before their recruitment, so their organizational identity is not unequivocal. That is also manifested in their choice of prison wing, which is usually a function of organizational affiliation. In effect, their choice is usually determined by social factors and their preference for the wing spokeswoman.

A twenty-two-year-old female Israeli-Arab student of *da'wah* (religious preaching) at the Islamic College said: "I don't like to participate in attacks. Why should a woman do it? I don't like the idea of a woman doing that. I don't want anyone to do it, but if they do, let it be the men. A woman is more delicate, more for staying at home. I don't think if she carried out an attack society will respect her. Allah gave her life. She is supposed to live it and not go out on terrorist attacks and things like that . . . I would ask a woman who carried out an attack why she did it, what her problem was. She was with a man who told her to do it. I would tell her not to do it."

She had the following to say about the generation gap and the Internet: "Fathers don't like their daughters to surf the Internet. So now they don't allow computers in their daughters' rooms, only in the living room, where everyone can see the sites they visit. Every father whose daughter surfs the Net feels uncomfortable, but they tell him she is a student and has to have an Internet connection." The father feels helpless because he cannot supervise his daughter. He understands nothing about computers, so not only does he restrict her outside the house, he tries to cut her communications lines inside as well. Nevertheless, between the computer, satellite television, and a mobile phone, his daughter is exposed to the outside world regardless of what her father wants, and the outside world is daring, limitless, and uninhibited. Daughters often chat and e-mail men without parental supervision, and sometimes the chats are erotic.

The stronger and more involved in society a family it is, the harder it will be for recruiters to enlist one of its daughters as a suicide bomber or integrate one into some other sort of terrorist activity. The strength of the family makes the recruiters wary of incurring their wrath. In one instance, they made a female terrorist sign a statement to the effect that she had left her house for training and volunteered for *istishhad* of her own free will, so that her family would not complain that they had recruited her and reduced her to having dealings with men, something that can lead to a blood feud. There were also cases in which girls were photographed with mobile phone cameras while associating with men to join a terrorist attack against Israel, but afterward became afraid the pictures would be made public and harm the family honor. Even pictures of women talking to men are sufficient grounds for blackmail against the young women themselves, or against their brothers, who then have to participate in attacks to preserve their sisters' reputations. Thus young women who want excitement or the company of men find themselves trapped.

A low social status also channels women into terrorism. A Palestinian man looks for a wife who is inferior to himself, even formally speaking. Many women who participated in terrorist attacks were motivated by the feeling that in any case, their lives were worthless, living as they do at the bottom of the social and family scale. When they finally do something exceptional, even if only for one brief moment, they become special and significant, at least in their own eyes.

In the world of terrorism, women support each other by providing places to sleep in women's dormitories at universities and by accompanying each other to terrorist attacks. Every time a woman fastened an explosive belt on the body of a female suicide bomber, she did it saying that she would be willing to carry out the attack herself. Willing, yes, but never actually doing it. A video from Turkey that showed a female suicide bomber strapping an explosive belt on herself was used as propaganda to recruit men. A statement made by another female suicide bomber from Turkey (PKK), whom I interviewed, indicated that when she refused to carry out a suicide bombing attack, her organization threatened her, telling her that she would die either as a heroine or as a frightened traitor.

Despite the on-camera praise, once the photographers have gone, a great deal of anger is directed at such women who trespassed into areas that do not belong to them. They are considered to have damaged the men's masculinity and to have personally disgraced them. There will always be uncomfortable questions about a female terrorist, even if they are not verbalized: What terrible thing did she do? What did she feel she had to atone for by carrying out an act which in fact was not required of her? Women and men are viewed differently. The man is considered "more masculine" after an attack, and as an object of veneration, a role model, but the woman is not considered "more feminine," but rather, if anything, less feminine. Such women will always be suspect. Was she raped? Did she commit adultery? Perhaps, instead of dying for the "good of the nation," would she have been killed to preserve the family honor? In addition, the presence of women involved in terrorism encourages the men to prove their masculinity, which is damaged when women take over men's "duties."

Often, the solution for such a woman, after she has been released from jail, is to marry another prisoner with whom a romantic liaison was formed in jail via notes and messages. Romance plays a great part in integrating women into terrorism. There are women who choose to carry out attacks because they love terrorists. They want to please and be physically close to them. Since physical proximity is impossible, being part of a terrorist group brings a kind of legitimacy to their spending time with the men they love, and the terrorists carry out attacks and use the women as they please.

In reality, using a woman as a living bomb is effective. She becomes socially unacceptable as having entered a world that does not belong to her and in which she has dealings with men. A Palestinian journalist I spoke to said that "men fantasize about why women do it, and there is a conspiracy of silence—terrorism, like smoking, is the job of a man."

As opposed to a father or brother in jail, who makes the family more respected, no one is proud when his sister goes to jail. What is absurd is that is exactly what happens when women are involved in terrorism. Women received contradictory messages: on one hand, a woman has to participate in the "struggle," and on the other, if she does participate, she is regarded as "damaged goods."

Another group exploited by terrorists is children, snatched from the schoolyard into the service of terrorism, cynically and cruelly abused by recruiters. They are taught at a young age to ape wanted terrorists, their local heroes. They are manipulated, given real guns to play with, and accompany and openly admire their heroes in the street. The wanted terrorists make them feel they are "men," and they have to play the role they are given.

Judges in the Israeli legal system have to decide about the emotional maturity of an underage terrorist, while Sheikh Yassin related primarily to the aspect of physical maturity as allowing or forbidding an underage individual to participate in a terrorist attack. Some of the adolescents are convinced to participate because the dispatchers assure them that as minors they are immune from legal prosecution.

The need to imitate a cousin or other relative who blew himself up and became a *shaheed* is mixed with the desire to avenge his death, so the theme of suicide bombing runs through families and is learned from observation and the constant presence of role models.

There was a period in the territories when the terrorist organizations did not reveal the names of the suicide bombers, to keep Israel from sending IDF bulldozers to destroy their houses as prevention and punishment. That changed, however, and then immediately after every attack the Palestinians broadcast the *shaheed*'s videotaped, preprepared "living testament." The video contributes to the intensity of the act and glorifies the suicide bomber himself. It not only commemorates the terrorist but is an effective tool in recruiting others. The motive is aggressive and even overcomes the need to protect the *shaheed*'s family from having its house destroyed, a sanction sometimes imposed on the families of suicide bombers. The only advantage the family receives from its son's death is that with his name on the *shaheed* roster, it will receive the promised money and recognition. In the final analysis, the video is not purely for purposes of *istishhad*, or for the sake of Allah or assuring a place in paradise for the *shaheed*'s family, but it is "self-sacrifice" with a high price tag, one agreed on beforehand in the coin of the realm in this world, not the next.

Young Palestinians are constantly exposed to violence and its aftermath, and they attend rallies and funerals. The place of young Palestinians in society and the family and the interaction between them and their environment also influence their enlistment in terrorist attacks. Within the terrorist group they feel liberated from the usual constraints, partake of a collective identity, and feel a sense of importance and belonging, of emotional fulfillment. *Shaheeds* wait impatiently for their first sexual experience, which will be with the virgins in paradise. Separating enlisted potential terrorists, both male and female, from their families is intended to give them a new identity and alternative family and a feeling of genuine belonging they might not have had previously.

The collective is more important in Arab society than the individual ego, and the general approach is that "*We* are important, *I* am not, and I am not in control of anything." Women and children occupy the lowest rung of the social ladder. When young Palestinian males are killed, there are many more to take their place. To prevent suicide bombing attacks, it is important to identify the motivational source and neutralize it.

Part of the strategy for preventing suicide attacks is to try and neutralize the secondary profits. Thus the media might report only that an attack had been carried out without specifying that it was a suicide bombing and without reporting the bomber's name, which would reduce their impact and provide fewer role models. It would also reduce the personal motivation of potential suicide bombers. Part of the war on terrorism is the media war. There are opposing vectors: the media want stories with headlines, which sometimes encourages terrorism. With the extensive media coverage of world events, can reporting be toned down and less detailed? In addition, the true story behind the suicide bomber's attack should be told, because sometimes telling the true story can delegitimize the terrorist act.

In addition to the sense of control and power, a suicide bombing attack gives the terrorist the status of being able to scorn the hedonists, those who like the "good life" of this world. The suicide bomber's approach, whether male or female, is "I will be considered an altruist in this world and a hedonist in the next." In Palestinian society, with its taboos and repressions, the woman's need for sensual love is delegitimized. The need is channeled into fantasies about paradise. Through that looking glass, every woman who carries out a suicide bombing attack will receive love, be redeemed, and be released from the oppression, humiliation, and shame of this world. Looked at from that angle, the suicide bombing attack seems worthwhile. The rewards of the Muslim paradise are free to both *shaheeds* and *shaheedas*, nothing like the coarse pleasures of this world and incapable of being described in earthly terms, which might offend some people. Everything impossible in this world is possible in the next. A woman's main reward is eternal virginity, critical in this world. Women might be persuaded to act differently if they could be convinced that by their killing people, Allah will send them to hell, not paradise. One would-be female suicide bomber said, "I wouldn't do it if I knew I would go to hell, and even after I did everything would be the same."

There are often contradictions between the dictates of the terrorist organizations and those of religion, especially regarding the dilemma over the place of women in the struggle, including mothers. There are the *fatwas* against suicide for personal reasons (issued, for example, by Sheikh Tantawi in 1996 and Sheikh Qardawi in 2003) and the question over whether carrying out a suicide bombing attack is, strictly speaking, suicide if it is part of a jihad for the sake of Allah. The general opinion is that a person who commits suicide for personal reasons does not fulfill his duty to society and thus defies Allah. However, *istishhad*, self-sacrifice for the sake of Allah, along with killing infidels, is not considered suicide.

Religion usually opposes suicide and considers it at best a waste of human life and at worst a mortal sin, but the artistic abilities of the radical Islamic sheikhs have allowed them to interpret it as they choose. Radical Islamic interpretations have prompted mass-murder suicide bombing attacks inspired by hatred. Both male and female suicide bombers quote specific passages from the Qur'an as moral justification for such attacks.

That is not the case, however, for the *shaheeda*. Her social duties and expectations are narrow and well defined. Her first duty is to marry and bear children. A woman who carries out a suicide bombing attack is perceived as having sinned, especially in a society in which the individual is unimportant as compared with the collective. The woman who blows herself up in a suicide bombing attack will never realize Arafat's dream of the Palestinian womb as the ticking demographic bomb that will annihilate the Jews in Palestine. In Iraq as well, cynical use is made of women's bodies. During the Iraq-Iran war women were urged to have more children for revenge against Khomeini and were told that every child they bore was a bullet in the chest of the common enemy.[3]

One Arab psychologist told me that Arabs, particularly Arab women, suffered from frustration, depression, a sensation of marginality, and helplessness. Female terrorists differ from them in that females are also obsessed with ideology, nationalism, and fundamentalist religion, which justify their participation in terrorism, and they feel Allah is with them. So they say, "I will be a *shaheeda* and die for the sake of Allah." However, often it is not sincere ideology but rather a rationalization for their behavior and the use of religion for political objectives. Often, belonging to or identifying with a group grants status. Sometimes a suicide bombing attack is a way to solve a personal problem, such as family honor, "immoral" conduct, or barrenness. Those women want the recognition and control lacking in their lives, and sometimes, it is a way of removing a stigma that is very strong in Arab society and would ordinarily destroy them.

My experience has shown that in many instances, suicide bombing terrorism is a family behavior pattern, a tradition passed down from one generation to the next. At first there is blind obedience to a source of authority (terrorists in the area, members of terrorist organizations), and then a process of imitation and identification begins. Sometimes one family will have young men, older men (brothers, cousins), and women all involved in terrorist attacks. Does the memory of the suicide bombers, their relatives, haunt them? It is not a question of a history or depression or something genetic, it is following the path of the "heroes." When it comes to women, it is not a question of individual stigma, but an obsessive thought process and a desire to be upgraded, to be worthy, to be considered worthy, and to change one's life beyond simply rising above personal and family problems, and even to express themselves and their uniqueness in an impressive way. The need to imitate nurtures society and creates a society predisposed to anomic suicide.

In certain societies where suicide bombing terrorism is common, there are reasons to assume that simply being born into the society will endanger the life of the newborn baby by virtue of exposure to dangerous propaganda and creating a proneness toward suicide through suicide bombing. It is like a disease caught in a plague spread by glorifying the *shaheeds* and *shaheedas*. It creates the emotional preparedness to obsessively tread the path of *istishhad* (self-sacrifice for the sake of Allah) with continuing thoughts of controlling life. It might be termed "shahadamania," the obsession with *istishhad*. "Mania is a condition manifested by psycho-motoric excitement and euphoria accompanied by uncontrollable babbling, marked by periods of great excitement and delusions,"[4] a situation often characterizing suicide bombers, as well as the excessive sexual appetite resulting from fantasizing about the seventy-two virgins waiting for the *shaheed* in paradise. In many instances the potential *shaheed* becomes more quiet and introverted the closer he comes to blowing himself up. Sometimes he recites Qur'an verses like a mantra. The promise of paradise conditions him psychologically, especially if he is an adolescent. The potential suicide bomber acts impulsively and moves automatically, reducing himself to the minimum, like a horse with blinders that restrict its field of vision and force it to focus on the road ahead. However, when circumstances change or a preventive action intervenes and interrupts his robotic behavior, the suicide bomber can no longer carry out the attack. For example, on the way to the site of the attack, the suicide bomber may chance to see a baby who reminds him of someone in his own family. At that point, he may then see his victims as human beings and change his mind about the attack.

Istishhad can be regarded as an obsessive way of thinking (*duda*, the worm that turns in his head). Suicide bombers who failed to carry out their attacks told me about the sensation that makes it possible for them to turn to a different reality (paradise). That obsessive behavior pursues the potential *shaheed* and becomes his whole world, driving away forbidden, embarrassing thoughts and behavior (*a'ib*), especially those connected with sex. After the explosion, when obsessive thoughts have become a practical issue, in the next world, that is, paradise, those embarrassing things will be permitted. It is a reiteration of what both the men and the women say, "What is forbidden in this world is permitted in paradise." The saying hints at a world of desires hidden in the sensual world of those young people and sometimes exposed to "the experiences of this world and their frivolities," such as women, wine, and free love as are found in Western cultures. The formulators of the Islamic moral code define those pleasures as "whoredom," forbidden in this world. Young people are forced to repress their forbidden desires and to make do with the promise that they will be completely fulfilled in the next world, in paradise with its flowing rivers of alcohol and seventy-two virgins who will satisfy their hidden desires forever. That future pleasurable meeting promises roles for women as well and gives "discounts" to their family members, who can also enter the *shaheed* club because they are related. By saying that what is forbidden in this world is permitted in the next, terrorist leaders enlist the fantasies of paradise to motivate a great number of shahadamanic suicide bombers. However, it still cannot be said that suicide bombers are mentally ill or cannot differentiate between right and wrong.

One of the female terrorists interviewed, who was twenty-six at the time of her trial, said that her father belonged to a family of refugees and that she herself was the youngest of eight siblings. Her father died of a heart attack two years before her arrest, which she blamed on the IDF and the stress of the situation. She was a heavy smoker but said she had not dared to smoke in her father's presence. When she decided to carry out a suicide bomb attack, she appealed to a woman friend who knew a terrorist operative and asked to meet him. The attack was planned down to the last detail, but she changed her mind at the last minute.

"There was someone who wanted to marry me and you killed him . . . I am accused of *istishhad* but I never wanted to kill myself, I don't know why people are saying that . . . Paradise is for Muslims and hell is for the Jews. We have Allah and we believe in him. There are a lot of good things about our religion. The most important thing is that after you die you see Allah and if he wills it, you see Muhammad as well. The men, the *shaheeds*, get seventy [*sic*] virgins."

This woman is an example of the destructive influence of the lack of a father in the patriarchal Palestinian society, which, as in many other cases, led to terrorism. In most cases parents act as restraining influences, and their awareness and supervision prevent the involvement of their children in terrorist activities. Most parents do not know that their children are going to blow themselves up and say that had they known, they would have prevented them. There were cases in Israel of parents who appealed to the Israeli security agency, the Shin Bet. Similarly, the London police were appealed to in 2005, before the series of attacks on the London Underground. The same thing happened with the attempted attack of the 2009 Christmas bomber on the plane from Amsterdam to Detroit: the father of the Nigerian terrorist, Farouk Mutlab, appealed several times to security personnel at the American Embassy in Nigeria, warning them that his son was going to do something. Mutlab was born into a polygamist family and felt isolated and that he had no one to talk to. Security personnel around the world have to learn to listen to parents who see changes in their children's behavior.

However, after an attack many parents express pride in what their children have done. That is all that is left to them, despite whatever plans they might have had for their offspring. The joy is greater when it was a "corrupt" daughter (and in any case, she was considered corrupt the instant she left the house without an escort and met with the guys), because the attack helped the family erase the shame. There were many cases where parents were furious with the dispatchers for having taken their children away, right out from under their noses, and cynically sent them to their deaths. A child who participated in a suicide bombing attack is a kind of "stupid bomb," because his death is even less significant and heroic than a woman's. I thought sorrowfully about the child who dreams of becoming a *shaheed* when he grows up, about the fact that he often does not wait until he grows up and has a better sense of judgment. He makes a wretched, childish decision and is supported in it by a cynical adult. The child does not have to grow up to become a *shaheed*; today he can blow himself up as a child.

Women do not participate in terrorism following a career in terrorism or criminal activities whose roots lie in a past full of such activity. They usually carry out just one attack, either a suicide bombing attack or some other which ends in imprisonment, such as a stabbing, or smuggling weapons, or even transmitting notes between prisoners hidden in the more intimate regions of their bodies. They sometimes engage in surveillance, money laundering, escorting suicide bombers to the site of an attack, and so on. There are women who even chose the site for an attack and strapped an explosive belt onto the body of a male suicide bomber. Generally speaking, the women are not recidivist, while the men who are involved in suicide bombing attacks or orchestrating other forms of terrorist attacks—and who survive—often are. They usually begin by throwing stones and Molotov cocktails and gradually turn to severe terrorist activities. That is especially true of those who become dispatchers. They are often in and out of jail but will end up serving many life sentences.

In their own eyes, and more so in the eyes of the society from which they come, women cannot be both "good" and terrorists at the same time, because a woman who deals with terrorism is already perceived as being in the company of men. She is considered unsupervised by the men in the family and as having violated the codes of behavior and modesty expected by the traditional Muslim society. I have no feminist cover with which to hide the small, frightened, anxious woman looking through the bars of her cell at a future wreathed in uncertainty, wondering when, if ever, she will be released and be able to realize herself by marrying and having children. That often returned to my thoughts when I observed the trials of women. I watched how they stretched their thin hands through the bars to have their handcuffs taken off when they were returned to their cells after the trial was over. Any woman who gets involved in terrorism and goes to jail knows that as far as the local market is concerned, she is damaged goods. Abu Tir, deputy head of the de facto Hamas administration, said, "Who needs a woman who gets out of jail and thinks she commands the house?"[5] His question revealed that in effect, as far as he was concerned, even if a woman was in jail, she was still just a woman.

The belief of some women that their status will be upgraded or that their pasts will be overlooked because of involvement in terrorism is a figment of their imaginations. The sense of power and freedom they had when they were recruited and the artificial "respect" they thought they had gained evaporated along with the feeling that they were unique. Their conceptions of themselves are mistaken, and such conceptions shatter in the harsh light of the society they live in, where their position is clearly defined as inferior and every step taken outside the accepted boundaries is liable to cost a woman her life. Muslim women are still not carried away by the waves of *mujahedeen* to Afghanistan, they do not go to fight in Afghanistan, and only a few have reached Iraq. One of those few was a European woman who converted to Islam. Even if they do participate in the waves of terrorism, they still adhere to their environments. Just as they were not mobile in their previous lives, they are not mobile as terrorists. (The Tamil Tiger from Sri Lanka who killed Rajib Gandhi was an exception.) Thus, in general women are involved in local terrorism and do not belong to terrorist organizations, which makes it even more difficult to track them.

A different kind of romanticism is the marriage of European women to radical Muslim men. The new husbands might be able to recruit their wives for terrorist activities. A situation may also arise in which a newly converted Muslim woman may want to prove her faithfulness to her husband and her new religion. In my assessment, the use of European women who convert to Islam will increase and will change the classic profile of the conventional female suicide bomber, territorially fixed and with limited mobility. The new model will be based on mobility seen as natural by them and their environments. The ability to move from one place to the other is better than the fixed situation of the female Muslim terrorist.

The "before" picture of the American "Jihad Jane," Muslim convert Coleen LaRose, is of a smiling, green-eyed, blond young woman, while the "after" shows her covered head to toe in a traditional black *burqa*.[6] This indicates that the more female suicide bombers there are, and the more women involved in terrorism, the more inertia and imitation will draw increasing numbers of women to the arena. A similar situation may arise when more European women who convert to Islam are channeled into terrorism and become role models for other Europeans who convert to Islam in an age when the search for significance and the value of life involves the choice of a new religion.

There is a certain polarity toward women in Arab society in that they are guarded and supervised at home, but in a suicide bombing attack they are left exposed for all to see, and that is an issue Arab society has yet to settle. Despite the moral difficulty, fundamentalist organizations such as the Palestinian Islamic Jihad have threatened to use women as "the smartest bomb." On May 20, 2007, the organization claimed that if Israel entered the Gaza Strip in response to the Qassam rocket fire targeting the southern city of Sderot, it would flood the country with women suicide bombers. Israel restrained itself until Operation Cast Lead, which began at the end of 2008. Despite the PIJ's threats, suicide bombers did not succeed in infiltrating Israel, thanks to the security fence.

Here is how an Israeli-Arab policewoman described Muslim women: "Beneath the surface, under her robe, a lot is going on. The Arab woman is like a cat trapped in a box . . . A security prisoner is a patriot. If she is pretty and educated, a match will be found for her in jail, between the men's and women's prisons. If not, maybe they will find a match for her outside . . . A security prisoner is perceived as an object of admiration, while a common criminal is perceived as a lowlife. There are people who are afraid of female terrorists and say, 'She's a man . . .' In our society a man looks for a woman who will be obedient and stroke him the way you stroke a cat, who will be a mother to his children, and he says to himself, 'Who needs such a headache? What about the future of the children?' Arab society is false and falling apart, and people try to imitate the bad things about Jewish society, not the good things. Arab society is weak, its education is weak, its religion is weak. It's falling apart. Superficially it is a religious, conservative community with robes and head coverings, but underneath there is nothing."

A Jerusalemite had this to say: "We never saw a security prisoner who was killed because of family honor. The opposite is true—they got married." Superficially, at least, such an approach is more sophisticated and respectful of security prisoners. The mechanism that channels women into carrying out security crimes sometimes solves family or other problems, which obviates the need to kill her. Sheikh Yassin defined the mechanism as "exceptional." For that reason, in many cases the prospective groom is a security prisoner and the initial relations are held indirectly through an intermediary while both sides are still in jail. It makes the time pass more easily.

Another told me that "all such women are called 'jail graduates,' and when the families of prospective grooms come to ask for her hand or examine her pedigree, that's what her title will be. Even if she was jailed for a nationalistic [*sic*] act, she still carries the stigma of a woman who was in jail."

Reports would seem to indicate that the general feeling in the Arab world is that girls and women are in danger because of modernization, including exposure to satellite television, the Internet, and cellular phones, and that Muslim society is helpless and has no real way of coping with the situation. Many older-generation Arabs feel they are losing their control over women, which makes them anxious.

According to Durkheim,[7] when people learn from early childhood that their lives are not important and to detest people who think they are valuable, they will inevitably reach a state in which they are willing to forfeit their lives on the slightest pretext. It is easy to sacrifice something that has no value. Like suicide committed deliberately, those customs are connected to the deepest moral values of primitive societies. Because such societies can exist only if the individual has no personal worth, it was necessary to train that person to be ready always to forfeit his life, and that is the source of the many cases of suicide that seem superficially to be spontaneous.

The act of a female suicide bomber is not spontaneous, even though it might seem to be. It is the sacrificing of human life, according to religious interpretation, on the altar of ideology and a twisted morality. Such a woman is finally taking charge of her own life, one might think, doing something active, even though it is a terrorist act. But that is not really the case, because she is acting impulsively in a way that is expected of her after she crosses societal boundaries. The victims are not the pick of the crop, but rather society's weak, damaged, and rejected.

Suicide bombing terrorism is becoming refined, and it is contagious. Women and children are culled as the modern fundamentalist Moloch's weakest victims. The day is not far off when there will be explosive tampons instead of explosive belts, and if that seems extreme today, it should be noted that no X-ray would ever reveal one. The Western world should prepare for what is coming.

NOTES

1. Emile Durkheim, *Suicide* (Hebrew) (Tel Aviv: Nimrod, 2002).
2. Durkheim, *Suicide* (Hebrew), 158.
3. O. Bengio, *Women in the Middle East: Between Tradition and Change* (Tel Aviv: Dayan Center for Middle Eastern and African Studies, Tel Aviv University, 2004).

4. Norbert Sillamy, *Dictionnaire de la Psycologie* (Hebrew), ed. Dorit Landes (Tel Aviv: Yedioth Ahronot Press, 1997).

5. Personal communication with the author, 2007.

6. Tom Leonard, "Blond-Haired 'Jihad Jane' Plotted Terror Attacks," *Telegraph*, March 10, 2010, http://www.telegraph.co.uk/news/worldnews/northamerica/usa/7415724/Blond-haired-Jihad-Jane-plotted-terror-attacks.html.

7. Durkheim, *Suicide* (Hebrew), 122.

Acknowledgments

My thanks to the members of the Israeli security establishment, especially the staff of the Prison Service, for allowing me to conduct my research inside the jails. A special thanks as well for the tireless work they do to preserve the safety and security of the civilians of the State of Israel.

Thanks to the publishers of Yediot Sefarim for bringing out the Hebrew version of the book, especially Dov Eichenwald, Kuti Teper, and Guy Raveh.

I am grateful to Susan McEachern, Janice Braunstein, and Karie Simpson of Rowman & Littlefield for their enthusiastic and efficient support in publishing my book. It has been a pleasure working with them.

Thanks to the IDC Herzliya, mainly the Institute for Counter-Terrorism (ICT), my academic home.

Thanks to Elizabeth Yuval for her excellent translation.

Thanks to Nina Rosenwald, a genuine Zionist and caring individual, for her friendship and support.

Thanks to Michelle, Sanford, and Howard Rosenbloom of the Ben & Esther Rosenbloom Foundation for their support, encouragement, and friendship.

Thanks to family friend Khaled Abu Toameh, *Jerusalem Post* correspondent, for his comments and criticisms.

Thanks to Professor Edna Erez, University of Illinois at Chicago, with whom I researched women in terrorism and crime, for her important insights.

Thanks to the Deborah Harris Agency for their continuing support of my professional efforts.

Thanks to Kim Cooper for her friendship and good advice.

Thanks to Abraham Wagner for his friendship and support.

Thanks to Professor Shlomo Giora Shoham, psychologist Baruch Tsadik, Professor Shmuel Moreh, Professor Moshe Addad, and Professor Yuval Wolf, whose innovative scientific work paved the way for me and many others.

Thanks to my friends and colleagues for their friendship and inspiration during my year as visiting professor at George Washington University: Franklin and Jackie Paulson, Lori and Jerome Marcus, Mazal Menasche, Vicky and Steve Wexler, Professor Bernard Reich, Professor Forrest Maltzman, Professor Walter Reich, Dr. David Ettinger, Shmuel Ben-Gad, Professor Susan Wiley, Zacharia Cotler, Professor Salman Elbedour, Dr. Mitchel Bard, and Jonathan Lord.

Thanks to Dr. Jerrold Post for his steadfast friendship and enormous knowledge.

Thanks to Daniel Pipes, scholar and president of the Middle East Forum, for his comments and for contributing the introduction.

Special thanks to Steve Joel Trachtenberg, former president of George Washington University for his openness and wisdom, and for guiding me in the right direction.

Last but not least, thanks to my father-in-law, the late Nahman Berko, and my mother-in-law, Nehama Berko, may she be blessed with long years, both Holocaust survivors, who inspired our entire family. Their great spirit, despite the loss of their families in Auschwitz, enabled them to build their home in Israel, to participate in founding a village [*moshav*] and building the country. They are a model for us all.

Thanks to my brothers and sisters, especially Hagit, and to my children, Tzlil, Yechiam, and Keshet.

An enormous thanks to Reuven, my beloved husband and partner, who supports and encourages me and helped me in editing the book. He is a Middle Eastern scholar with amazing knowledge and professional experience.

Glossary

Abdullah Azzam	Al-Qaeda ideologue.
a'ib	Shame.
"Allahu akbar"	"Allah is most great." Also used as the last words of a suicide bomber before blowing up.
amaliyyat istishhadia	Suicide bombing attacks.
a'rd	A woman's honor, which can never be extended or regained.
a'wra	The shame of a woman's genitalia.
baklawa	A type of Eastern pastry.
banat	Girls (plural of *bint*).
dardali	Weak, insignificant.
da'wah	Religious preaching.
"Eid sa'eed"	"Happy holiday."
fallaha	A female farm worker.
fallahin	Farm workers.
Fatah	A Palestinian terrorist organization.
Fatah Tanzim	Fatah's military terrorist wing.
fatwa	Islamic religious edict.
fitna	Sibling/family rivalry.
ful	Broad beans.

Green Line	The demarcation lines set out in the 1949 Armistice Agreements between Israel and its neighbors.
hadith	The oral tradition regarding the deeds of Muhammad.
halawat	Cookies distributed on festive occasions.
Hamas	A radical Islamic Palestinian terrorist organization currently ruling the Gaza Strip; an offshoot of the Muslim Brotherhood.
hamoula	Extended family.
Hanafi	One of the schools of Islam; relatively moderate.
haram	Forbidden; it's a pity.
Hezbollah	A Shi'ite terrorist organization funded and armed by Iran and entrenched in southern Lebanon.
hijab	The head scarf worn by Muslim women.
hudna	Temporary cease-fire of unspecified duration.
huriyat	The virgins of the Muslim paradise (plural of *huriya*).
imama	Female preacher.
intifada	Popular uprising.
istishhad	Self-sacrifice.
jahil	Ignorant.
jahilia	The period of ignorance before Islam.
jawaz muta'a	A "pleasure marriage," a short-term marriage acceptable in some Arab countries.
Jenin	A city in the West Bank.
jihad	Holy war.
jilbab	A loose traditional Arab dress.
khalas!	Enough!
kharta	Bullshit.
Khomeini	Leader of the Islamic Revolution in Iran, 1977.
kibbutz	A collective Israeli village.
labaneh	Homemade sour cheese.
Lod	A mixed Jewish-Arab city in central Israel.
mabsout	Happy (masculine singular).

majnuna	Deranged, crazy.
maqluba	A chicken, rice, and eggplant casserole.
masbaha	Worry beads.
Masih ad-Dajjal	The false Messiah.
maslakha	Personal advantage.
metalaka	Divorcée.
Muqata'a	The Palestinian Authority administration complex in Ramallah.
muqawamah	Struggle.
Nablus	A city in the West Bank, known during the second *intifada* as the suicide bombers' capital.
nargila	Hookah.
nazal amaliyyah	Leaving for a terrorist action.
Qalqilya	A city in the West Bank.
Qassam rockets	Homemade Hamas rockets.
Ramadan	A holy Muslim month of fasting.
Ramallah	A city in the West Bank where the Palestinian Authority (PA) is headquartered.
rasul	The prophet Muhammad.
saif	Sword (of the prophet Muhammad).
"Sauda tuchkum ala'alam?"	"A black woman running the world?"
shabab	A group of friends, usually young and exclusively male.
shahada	The Islamic creed: "There is no God but Allah and Muhammad is his prophet."
shaheed	A martyr for the sake of Allah (male).
shaheeda	A martyr for the sake of Allah (female).
sharaf	A man's honor, which can grow throughout his life.
Shari'a	Islamic religious law.
sharmouta	Whore.
shekel	The Israeli currency.
Shi'a	A school of Islam.
shuhada'a	Martyrs for the sake of Allah.

siwak	A special toothbrush made of wood, similar to that used by the prophet Muhammad.
Sunnah	A school of Islam.
tabun	A convex metal plate placed over a source of heat.
tahadiya	Lull in the fighting.
tyamanu	Everything should be done from the right (as opposed to left) side or with the right hand.
umi	My mother.
Usra	A Muslim Brotherhood cell (singular of *usar*).
waqf	The land of the Muslim endowment.
watan	Homeland.
Ya ebni	"My son."
za'im	A leader.

Selected Bibliography

Ali, Farhana. (2006). "Rocking the Cradle to Rocking the World: The Role of Muslim Female Fighters." *Journal of International Women's Studies* 8(1):21–35.

Anderson, Margaret. (2005). "Thinking about Women." *Gender & Society* 19(4):437–55.

Barrett, Frank. (1996). "The Organizational Construction of Hegemonic Masculinity: The Case of the US Navy." *Gender, Work and Organization* 3(3):129–42.

Bengio, O. (2004). *Women in the Middle East: Between Tradition and Change*. Tel Aviv: Dayan Center for Middle Eastern and African Studies, Tel Aviv University.

Berko, Anat. (2002). *The Moral Infrastructure of Chief Perpetrators of Suicidal Terrorism: Cognitive and Functionalist Perspectives*. Unpublished dissertation (Hebrew), Bar Ilan University.

———. (2007). *The Path to Paradise: The Inner World of Suicide Bombers and Their Dispatchers*. Translated by Elizabeth Yuval. Westport, CT: Praeger.

Berko, Anat, and Edna Erez. (2007). "Gender, Palestinian Women, and Terrorism: Women's Liberation or Oppression?" *Studies in Conflict & Terrorism* 30(6):493–519.

———. (2008). "Martyrs or Murderers? Victimizers or Victims? The Voices of Would-Be Palestinian Female Suicide Bombers." In Cindy Ness (ed.), *In the Name of the Cause: Female Militancy and Terrorism in Context*. New York: Taylor and Francis.

Berko, Anat, Edna Erez, and Julie Globokar. (2010). "Gender, Crime and Terrorism: The Case of Arab/Palestinian Women in Israel." *British Journal of Criminology* 50(4):670–89.

Berko, A., Y. Wolf, and M. Addad. (2005). "The Moral Infrastructure of Chief Perpetrators of Suicidal Terrorism: An Analysis in Terms of Moral Judgment." *Israel Studies in Criminology* 9:10–47.

Berko, Reuven. (2011). *The Islamic Operational Code from Teaching of Sheikh Muneer Algadban as a Guide for Islamic Fundamental Movements*. Unpublished dissertation (Hebrew), University of Haifa.

Beyler, Clara. (2004). *Messengers of Death: Female Suicide Bombers.* New York: McGraw-Hill.

Bloom, Mia. (2005). "Mother. Daughter. Sister. Bomber." *Bulletin of the Atomic Scientists* 61(6):54–62.

———. (2007). "Female Suicide Bombers: A Global Trend." *Daedalus* 136(1):94–103.

———. (2011). *Bombshell: The Many Faces of Women Terrorists.* Toronto: Penguin Canada.

Brunner, Claudia. (2005). "Female Suicide Bombers–Male Suicide Bombing? Looking for Gender in Reporting the Suicide Bombing of the Israeli-Palestinian Conflict." *Global Society* 19(1):29–48.

Cook, David. (2005). "Women Fighting in *Jihad?*" *Studies in Conflict and Terrorism* 28(5):375–84.

Crenshaw, Martha. (1995). *Terrorism in Context.* University Park: Pennsylvania State University Press.

Cunningham, Karla. (2003). "Cross-Regional Trends in Female Terrorism." *Studies in Conflict and Terrorism* 26(3):171–95.

———. (2007). "Countering Female Terrorism." *Studies in Conflict and Terrorism* 30(2):113–29.

Davis, Jessica. (2007). "Women and Terrorism in Radical Islam: Planners, Perpetrators, Patrons?" Centre for Foreign Policy Studies, graduate symposium, Dalhousie University, Nova Scotia. http://centreforforeignpolicystudies.dal.ca/pdf/gradsymp06/Davis.pdf.

De Cataldo Neuberger, Luisella, and Tiziana Valentini. (1992). *Women and Terrorism.* Translated by Leo Michael Hughes. New York: St. Martin's.

Dershowitz, Alan. (2002). *Why Terrorism Works: Understanding the Threat, Responding to the Challenge.* New Haven, CT: Yale University Press.

Deutsch, Francine. (2007). "Undoing Gender." *Gender & Society* 21(1):106–27.

Durkheim, Emile. (1997). *Suicide: A Study in Sociology.* New York: Free Press. Originally published 1897.

Durkheim, Emile. (2002). *Suicide* (Hebrew). Tel Aviv: Nimrod.

Eager, Paige W. (2008). *From Freedom Fighters to Terrorists: Women and Political Violence.* Aldershot, UK: Ashgate.

Erez, Edna, and Anat Berko. (2010). "Pathways of Arab/Palestinian Women in Israel to Crime and Imprisonment: An Intersectional Approach." *Feminist Criminology* 5(2):156–95.

Al Ghadban, Muneir Muhammad. (1983). *Al Manhaj-ul-Harki Le Seerat-un-Nabawiyyah* (Arabic). Maktabat al-Manar, Jordan: Zarqa.

Galvin, Deborah M. (1983). "The Female Terrorist: A Socio-Psychological Perspective." *Behavioral Sciences and the Law* 1(2):19–32.

Ganor, B. (2005). *The Counter-Terrorism Puzzle: A Guide for Decision-Makers.* New Brunswick, NJ: Transaction.

Gerda Lindner, Evelyn. (2001). "Women and Terrorism: The Lessons of Humiliation." *New Routes: A Journal for Peace Research and Action on Women and Peace* 6(3):10–12.

Gunaratna, R. (2002). *Inside Al Qaeda: Global Network of Terror.* New York: Columbia University Press.

Harel, Amos, and Avi Issacharoff. (2004). *The Seventh War* (Hebrew). Tel Aviv: Yedioth Ahronoth Publishing.

Hasso, Frances. (2005). "Discursive and Political Deployments by/of the 2002 Palestinian Women Suicide Bombers/Martyrs." *Feminist Review* 81(1):25–51.

Heifetz-Yahav, Deborah. (2004). "Non-mediated Peacekeeping as a Cultural Performance of Masculinity." In David Last (ed.), *Social and Culture Change: Challenge and Change for the Military.* Montreal: McGill-Queen's University Press.

Hoffman, B. (1998). *Inside Terrorism.* London: Victor Gollancz.

Holt, Maria. (2003). "Palestinian Women, Violence and the Peace Process." *Development in Practice* 13(2–3):223–38.

Israeli, Raphael. (2004). "Palestinian Women: The Quest for a Voice in the Public Square through 'Islamikaze Martyrdom.'" *Terrorism and Political Violence* 16(1):66–96.

Jacques, Karen, and Paul J. Taylor. (2008). "Male and Female Suicide Bombers: Different Sexes, Different Reasons?" *Studies in Conflict and Terrorism* 31(4):304–26.

———. (2009). "Female Terrorism: A Review." *Terrorism and Political Violence* 21(3):499–515.

Kandiyoti, Deniz. (1994). "The Paradoxes of Masculinity," in *Dislocating Masculinities: Comparative Ethnographies,* edited by Andrea Cornwall and Nancy Lindisfarne, 197–213. London and New York: Routledge.

Katz, Sheila. (1996). "Shahada and Haganah: Politicizing Masculinities in Early Palestinian and Jewish Nationalisms." *Arab Studies Journal* 4(2):69–81.

Kedar, Mordechai. (2007). "Gap of Values: Gender and Family Issues as Source of Tension between Islam and the West." Herzliya: Institute for Policy and Strategy, Inter-Disciplinary Center.

Korbin, Nancy (2005). "Countering Terrorists' Motivations." Paper presented at the Annual Conference of the International Policy Center for Counter-Terrorism, The Interdisciplinary Center, Herzliya, Israel.

Manji, Irshad. (2005). *The Trouble with Islam: A Muslim's Call for Reform in Her Faith* (Hebrew). Or Yehuda: Kinneret Zmora-Bitan Dvir.

Merari, Ariel (2004). "Suicide Terrorism in the Context of the Israeli-Palestinian Conflict." Paper presented at the Suicide Terrorism Research Conference, National Institute of Justice, Washington, DC, October 25–26, 2004.

Moghadam, Assaf. (2006). *The Roots of Terrorism.* New York: Infobase.

Moghadam, Valentine. (2000). "Gender, National Identity and Citizenship: Reflections on the Middle East and North Africa." *Hagar* 1(1):41–70.

Motzafi-Haller, Pnina. (2000). "Reading Arab Feminist Discourses: A Postcolonial Challenge to Israeli Feminism." *Hagar* 1(2):63–89.

Naaman, Dorit. (2007). "Brides of Palestine/Angels of Death: Media, Gender, and Performance in the Case of the Palestinian Female Suicide Bombers." *Signs: Journal of Women in Culture and Society* 32(4):933–55.

Nacos, Brigitte L. (2005). "The Portrayal of Female Terrorists in the Media: Similar Framing Patterns in the News Coverage of Women in Politics and in Terrorism." *Studies in Conflict and Terrorism* 28(5):435–51.

Ness, Cindy D. (2005). "In the Name of the Cause: Women's Work in Secular and Religious Terrorism." *Studies in Conflict and Terrorism* 28(5):353–73.

Pape, R. (2005). *Dying to Win: The Strategic Logic of Suicide Terrorism.* New York: Random House.

Patkin, Terri T. (2004). "Explosive Baggage: Female Palestinian Suicide Bombers and the Rhetoric of Emotion." *Women and Language* 27(2):79–88.

Post, Jerrold M. (2007). *The Mind of the Terrorist: The Psychology of Terrorism from the IRA to al-Qaeda*. New York: Palgrave Macmillan.

Post, Jerrold, and Anat Berko. (2009). "Talking with Terrorists." *Democracy and Security* 5(2):145–48.

Reuter, C. (2004). *My Life Is a Weapon: A Modern History of Suicide Bombing*. Princeton, NJ: Princeton University Press.

Risman, Barbara. (2004). "Gender as a Social Structure." *Gender & Society* 18(4):429–50.

Rourke, Lindsey A. (2009). "What's Special about Female Suicide Terrorism?" *Security Studies* 18(4):681–718.

Rubenberg, Cheryl A. (2001). *Palestinian Women: Patriarchy and Resistance in the West Bank*. Boulder, CO: Lynne Rienner.

Schweitzer, Yoram. (2006). "Palestinian Female Suicide Bombers: Reality vs. Myth." In *Female Suicide Bombers: Dying for Equality?* edited by Yoram Schweitzer, 25–42. Tel Aviv: Jaffee Center for Strategic Studies, Tel Aviv University.

Skaine, Rosemarie. (2006). *Female Suicide Bombers*. Jefferson, NC: McFarland.

Speckhard, Anna, and Khapta Akhmedova. (2006). "Black Widows: The Chechen Female Suicide Terrorists." In *Female Suicide Bombers: Dying for Equality?* edited by Yoram Schweitzer, 63–80. Tel Aviv: Jaffee Center for Strategic Studies, Tel Aviv University.

Sillamy, Norbert. (1997). *Dictionnaire de la Psycologie* (Hebrew), edited by Dorit Landes. Tel Aviv: Yedioth Ahronot Press.

Stern, J. (2004). *Terror in the Name of God: Why Religious Militants Kill*. New York: HarperCollins.

Tickner, J. Ann. (2002). "Feminist Perspectives on 9/11". *International Studies Perspectives* 3:333–50.

Tzoreff, Mira. "The Palestinian *Shahida*: National Patriotism, Islamic Feminism, or Social Crisis." In *Female Suicide Bombers: Dying for Equality?* edited by Yoram Schweitzer, 13–24. Tel Aviv: Jaffee Center for Strategic Studies, Tel Aviv University.

Victor, Barbara. (2003). *An Army of Roses: Inside the World of Palestinian Women Suicide Bombers*. New York: Rodale.

Von Knop, Katharina. (Spring 2006). "The Multi-faceted Roles of Women inside al-Qaeda." *Journal of National Defense Studies* 6:139–75.

———. (2007). "The Female Jihad: Al-Qaeda's Women." *Studies in Conflict and Terrorism* 30(5):397–414.

Wadud, Amina. (1999). *Qur'an and Woman: Rereading Sacred Text from a Woman's Perspective*. London: Oxford University Press.

Wagner, Abraham. (2007). *Meeting the Terrorist Challenge: Coping with Failures of Leadership and Intelligence*. New York: HarperCollins.

Weinmann, Gabriel, and Conrad Winn. (1993). *The Theater of Terror: The Mass Media and International Terrorism*. New York: Longman.

Zedalis, Debra. (2004). "Female Suicide Bombers." Master's thesis, US Army War College. Available online at http://www.dtic.mil/cgibin/GetTRDoc?AD=ADA424 180&Location=U2&doc=GetTRDoc.pdf.

Index

Abdallah, 9, 11

Abir, 15–17, 135–36, 142, 159–61

Abu Ayisha, Darin. *See* Darin

Academic Star, 40

adolescents, as suicide bombers, 59–72; advantages of, 63; Fawaz on, 73–74, 76; Qatada on, 69–70

Ahmadinejad, Mahmoud, 82

a'ib, 86; definition of, 183

Akhlas, 133–34

Akram, 133–40

al-Banna, Hassan, 100

al-Ghadban, Muneir, 4, 12n7

Ali, Farhana, 5

Al-Jazeera, 105, 169. *See also* media

al-Malaika, Naziq, 10–11

Al-Qaeda, 4–5, 100; attitudes toward women, 5–6; Tir on, 41

altruistic suicide, 3, 166

al-Zawahiri, Ayman, 5–6, 100

amaliyyat istishhadia, 149; definition of, 183

Amjad, 60–61

Ammar, 4

Arab society. *See* Palestinian society

Arab Spring, 12n1, 100, 169

Arafat, Suha, 68

Arafat, Yasser, 82, 103, 119

a'rd, 10; definition of, 183

Asaliya, Souhila, 54–55, 57

Asaliya, Ziyad, 53–58

Atoun, Ahmed, 40

a'wra, 56, 166; definition of, 183

Ayash, Yahiya, 45

Ayisha, 77–80

Azzam, Abdullah, 100, 183

baklawa, 129, 142; definition of, 183

banat, definition of, 183

Barak, Ehud, 82

Barghouti, Marwan, 152

Bassam, 46–48, 78

Bechor, Guy, 28

Ben-Gurion, David, 159

bin Laden, Osama, 100, 103, 149

burqa, 178

Caliph, 56

camouflage, 81–82

children: in jail, 45, 47, 130; Nabil on, 148; Rania on, 49; Salima on, 108–9; Suad on, 51; and terrorism, 34–35, 71, 171–72, 176. *See also* adolescents

Christianity: Hamas and, 43n1; Nabil on, 67–68; Qatada on, 67; Riyad on, 101; Silvia and, 139; Tir on, 38
clerics, on female suicide bombers, 99–105, 149–50
communication, with terrorists, 125–32

Daoud, 11
dardali, 135; definition of, 183
Darin, 9, 135, 141–46, 152–56, 160
da'wah, 100, 169; definition of, 183
death: Riyad on, 84–85; Tawfiq on, 104
debt, suicide bombers and, 84
democracy, 28; Asaliya on, 54
Dichter, Avi, 5
disabilities, and recruitment, 121–22
dispatchers, xiv, 2–3, 9, 99, 167; and adolescents, 74; and mother figures, 21–22; Nabil, 9, 16–17, 51–52, 67–68, 130, 135–36, 138, 141–63; and recruitment, 84; romantic relationships with, 16–17, 51–52, 89–98, 136
divorce, 4, 6, 62, 75; Ayisha on, 77; Fadwa on, 92; jail and, 32–33; Nabil on, 161; Nawal on, 116; Salima on, 109
domestic violence, 1–2, 6; Nasser on, 71–72. *See also* rape; sexual violence
Durkheim, Émile, 3, 166, 179

education: adolescents and, 59–60, 63; Ayisha on, 79; Fadwa on, 94; Jemilla on, 19; Nabil on, 141–42; Qatada on, 67; Rania on, 48; Tawfiq on, 103; Tir on, 35–36; of women, 19, 35–36, 48, 79, 94
Egypt, 12n1, 100–101, 169
"Eid sa'eed," 111; definition of, 183
el-osur, 100
Erez, Edna, 4
exposure, 167; Asaliya on, 55–57; avoidance of, 3, 34, 51; Ayisha on, 80; Fawaz on, 76; media and, 104; Nabil on, 150, 152; Qardawi on, 149–50; Riyad on, 57

Fadlallah, 139
Fadwa, 89–98
Fahima, 91
fallaha, 108; definition of, 183

fallahin, 108; definition of, 183
family relationships, 2, 10–11, 167–68, 170; Atoun on, 40; Ayisha on, 79–80; divorce and, 78; Fadwa and, 89, 91–93; Fawaz on, 73–77; Hassan on, 62–64; Jemilla on, 17–21, 24–25; Nabil on, 143, 146–47, 152; Nawal on, 113–15; and prevention, 176; Qatada on, 67, 69; Rania on, 49; and recruitment, 160; Salima on, 108–9; Tir on, 35–36. *See also hamoula*
Fatah, 24, 27–28, 70; definition of, 183; Nabil on, 142; Suad on, 52
Fatah Tanzim, 24, 107; definition of, 183
fate, Samira on, 28
father figures: Fadwa and, 92–93; lack of, 175–76; Nawal on, 114
fatwa, 34, 56, 149, 173; definition of, 183
Fawaz, 73–77, 79–80
female suicide bombers: advantages of, 5, 11, 56; aftermath for, 171, 178–79; Asaliya on, 55; attitudes toward, 1–13, 165–80; clerics on, 99–105; demographics of, 117–18, 120; Fawaz on, 76; global, 4–5, 177; Hassan on, 66; interrogation of, 117–23; lawyers on, 133–40; Marwan on, 104–5; motives of, 3–4; Nabil on, 142, 145, 149–51, 154; Nasser on, 72; Qatada on, 69; Riyad on, 83; self-portrait of, 50f; Tawfiq on, 102–4; trends in use of, 5. *See also shaheeda*
feminism: versus female roles in terrorism, 9–10, 177; Jemilla on, 18–19; versus research, 53
fitna, 83; definition of, 183
Fogel family, 55
Fuad, 136–37
ful, 109; definition of, 183

Gaza Strip, 12n1, 15–16, 100–101; Nabil on, 145–46; Tir on, 36
gaze. *See* exposure
gender roles/expectations, 7–8, 11; Asaliya on, 55–56; and children, 78; factors affecting, 10; Fadwa on, 91; Jemilla on, 18–19, 23–24; lawyers and, 136–38; and

motivation, 6–7; Suad on, 51; Tir on, 32–34, 38–39
Goldwasser, Ehud, 42
Grad rockets, 102
Green Line, 55; definition of, 184
groom syndrome, 3

hadith, 83; definition of, 184
Hai, Meir, 55
halawat, 155; definition of, 184
Hamas, 4, 8, 12n1, 15, 27–29, 29n1, 101; definition of, 184; demands of, 34; Fawaz on, 73; Rajoub and, 42; Suad on, 51–52; Tir and, 31–43
hamoula, 7, 10–11; definition of, 184; divorce and, 78; Jemilla on, 20; and motivation, 16–17; Nawal on, 115. *See also* family relationships
Hanafi, 101; definition of, 184
Haniya, Ismail, 36, 40–41, 99
haram, 39; definition of, 184
Haran family, 42
Hassan, 61–66
Hebron, 42
Hezbollah, 28, 42; definition of, 184
hijab, 3, 8; definition of, 184; Sabiha on, 46
Hilal, Abu, 149
Holocaust, 82
honor killings, 8, 10–11, 68
Houda, xiii, 2, 6, 8, 17, 24, 108, 110; Akram on, 134–35; interrogation of, 121; Nabil on, 161; release of, 29n1; Tir on, 39
houris, 37, 51; definition of, 184. *See also* paradise
hudna, 28, 34; definition of, 184
human shields, 147, 159
huriyat, definition of, 184
Husseini, Feisal, 68
hymen, reconstruction of, 26–27, 47

Ibn Battuta, 102
Ibn Taymiyyah, 101
ibn Yasir, Sumayyah Um Ammar, 4
Idris, Wafa, 4, 6, 79, 119, 143, 149, 154
Ikhlas, 9, 11
imama, 5; definition of, 184

infertility, 4, 6, 154–55
Internet: influence of, 169–70; and recruitment, 169
interrogation, of women, 117–23
interviewing process, 53, 125–32
intifada, 18, 35, 119; definition of, 184
Iran, 36, 56–57, 82, 169
Iraq, 5, 9, 18, 32, 101, 118; Samira on, 28; Tir on, 41
istishhad, 62, 102, 155, 173, 175; definition of, 184

Jabbar, 61, 64–65
jahil, 36; definition of, 184
jahilia, 9; definition of, 184
jail: aftermath of, 171, 178–79; behavior in, 26–27; conditions in, 2, 15–17, 33–34, 110; and education, 60, 63; family and, 20; Fawaz on, 76; hopes of early release from, 23; versus interrogation, 121; and interviewing, 131; Nabil on, 150; Nawal on, 113–16; power relationships in, 17, 24, 34; Qatada on, 70; and reputation, 7–8, 16; romantic relationships in, 161; Sabiha on, 46–47; Salima on, 109–10; Tir on, 33–34, 36; visitation rules, 64
Jamil, 61–62, 65
Jaradat, Hanadi, 82, 118, 120, 133, 149, 162
Jaradat, Muhammad, 118, 133
jawaz muta'a, 136; definition of, 184
Jemilla, 17–27, 110–11
Jenin, 11, 100; definition of, 184
Jews: Qur'an on, 100–101; Rihad on, 82
Jibril, Ahmed, 72n2
jihad, 56; definition of, 184; global, 100; Riyad on, 83, 99–101
Jihad Jane, 178
jilbab, 3, 8; definition of, 184
Johnston, Alan, 51
Jordan, 138, 169
Judaism, Tir on, 37–38

Karmi, Rayid, 133
khalas, 155; definition of, 184
kharta, 27; definition of, 184
Khomeini, 71, 184

kibbutz, 94; definition of, 184
Kuntar, Samir, 42

labaneh, 55; definition of, 184
LaRose, Coleen, 178
lawyers, on female suicide bombers, 133–40
Layla, 51–52, 135
leadership, Asaliya on, 54
Lebanon, 42
legal system, Israeli, 7; and adolescents, 70, 171–72; and Fadwa, 89–90; Nawal on, 114. *See also* jail
Lod, 89, 91; definition of, 184

mabsout, 25, 35; definition of, 184
Mahmoud, 65
majnuna, 104; definition of, 185
Manal, 135
maqluba, 55; definition of, 185
marriage: Asaliya on, 56; Nabil on, 147–48, 159, 161–62; Nawal on, 115–16; Rania on, 49; Salima on, 108–9; and suicide attacks, 177–78; Tir on, 32–33, 36, 42–43
marriageability, 7–8, 16, 33, 43, 178–79
Marwan, 6–8, 104–5
masbaha, 107; definition of, 185
Mashaal, Khaled, 99, 147
Masih ad-Dajjal, 38; definition of, 185
maslakha, 41; definition of, 185
media, 167; and exposure, 104; and gender roles, 9–10; and motivation, 60, 104–5; Nabil on, 142, 144, 148, 162; and prevention, 172–73; Rania on, 48; and social structures, 40
metalaka, 6; definition of, 185
Monir, 60
Morsi, Mohamed, 100–101
motherhood: Fawaz on, 76–77; Hassan on, 62–63; Jemilla on, 22, 25; Qatada on, 69; Rania on, 48–49; Salem on, 166; Salima on, 108; versus suicide attacks, 173–74; Tawfiq on, 104; terrorists and, 21–22; Tir on, 38–39
motivation, xiv, 3–4, 166, 173; abuse and, 116; Ayisha on, 79; family and, 16, 172,

176; interrogation and, 120–22; Jemilla on, 21, 24–25; Nabil on, 153; parents and, 2
Mubarak, Hosni, 169
Mugrabi, Dalal, 119
Muhammad (dispatcher), 89–98
Muhammad (prophet), 4, 38, 83
Muneira, 1–3, 47
Muqata'a, 147; definition of, 185
muqawamah, 33; definition of, 185
Muslim Brotherhood, 28, 100, 149
Mutlab, Farouk, 176

Nabil, 9, 16–17, 51–52, 67–68, 130, 135–36, 138; artwork by, 151*f*, 157*f*; interview with, 141–63
Nablus, 6, 62; definition of, 185
Najar, 99, 161
nakedness. *See* exposure
nargila, 7; definition of, 185
Nasrallah, Hassan, 37, 41, 71, 100
Nasser, 71–72
Nawal, 110, 113–16
nazal amaliyyah, 62; definition of, 185
Netanyahu, Benjamin, 169

Obama, Barack, 138
obsession, 174–75; Ayisha on, 79
older women: attitudes of, 5, 20; in jail, 47; Marwan on, 104–5; Nabil on, 161; and preparation, 144; Qatada on, 70; and suicide attacks, 61, 99; Tawfiq on, 104
Operation Cast Lead, 12n1, 29, 70, 101, 178

Palestinian Prisoner's Club, 64
Palestinian society: and collective, 172; and education, 63; Jemilla on, 25; Tawfiq on, 102–3; and women, 1–13, 78, 109, 119, 139, 162, 167–68
paradise, 175; Amjad on, 60; Ayisha on, 80; Fawaz on, 75–76; Hassan on, 65; Jemilla on, 21, 26; Nabil on, 148, 158; Qatada on, 69; Rania on, 49; Riyad on, 85–86; Sabiha on, 46–47; Suad on, 51; Tir on, 37, 43; women on, 86–87
parents. *See* family relationships

Pipes, Daniel, ix–xi
Popular Front for the Liberation of Palestine, 18–19, 21–22, 72n2
Powell, Colin, 137
power relationships: in interview, 128; in jail, 17, 24, 34

Qalqilya, definition of, 185
Qardawi, Yussuf, 149–50, 173
Qassam rockets, 35, 102, 104, 161, 178; definition of, 185
Qatada, 66–71
Qutb, Sayyid, 100

Rabin, Yitzhak, 42
Rachel, 89–90
racism, 86, 137, 139
Rahman, Abdul, 121
Rajoub, Naif, 41–42
Ramadan, 135, 149; definition of, 185
Ramallah, 6, 91; definition of, 185
Rania, 47–48, 52, 136
rape: jail and, 123; as leverage, 5, 9, 136; as motivation, 1, 6–7; Nabil on, 68; Nawal on, 113–15; Qatada on, 67; Tir on, 35
Rasha, 11
rasul, 46; definition of, 185
reality TV, Atoun on, 40
recruitment, 84, 136; of adolescents, 60–65, 75–76; disabilities and, 121–22; family relationships and, 16–17, 160; Internet and, 169; Nabil on, 142–43, 148; Riyad on, 85; romantic relationships and, 90; Tawfiq on, 102; women and, 5, 20
Regev, Eldad, 42
reputation: Akram on, 133–34; jail and, 16; and motivation, 6–7; threats to, 8–9, 50, 104, 170–71
research process, 53, 125–32
Rice, Condoleezza, 137–38
Riyad, 57, 81–86, 99–102
Riyashi, Rim, 39, 52, 149
romantic relationships: in aftermath, 171, 178–79; Akram on, 133–40; with dispatchers, 16–17, 51–52, 89–98, 142–43; European women and, 177–78; with

interrogators, 121; in jail, 161; Nabil on, 152–53, 158–60; with terrorists, 23, 39, 120–21
rumor, 8–9, 50

Sabiha, 45–52, 78
Safia, 114
saif, 155; definition of, 185
Salah, Muhammad, 36–37
Salem, 165–66
Salima, 107–10
Samir, 136–37
Samira, 27–29, 45, 47–48, 77–78, 111; Akram on, 134–35
"Sauda tuchkum ala'alam?," 138; definition of, 185
Sawid, 140, 158
sexuality: Fawaz on, 75–76; Jemilla on, 19, 26–27; as motivation, 7, 172, 174–75; Riyad on, 86; Tir on, 35, 39; women on, 86–87
sexual violence: as motivation, 7; Nabil on, 150, 152–53; Nawal on, 116. *See also* rape
shabab, 39, 66; definition of, 185
Shafika, 92
Shafiqa, 139–40
shahada, 84–85; definition of, 185
shahadamania, 79, 174–75
Shahade, Salah, 159
shaheed, 3; Asaliya on, 56; definition of, 185; rewards for, 12n3; Riyad on, 83–85; Tir on, 37
shaheeda, 4, 6; Asaliya on, 54; attitudes toward, 1–13, 165–80; definition of, 185. *See also* female suicide bombers
Shalit, Gilad, 8, 15–16, 23, 29n1, 51–52, 98
sharaf, 10; definition of, 185
Shari'a, 26; definition of, 185; and divorce, 32–33
sharmouta, 6, 167; definition of, 185
Sharon, Ariel, 36, 97
shekel, 64, 70, 76, 108; definition of, 185
Shi'a: Asaliya on, 57; Atoun on, 41; definition of, 185; Qatada on, 71; Tir on, 36–37, 41
Shlomo, 117–22
shuhada'a, 75; definition of, 185

Silvia, 138–39
siwak, 81, 84–85; definition of, 186
Soroka Hospital, 1
state, Israeli: Asaliya on, 54; Hamas and, 34, 42; Nabil on, 147; Qatada on, 69; Qur'an on, 100; Tir on, 32, 37–38
Suad, 50–51, 136
suicide: altruistic, 3; Amjad on, 61; Asaliya on, 55; nature of, 166
suicide bombers: identification of, 81–82, 165, 175; Nabil on, 159; prevention of, 172–73. *See also* female suicide bombers
Sunnah/Sunnis: Asaliya on, 57; Atoun on, 41; definition of, 186; Suad on, 52; Tir on, 36–37, 41

tabun, 109; definition of, 186
tahadiya, 29; definition of, 186
Taliban, 103
Tawfiq, Abu, 62, 102–4
Tir, Abu, 6, 11, 31–43, 125–26, 177
Tivka, 26
Toledano, Nissim, 42
training, 8
tyamanu, 54, 81; definition of, 186

umi, 21; definition of, 186
Umm el-Fahm, 53
United States: Samira on, 28; Samir on, 137; Tir on, 41
Usra, usar, 100; definition of, 186

video statements, 172
violence: in past, 1; Tawfiq on, 102. *See also* rape; sexual violence
virginity: imitation of, 26; Nabil and, 154; Sabiha on, 47

waqf, 99; definition of, 186
watan, 39; definition of, 186

Ya ebni, 22; definition of, 186
Yair, xiii
Yassin, Ahmed, 9, 11, 22, 35–37, 121, 128, 171–72, 179
Yosef, 117–18, 120
Yossi, 94–98
Youmana, 3
Yusuf, Muhammad Bassam, 137

za'im, 39; definition of, 186